IN THE BUCKET

REMASTER THE LOST ART OF MARKETING

Prof. Cyrus M Gonda
Dr. Kalim Khan

IN THE BUCKET

REMASTER THE LOST ART OF MARKETING

Prof. Cyrus M Gonda
Dr. Kalim Khan

First Published in India 2010

Published in India by:
EMBASSY BOOK DISTRIBUTORS
120, Great Western Building,
Maharashtra Chamber of Commerce Lane,
Fort, Mumbai - 400 023.
Tel : (+91-22) 22819546/32967415
Email : info@embassybooks.in
Website: www.embassybooks.in

ISBN: 978-93-81860-63-2

Printed in India by Decora Book Prints Pvt. Ltd. Mumbai.

DEDICATION

To an Angel, Abdul Gafoor,

who though shortlived, bought

all the joys and Love in Life.

KALIM KHAN

For my ever loving parents

and my grandparents,

whose blessings are responsible

for this work seeing light of day.

CYRUS M GONDA

Endorsements for

SEAL THE HOLE IN THE BUCKET

An amazing book on Customer Experience Management. I just couldn't put it down once I started. ***It is among the best books on the vital subject of marketing that I have read in a long time.*** What's interesting is that as I read along, I could relate to similar instances which happen with regularity in the corporate world. We at Antal, having offices in twenty eight countries, and being one of the world's leading executive recruiters, can identify with the concept, the philosophy, and the examples that this superb book so eloquently brings out. This book applies to everyone in business, whether in India or globally, who wishes to get a leading edge over their competition.

- Douglas Bugie, CEO, Antal.com (Antal International Network)

(Doug is among the top 100 most influential people in the Recruiting Industry worldwide according to Recruiter Magazine.)

This book slices through the prevailing jargon and gets to the heart of marketing management. The language is lucid, the examples are exceptional, the message for marketers is memorable.

Cyrus and Kalim are amongst India's youngest and brightest brains in the field of Customer Experience Management.

- Murali Gopalan, Business Editor, The Hindu Business Line

Try describing God or love, and you can write volumes.

Similarly, Marketing Management and Customer Service too are topics on which one can carry on endlessly. But hats off to Cyrus and Kalim. With this book, they have hit the nail just at the right spot. Their examples are apt and I doubt they could be bettered. A must read for all, especially the Hospitality and professionals from any Service Industry. I enjoyed reading it thoroughly. ***Follow the message of this book and watch your profits soar.***

- Rakesh Rawat, General Manager, The Orchid, Mumbai (Asia's first 5 Star 5 Globe Ecotel)

I know Cyrus Gonda since a long time, as he has been associated with me, at Burgmann India, as a Visiting Faculty, to train our employees on various Soft Skills.

I had a chance to discuss and read the work of Mr. Cyrus M. Gonda and Mr. Kalim Khan on Customer Retention.

Their work on Customer Retention includes examples of original best practices. It covers every significant intellectual, practical and factual area on Customer Retention.

Their work can be considered as a guide to building Customer Retention Strategies and programmes.

Their writing style is very light with a lot of common sense.

- Umar Balwa, Managing Director, Burgmann India

'Seal the Hole in the Bucket' fills the need for a book anyone can use to create an effective marketing and customer retention strategy. It simplifies and demystifies marketing strategy in brilliant fashion. The power of this book lies in the fact that even a non MBA will find the concepts easy to understand and apply. This feat has been achieved by including some stunning examples which will leave a lasting impression for the marketing practitioner. This book can help anyone put together an effective retention strategy. I highly recommend this book to anyone who wants to create a customer oriented strategy that really works and is easy to measure. Abounding with relevant proverbs and quotations, this book certainly manages to put all focus back onto the customer. So if you're into dealing with customers and generating profits for your company/enterprise, this book is must for you.

- Krishna Durbha, Head (Value Added Services),
Reliance Communications

Dr Khan's and Prof. Gonda's new work is a wonderful gift for all practitioners of marketing. Unlike most works written by academics, here is a book that is uncluttered by jargon, rich in anecdote from every product and service category, and all in all a delightful and absorbing read. Even as you relish the book, the authors successfully kit you out with a brimful of practical suggestions that you can readily bring to bear on your own brand marketing charter.

- Paritosh Joshi, President, New Ventures, Star TV

Walls of progressive companies are adorned with posters stating that it takes 3 to 5 times "more" money to acquire a customer than to retain him. While this is now common knowledge, there is little awareness and consistency about "what" companies need to do to "plug the leaking bucket". This book attempts to provide clear and concise steps towards achieving that objective which is critical for the survival of every business.

- Chandrashekar Pitre, Senior Director Marketing, South Asia, DHL Express

Dr Khan and Professor Gonda lend a refreshing perspective to the idea of loyalty and customer retention. Thought provoking yet practical.

- Shiv Maulee, Chief Client Officer, Millward Brown India

Contents

ACKNOWLEDGEMENTS

This page itself could be a book if we were to write the names of all those who have directly or indirectly contributed in their own unique way. A very big thank you to all these special well wishers.

This book is a direct outcome of the co-operation received from Rizvi Institute of Management Studies and Research. Our faculty colleagues, students and the staff have been a constant source of support in this work. Very frankly this attempt wouldn't have been possible without the Institute.

We would like to thank all those who have helped us in the proof reading and editing the manuscripts of this book. Prof. Mohammed Osaid Koti and his students Rushabh Turakhia and Priya Juneja deserve a special mention in this regard. We would also like to thank our students Ashfaque Shaikh, Aamir Ayubi, Zafar Geelani and Manzar Ghansar for being such wonderful support. Prof. Sudhendhra Sharma deserves a special mention for painstakingly proofreading the manuscript and offering valuable suggestions.

We can never forget all our students, past and present, whose love has been a very strong motivator in all our academic impetus. We would like to thank each one of them who have been a part of our academic journey.

Heartfelt gratitude is also due to all our corporate partners for whom we have been conducting training workshops and undertaking consulting assignments over the years.

We are highly indebted to the team of Sohin Lakhani and Varsha Shah of Embassy Book Distributors and our dear critic Rafiudeen Shaikh of Ensign Book Stores, for their honest feedback and suggestions towards improvement of the manuscript.

We would also like to acknowledge the efforts of Dr. C.G. D'lima for being an outstanding mentor and guide.

We shall forever be grateful to Dr. A. H. Rizvi, President, Rizvi Education Society for all his generosity and unconditional support.

Special thanks are due to our respective families. It is their presence which has been the strongest reason for all our endeavours till date.

Finally we would like to thank the Almighty for all His blessings and mercies bestowed upon us.

FOREWORD

The Indian market has changed dramatically in the last two decades. We have moved from a country of shortages to a country of surplus in most consumer goods markets. Most monopolies, public or private created by artificial forces have either disintegrated or have been overhauled. A number of forces came together to create this strong growth in Indian consumer markets.

1. The advent of free television spurred audio visual literacy of brands. Television enthused many rural consumers to move from commodities into brands.

2. The process of liberalization created the framework for sustained growth.

3. The Indianisation of advertising created emotional bonds with brands, Indian advertising professionals built strong local brands leveraging on local understanding.

4. The development of basic infrastructure like roads, communication, banking facilities helped spur commerce to many corners of the country.

Competition in the Indian market is across a wide price value spectrum. There are three broad brands of value in the market place. At the bottom is the "I pay less, but I get less" segment. Consumers here are mostly cash strapped but want to tap into brands and their promise. Hence they buy small sachets of brands in various categories, fully recognizing that they might be paying more on a per gram basis for these packs. Then is the mid segment "worth the price". This is a traditional paisa vasool behavior. At the top end is the "I pay more and I get more" segment. The bulk of the get more is in the emotional surplus area.

The marketing success stories of the 80s and 90s were to do with satisfying the "I pay less but I get less" consumer. Most marketers and firms developed sachet strategies, developed trade networks and spruced up small town and rural communication to grow markets. Consumer understanding centered around disposable incomes, barriers and triggers to category purchase and role of brands in the consumer life space. As a result, most categories today have high degree of penetration in both urban and rural markets. The lessons from consumer goods markets were successfully adopted by other industries with the same results.

The last five years have seen something different. India has moved from being a penetration led market economy to a consumption economy. This has happened as a result of demographic dividend, i.e., younger consumers coming into the consuming economy, younger consumers' willingness to spend on products that made them look and feel good, the adulation of celebrities in every sphere by the media feeds a bunch of wants and desires hitherto untapped by marketers, the development of large format retail stores that gave consumers significantly improved experience in almost every category. The drivers are more sensory in nature now.

This new scenario calls for a different marketing mindset, that is one of retention and not penetration. Retention will mean more consumer and customer education, will mean better management of the consumer relationship after the purchase has been made, it will mean more dialogue with the consumer. In short, getting the same consumer to buy the same brand again is the challenge. This is labeled retention by many.

We see the retention concept unfolding in mobile devices as millions have come into the mobile fold in the last five years. The Nokia way of addressing retention is through constant feature upgrades, through constant new technology and by focusing on what consumers can do with phones in the area of applications and hence solutions. **I am happy to see Dr. Kalim Khan and Prof. Cyrus Gonda address the concept of consumer, customer and retention in this second book of theirs. I am sure you will enjoy their stimulating presentation of these concepts.**

- Shiva Kumar, Managing Director, Nokia India

PREFACE

This is a book dedicated to all honest and hard working individuals engaged in any business activity across time and place. It is commerce that makes the world go round. And without the essential ingredient of customers, commerce would not exist.

Although the world of commerce has embraced technology and modern means of communication with open arms, businesses and brands continue to falter and in many instances, find it difficult to survive. Many reasons for this could be identified, but a primary reason, indeed, a root cause, is that customers of these businesses do not receive the attention they rightfully deserve.

Customers who do not get the attention that they rightfully deserve from an organisation, will never be retained customers with that organization.

And it is only repeat, retained clientele, and a regular customer base which results into an organisation being profitable and successful over a period of time.

Without getting into more detail at this stage, let us introduce the basic but vital premise of this book – that the philosophy of customer retention is infinitely more important and contributes much more to an organisation's success, than does the philosophy of customer attraction.

This book focuses, with the help of a model we have developed, on WHY retention should be given more importance, and once that basic postulate is established and confirmed, the HOW of retention is elucidated in great detail, in simple language, with real life personal examples and case studies of the best brands, large and small, worldwide.

It is our sincere desire that you first and foremost enjoy the book, and absorb and implement its brief but crucial message, which we humbly believe is a recipe for success for brands and organisations in bad times and good.

We wish each reader heartfelt success in his or her personal and professional endeavours, and may his or her brand be identified as the benchmark of excellence against which other brands are measured.

We pray that your customers approach and patronise you and the organizations you represent with a joyous smile on their faces.

PROLOGUE TO PART ONE

Every business has two financial objectives: one is to make money, the other; more elusive, is to make money consistently.

- Dave Linigerr (Founder – Re/Max)

As mentioned in the preface, this book is a combination of the WHY and the HOW of customer retention.

Any individual who has invested in the stock market, bet on a race horse, or played in a casino is aware that winning once is easy. But sustained winning over a period of time, while elusive to most, is the only route to survival.

Part One of this book contains the Brains Trust Customer Consumer Model, developed by us at Brains Trust Management Consultancy. Over the years, we have come to the conclusion that no clear definition of the terms **customer** and **consumer** exist from the point of view of business in general and marketing in particular.

This has led to ambiguity, and when ambiguity exists, focus is lost.

Not only is focus lost on these two terms, but also on related terms, such as customer retention and customer attraction. And when focus is lost, resources which need to be allocated by organizations and brands towards customer retention and customer attraction could well be distorted.

Thus in Part One, the WHY and the WHAT and the IMPORTANCE of following customer retention as a strategy for any organization or brand is thoroughly explained.

After perusing the six chapters in Part One, the reader will be able to:

- Clearly distinguish between the two terms – Customer and Consumer.
- Clearly understand the exact meaning of that critical yet elusive term – Strategy.
- Understand the four possible strategies that any organization could possibly adopt towards its customers.
- Realise the multiple advantages of channelising the lion's share of resources of the organization towards Customer Retention rather than towards Customer Attraction.
- Understand the importance of getting back to the basics of marketing and business and the benefits of entering an era of Marketing Renaissance.

On with the show, and may it bring you revenue consistently in your business for a lifetime.

An out-of-touch management invariably results in an out-of-sight customer base.

- Cyrus M Gonda, Kalim Khan

CUSTOMER AND CONSUMER

Confusion Galore

Worry about being better; bigger will take care of itself. Think one customer at a time and take care of each one the best way you can.

- Gary Comer, Founder of Land's End

Who is a Customer? Who is a Consumer?

Have you got the difference right?

If your answer is, "The ***customer*** is the one who ***buys***", and, "The ***consumer*** is the one who ***consumes***", then you are in line with the majority who actually believe this to be the difference. This is the most common, popular and wide spread distinction and we label this as ***Current, Conventional Marketing Thinking.*** If this was the distinction that you thought of, then the silver lining is that you are not the only one who defines the two terms in this manner. But not only is this distinction erroneous, it also has caused colossal damage to the principles and practices of the entire discipline of marketing. The reason for this book being on the shelf is to clear this myth, and many more misconceptions going around in the garb of marketing today.

It is amazing to see many of the current lot of best practitioners of marketing faltering in their understanding of these most elementary concepts in the field of marketing. We believe that the entire essence of understanding the discipline of marketing emanates from understanding the difference between these two terms (customer and consumer), that have often been interchangeably used, misused and abused.

What makes matters worse is that besides the above mentioned incorrect distinction, there are multiple other contradictory definitions for these two basic terms, namely 'Consumer' and 'Customer', floating around. There are even some text books which claim that a Consumer is a first time buyer and a Customer is a repeat buyer, without assigning any reason for this explanation.

Students, teachers, practitioners and even professionals have time and again applied the current, conventional but incorrect connotations to these terms which ultimately form the crux of any strategy building exercise in marketing. Thus, if there is a flaw in the understanding of these terms, strategy based thereon would be misleading, and any decisions taken and applications made based on these would be nothing short of catastrophic.

The next question obviously is, if the above explanations of the two terms are incorrect, what, then, ***is*** the difference between the terms Customer and Consumer?

Before we get to that, let us understand ***why*** the current, conventional thought process about these two terms is misleading and erroneous. If, as erroneous current thinking goes, the distinction between the two would be that the customer is the one who buys, and the consumer is the one who uses, then the following vital issues are left unanswered, and more so open ended and ambiguous:

1. If one set of people buy, and the other set use, and the demarcation is done on this basis, then on which set of people should the company lay emphasis? This is not clarified in the current distinction. If the answer is that emphasis should be on the customer (that is the one who primarily buys, not uses, as per the current definition), then product attributes, usage and feedback on product for the organization have no value, as these would be of importance to the user, not to the purchaser. And if it is the consumer who should be the focus, (that is the user and not the buyer, as per the current thought process), then attributes such as point of purchase displays, price, packaging and promotion have no role to play, as the user is not affected by these. And if you say both sets of people should be the focus, (to tread the path of

neutrality), then why strive to differentiate between the two in the first place.

2. Is every Consumer a Customer or is every Customer a Consumer? Try taking a stance using the currently prevalent erroneous distinction. Ambiguity will be your only answer.

3. Another problem that arises when the term ***customer*** is not specifically defined, but is loosely termed to mean - ***someone who purchases or uses,*** goes as follows. Such an incomplete definition of the term 'customer' immediately eliminates and discards individuals who have had opportunities to ***interact*** with the brand, but have not purchased or consumed its goods or services. Under the current, conventional definition of the term ***customer,*** such an individual would never be considered as a customer. He would neither be given the attention nor the importance he deserves if he is just considered as a browser or a window-shopper.

   For example, in a Business to Business situation, if a sales presentation is made to a potential client, and he decides to avail of your competitor's goods or services, the potential client would not be considered as a customer, as neither has he bought, nor has he consumed the offerings of your brand. As you will clearly see in later tenets in Part Two of this book, (for example, Tenet Five commences with a very strong real life example of this), ignoring such an individual or organization because he doesn't fit into the current, conventional definition of ***customer,*** could be one of the biggest errors any brand or organization could ever make.

4. Therefore, on the basis of the issues raised above, the currently accepted distinction leads to subjectivity, and definitions, even in the field of marketing, can never be subjective. To substantiate this point, let us consider the following examples. First consider a product category like baby oil. (By the way in most of the training programmes we conduct on marketing, this is one of the most common examples given by the participants to justify erroneous conventional thought process). As per conventional distinction, the mother should be the customer because she buys, and the baby the consumer. But what if the mother also uses the same baby oil, does she then convert from being a customer to a consumer?

Or, assume, ***A*** buys a bike and gifts it to ***B***. Again, according to convention, ***A*** becomes the customer because he buys, and ***B*** is the consumer because he uses it. Now, if ***B*** were to return the bike to ***A***, could be for any reason, say for ***B*** leaving town, then ambiguity glares again as to the status of the two.

Or take the example of a dentist who orders magazines for his waiting room. He may or may not read the magazines, his patients may or may not read them. Assuming no one ever reads, (uses), the magazine, does this magazine ***have*** any consumer in this case?

So ***what*** then should be the correct difference between a Customer and a Consumer, which satisfactorily and clearly addresses the above issues?

Even dictionary searches for these two terms lead to ambiguity, with the two terms being explained interchangeably. This is because the dictionary differentiation has not been made from a marketing perspective.

Let us now steer away from all these ambiguities and give you the real meaning of these two terms from the perspective of marketing with logical justifications and explanations for the same.

At ***Brains Trust Management Consultancy,*** (of which we two authors are the founders), our efforts have always been to ensure solid marketing practices with a strong emphasis on basics in marketing.

The Brains Trust Definition of Customer and Consumer

"A ***Customer*** is an individual, group or entity which has patronized or availed or experienced the products or services of a particular brand."

This includes either the purchase, and/or the usage/experience; because our definition is ***not*** based on who buys and who uses. Thus a customer is one who has had any form of ***interaction*** with the brand, be it through self purchase or experience or otherwise.

"A ***Consumer*** is a set of ***all customers***, irrespective of the brand, who patronize, avail or experience the products or services provided by an entire sector or industry."

In short, a CUSTOMER generates revenue for a BRAND, whereas the CONSUMER generates revenue for the INDUSTRY.

Hence all customers have to be consumers to that industry, but all consumers of that industry need not be customers for a particular brand.

Let's take an example to illustrate the difference from the perspective of our definitions.

Do you have or use a cell phone? If yes, then you are a consumer for the cellular industry at large. But you are a customer for the brand of the mobile phone that you use. Hence if it is a Nokia, you are a customer to Nokia. It really doesn't matter if the cell phone was purchased by you, gifted to you, won in a competition, purchased second-hand or even borrowed temporarily from a friend, or a fairy tale Santa Claus present. It also doesn't matter who else uses the cell phone. Whether it's used by you, your mom, your girlfriend or any other individual. And for all those who use and experience it, they are all customers to Nokia.

A word of caution here would do well. We do not intend to imply that out of the two, either the buyer or the end user, only one of them should be the focus for a brand. That is not our intention. The definition from our end is developed to ensure that the differentiation between the terms Customer and Consumer is not based on the Buyer and the User relationship, and to remove the vagueness and ambiguity attached with differentiation based on parameter of purchase, so that strategy formulation for the entire organization can be done in a highly focused manner.

We could substantiate our difference using the following examples and case studies which will eliminate all existing ambiguity.

An example from the world of retail. If a person buys a gift voucher from Shoppers Stop and gifts it to someone, then according to the currently prevalent definition, the person who has bought the voucher is the customer and the person who is the recipient of the voucher as a gift is not. Does that mean that the recipient doesn't get customer service? (The recipient can't be called a customer according to the current definition, as he has not purchased the voucher.) In fact, the recipient is the one who needs Customer Service the most when he goes to encash the voucher at the mall. (When he does so, it isn't termed as consumer service, is it?)

Currently, the add-ons, (that is the complementary words such as service, feedback, loyalty, etc.), attached to the two words Customer and Consumer, are subconsciously being used correctly, but for the wrong reasons. Let's see why we at Brains Trust say so. According to the traditional definition, if **A** buys a book, he is termed as a customer. (The traditional definition says that the customer is one who buys or purchases). Let us say he doesn't read or use the book at all but gifts it to **B**. According to traditional definition, **B** will be termed as the consumer because he uses the book but has not bought it. Now assume **B** has a problem with the book for whatever reason. The printing is not proper or a page is missing, and he comes to the bookstore to exchange the book. For the bookstore, **B** would be termed as an upset customer, and he would be termed as a customer with a complaint, and the bookshop would be getting customer feedback from him, and they would be redressing a customer grievance.

Now look at the glaring discrepancies in the traditional definition of the terms customer and consumer, and the add-ons currently being associated and used with them. We saw that as per the current definition, **B** would be classified as the consumer and not the customer, (he's the user, not the buyer). So **B's** complaint should, according to current definition, actually have been termed a consumer complaint, and **B** should be termed as an upset consumer, or what B says should be termed as consumer feedback.

It is not.

What all this means is that, subconsciously, the add-ons to the two terms have always been correctly formulated and used, but the two terms themselves have been misunderstood.

Conventional, (and incorrect) labeling of the term consumer has been done on the misunderstanding that he consumes and therefore should be termed a consumer. Extending that same logic, the term customer ought to have arisen because the product or service offering ought to be customised for every purchaser. Such is definitely not the case. If a consumer consumes, for every customer you ought to customize. Right?

Not so. It doesn't happen that way.

According to our definition, a person who is availing of goods or services from a particular organization, whether he has paid and purchased them himself, or someone else has paid on his behalf, is clearly a customer for that brand or organization. ***The focal point on which we base our differentiation is whether he uses a product or service of a particular brand or that of a competing brand.***

Thus, according to our definition, **B** in the above bookstore example would rightly fit into the definition and category of customer, because we believe and state that the difference between customer and consumer has got nothing to do with who is the buyer and who is the user.

Or take for example when a newspaper claims that it sells a million copies, but five million people read it. According to our definition, the number of customers the newspaper has is five million and not one million, as all these five million individuals experience the newspaper.

Another example. If **Mr. C** is hosting a party at a restaurant, and he takes a group of friends with him as guests, will only **Mr. C** be called the customer and all the others along with him termed as consumers? (According to current, conventional definition, this ought to be the case, because only **Mr. C** is paying, remember?) Now what if this entire group, (**Mr. C** included), all decide to all go Dutch and pay their own bills, will they suddenly all become customers? No way. (But that is what the traditional definition says.) According to our definition, they are all customers, in both instances, whether **Mr. C** is footing the entire bill, or whether they all pay for themselves, because in both instances, all of them are experiencing the brand, and each of them is getting habituated or accustomed to the Brand. That's where the root of the word customer comes from. From the words habit and custom. Supporting or patronizing or giving your custom to a particular business establishment. And not the industry as a whole.

It is ridiculous to believe that a kid going with his parents to a favourite restaurant dozens of times, is not termed as its customer, simply because he doesn't pay the bill.

So a customer could be any individual who buys (pays the bill), but doesn't experience; buys and experiences; doesn't buy but experiences a brand.

The implication and business applicability of our definition is, a person who experiences or has a touch point with a brand or an organization, whether he purchases and pays or uses or otherwise, is EVERY BIT AS IMPORTANT for the organisation as the one who currently pays the bill, because he could be instrumental in getting himself and others with him to experience and purchase the brand the next time.

The following are rationale which will further cement our emphasis on evolving clear definitions and establishing the logic and accuracy of our definitions of the two terms:

1. In a discipline such as Marketing, which is crucial to business success, clarity of thought is vital for accurate strategy formulation and decision making. Objectivity and clarity is always rated at a higher level as compared to subjectivity and vagueness; as objectivity eliminates ambiguity. This is the reason why every science strives to become a perfect and pure science by becoming as objective as possible. According to the current definitions used, a customer who buys may also be termed a consumer if he uses, and a consumer who uses may also be a customer, if he buys. This vagueness and overlap does not make for coherent decision making at any level at any point in time.

2. There are certain complementary terms attached to customer and consumer, as per current usage. These terms have a perfect fit with the definitions developed by us at Brains Trust. The word customer has always been associated with the following prefixes and suffixes.

    - Customer Touch Point
    - Customer Training
    - Customer Value
    - Customer Centered Organisation
    - Customer Service Representative
    - Customer Handling
    - Customer Lifetime Value

- Customer Loss Rate
- Customer Loyalty
- Customer Partnering
- Customer Consulting
- Customer Defection
- Customer Evangelist
- Customer Experience Management
- Customer Feedback System
- Customer Portfolio
- Customer Switching
- Customer Retention
- Customer Satisfaction
- Customer Delight
- Customer Visit
- Customer After Sales Service
- Customer Attrition
- Customer is King
- Customer Helpline
- Customer Helpdesk
- Customer Service
- Customer Relationship Management
- Customer Loyalty Programme
- Customer Complaint
- Customer Care Department
- Customer Loyalty Programme
- Customer Orientation
- Customer Convenience and not Consumer Convenience
- 'Understand your Customer', is the phrase correctly used, and not Understand your Consumer.

Check all the above terms with the prefix or suffix, "Customer." The terms fit in to a "T" with our definition of Customer. All the above terms are meant for or indicate a set of people who purchase from, patronize, use or experience the Brand, and not necessarily only those who have bought or purchased. For example, when we talk of a customer complaint, then whose complaint should a brand resolve? Only the complaint of a person who has purchased? Or the complaint of someone who has a problem as a user of the brand, irrespective of whether he has purchased or not? The answer is obvious.

Customer Satisfaction thus means satisfying every individual who has a touch point with the brand, whether he is the buyer or the user.

Similarly, the word Consumer has been related and linked with certain prefixes and suffixes to form the following terms.

- Consumer Price Index
- Consumer Electronics
- Consumerist Movement
- Consumer Court
- Consumer Protection Act
- Consumer Awareness Forum
- Consumer Activism
- Consumer Guidance Society
- Consumer Behaviour
- Government ensures that duty cut benefits are passed on to Consumers

Again, all the above terms indicate a fit with the entire industry at large, and not with a particular individual brand or organization. For example, Consumer Protection Acts or Consumer Guidance Societies are attempts to protect all buyers and users of an entire industry, irrespective of the brand they experience or patronise.

Thus all the terms you see above as being used today, if understood with respect to our definitions, make perfect sense. People don't go wrong with the usage and application, but they tend to be confused with the definitions of the two words. By default, people's usage of the terms is correctly in place. You will never find the terms incorrectly used as part of a phrase. But if you observe how they are used in the context of currently prevailing definitions of consumer and customer, there would be multiple contradictions.

3. Lastly, take one of the most commonly used acronyms in the discipline of marketing - FMCG. What does this acronym stand for? You're right. It stands for Fast Moving Consumer Goods. (Not Customer.) Now think of some examples of FMCG products. Did we hear it right? Some immediate answers that must have occurred to you would be soap, toothpaste, shampoo, beverage, confectionery, lotion, etc. Isn't it surprising that you didn't think in terms of Lux, Colgate, Head and Shoulders, Nestle, Pepsi, or any other specific brand? That's our point. Since the "C" in FMCG stands for Consumer, all the examples that occurred to you were pertaining to the broad industry or sector and not to a specific brand. By the same logic, the other way around, you wouldn't have heard anyone claiming, "I am a customer of soap." The statement would definitely be, "I am a customer of Lux."

Need we say more.

Chapter 2

THE MYTH OF STRATEGY

Wish the term STRATEGY had been better understood

I have made this letter longer,
because I have not had the time to make it shorter.

- Pascal

(The above brilliant quotation tells us that it is easy to write paragraphs and volumes, but it is much more difficult to be clear, concise, specific and to the point; which is what is essential in strategy formulation.)

As someone rightly said, ***an organisation's strategy statement should be concise enough to be written on the back of a bus ticket.***

With the ambiguity over the terms, customer and consumer, having been clarified, let's shift our focus to another term - Strategy. This term needs to be clearly understood before we proceed with the rest of the book, for reasons which will soon become evident.

Today, the term strategy is thrown around loosely and is regularly (mis) used to indicate the next immediate course of short term action. The following examples of the incorrect usage of the term strategy may help clarify the point pertaining to its current misuse:

- An advertising manager talks of his next advertising campaign as his next strategy.
- A salesman speaks of the strategy he would adopt to convince a client to clinch a sale.
- A candidate going for a job interview mentions the strategy he would use to impress the interviewer.

The above are not strategies, but actually all short term plans and actions decided and implemented at the operational or tactical level.

The correct meaning of the term strategy has nothing to do with planning or action. Strategy is purely a vision, an aim, a goal, a direction you wish to take as a guiding path.

As an example, two five star hotels in the same luxury category and price range may have totally different organizational strategies they wish to adopt.

One hotel may want to be known for its professional attitude and approach, perfection in functioning. (That's its strategy or goal.) This strategy, if properly executed, will now ensure that this hotel focuses on precision in service, absolute punctuality, and thus caters to a specific audience - the very demanding business traveler.

The other hotel, equally impressive in dimension, facilities and lay out, may wish to adopt, (be known for or aim for), a strategy of warmth and friendliness, where it exudes a family type of atmosphere, preferred by the tourist on holiday.

Thus the plans and actions these two hotels would undertake and the tactics they would adopt would be in line with their decided strategies. ***But these plans, actions and policies, are not strategies by themselves.***

In short, ***strategy indicates what your organisation would like to be known for.***

For example, the brilliant, recently launched television channel, ***Colors***, which is giving all established channels a run for their money, has adopted the organsiational strategy of taking up programming content related to social causes and issues.

Or the ***Grameen Bank*** of Bangladesh, whose founder has been awarded a Nobel Prize for successful implementation of its crystal clear strategy of providing loans and financial assistance to the poor, eliminating the need for collateral, and operating on the principles of mutual trust and accountability. A very clear example of focused strategy.

To further clarify, consider another case; that of the Newspaper Industry.

One newspaper could want to follow the strategy of glamour and hype, appealing to a teenage audience. Whereas it's competitor could focus on a strategy of hard hitting honest and basic journalism. Both now have different goals, aims and directions. Both would like to stand for or be known for different things. (This is strategy.) And the actions they take to reach these goals, be it within individual departments, or as an organization as a whole, are the plans, policies and sets of actions. But these plans, policies and sets of actions are NOT strategy.

Consider the organisation - ***3M***. It follows an organization wide strategy of ***innovation***, because of which it has in place certain policies and plans. Since the organisational strategy of ***3M*** is to be known for innovation, all organizational and individual departmental policies of ***3M*** are oriented towards this end. The organization and all its component parts are very clear and focused and work towards a common aim. (This is the advantage of clearly defining organizational strategy.)

In order to ensure that new products keep getting developed, (i.e. to ensure that the strategy of innovation is actually implemented), ***3M*** as an organisation has a policy that a certain amount of it's turnover every year ***has*** to be generated from products that have been recently developed - in the last couple of years. In order to achieve this objective, the staff at ***3M*** is given the freedom to experiment for a few hours a day on their own in the organisation's laboratory, using organizational facilities and material, and are encouraged to develop new products. Another policy of ***3M*** is, if the immediate superior of the employee who has developed a new product, does not encourage that employee to continue working on it further, that employee can bypass his superior and go to his superior's superior, with no fear of negative repercussions.

All these are not strategies but policies, though the common misnomer of strategy is normally assigned to such actions.

These are action plans and policies to achieve the organizational strategy of innovation.

Strategy is a long term organisational vision and ***cannot*** change from day to day.

It cannot be decided by middle management.

Thus strategy is a long term goal decided by top management.

Strategy by definition defines a ***holistic organizational view***, and therefore corporate strategy ***cannot be linked to individual departments.***

Individual departments and units of an organization cannot by definition have their own individual strategies. This is so ridiculous a concept, it is laughable. The moment individual departments start initiating their own strategies, confusion prevails. Synchronicity and the common thread linking the organisation is lost.

Thus terms like Marketing Strategy, H R Strategy, Advertising Strategy are incorrect and cannot be used. Strategy has to be defined for the organisation as a whole.

What individual departments have are in reality plans, policies and action statements, which are followed to meet the organisational strategy as a holistic entity. Actions taken to reach the goal are not part of strategy.

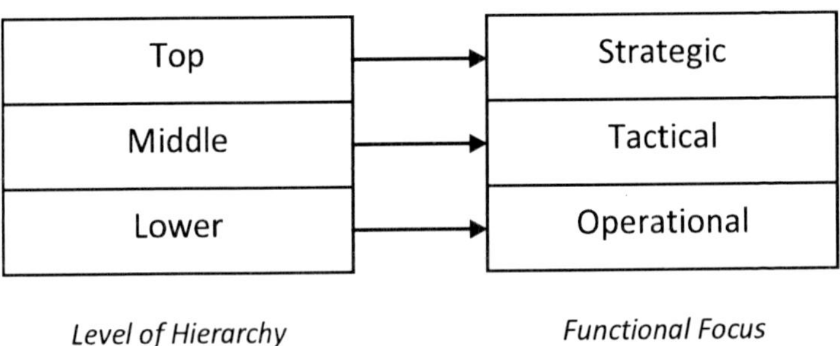

Thus:

Plans are a roadmap for the strategy proposed.

Policies are operational guidelines.

Actions are activities undertaken as per the plans and within the sphere of the policies.

To illustrate how widespread and endemic the misuse of the term strategy is, it would be interesting to note that some intellectuals in the University of Mumbai have developed a University paper titled Marketing Strategy for the MBA Course. The term Marketing Strategy is an oxymoron. You simply cannot have a separate Marketing Strategy. There can only be an overall organisational strategy.

If such is the case, it is no wonder that basic definitions among leading professionals are warped.

Just to reiterate, strategy thus purely indicates the vision that the top management has for its organization in entirety in clear terms.

According to Charles Kepner and Benjamin Tregoe, the acknowledged experts in the field of strategic management, ***strategy*** is defined as, ***"The framework which guides those choices that determine the nature and direction of an organization. It should provide a picture of the organization as it wants to look in the future. It is vision directed at WHAT the organization should be and NOT HOW the organization will get there."***

We don't think that there could be any definition of strategy which clarifies the term as well as the above definition by Kepner and Tregoe.

Importance of formulating a clear Organisational Strategy

The importance of understanding what strategy actually is, and the criticality of formulating a crystal clear strategy for an organisation, is that once strategy is clear, the entire weight and resources at the command of the top management of the organization can now be directed towards achieving this organizational strategy through plans, policies and actions.

Also, all the organizational departments and resources would now work in unison towards the same common goal, and not at cross purposes as normally happens, when individual departments formulate and implement their own strategy.

Therefore, any clear strategy statement needs to comprise of the vision and the specific advantage in a selected domain that an organization or brand will offer its *customers*. (The right word is *customer*, and not *consumer*.)

In order to understand whether an organization has a clear, well defined strategy, the following questions need to have clear and specific answers.

Questions

- Are you aware ***where your*** organization is headed?
- Can ***you*** define your organizational strategy in ***one crisp, clear sentence?***

Why do we feel that the above two questions are of prime importance? Simple. Because research has proven that most individuals in top management are unable to clearly state the strategy of their own organization. And if this were not catastrophic by itself, the bigger misery is that different executives in the same organization have different answers as to what the strategy of their organization is. Different organizations in the same industry see themselves at different points in the future and thus have to make trade offs and give up certain opportunities in order to gain others to reach that point.

What USPs your organization will ultimately be known for will be the basis of strategy formulation.

Any organization, indeed any entity, needs to have a clearly defined goal.

Take the fast paced result oriented game of soccer. We all know how the game is played. Just for a moment, imagine the same game of soccer now being played with ***one*** change. ***We remove the goalposts.***

Let everything else remain the same. The stadium, the thousands of spectators, the referee, the two linesmen, the two teams with eleven players each, the red cards, the yellow cards, the two halves of forty five minutes, all the other rules, *let everything else remain the same.* We just remove those two small goalposts.

The game will be finished before it even commences. The highly skilled players will be scattered around the field wondering what they are supposed to be doing. *There is no goal, nothing to aim at.*

The same thing happens to organizations which have brilliant staff but no clear organizational goal or strategy.

Now take a break and calmly think, "Can you *clearly* define the strategy of your organization as a whole." (And not individual departmental strategies, because such a term by itself is incorrect.) It is well worth the effort.

Our understanding of the reasons as to why this myth regarding strategy being mistaken for plans and action commonly exists and frequently occurs, are as follows:

1. Individuals tend to mix up operations as strategy, as this is the terminology commonly though incorrectly being used.
2. For strategy to *genuinely be termed* as strategy, there needs to be considerably less attrition and more continuity at the top level of the organizational hierarchy. When executives keep shuffling and rotating from organisation to organization and even industry to industry like a pack of cards in a deck, each coming with their own perspective; continuity in vision, culture, aims and long term objectives is lost. Strategy by its nature requires long term commitment to a philosophy, and a constant steady goal for it to bear quality fruit. If people keep leaving organisations at the rate which is currently happening, their focus ***cannot*** be long term and all activities they undertake within their short tenure will be at an operational level, and ***not at a strategic level.*** For example, if a CEO joins and leaves an organisation within two years, (as is the norm today), the questions to be answered are:

    a. What strategy can be understood and envisaged within that relatively short period?

    b. Did the CEO have strategies in mind in the first place,

or to put it rather bluntly, did he think in terms of a long term tenure with the organisation and therefore a long term relationship with current customers as an ideology? (Only then can genuine innovation and continuous improvement be a norm in the organization, else the focus will be on short term survival activities.)

c. What is the assurance that the person who takes over in a decision making position is in sync with his predecessor? This is absolutely essential for continuity of strategy to be entrenched.

d. Are the changes a new CEO makes undertaken for the sake of *progress*, or rather just an attempt to show that *some changes* have been done, as happens in many instances, thus confusing all stakeholders in the bargain.

Our belief at *Brains Trust* is that *clear organisational strategy* is a very strong function and result of the stability in terms of tenure of top management. The long tenure creates a bond that forges a relationship with all stakeholders concerned and therefore every action and operational task is in line with the long term intent of the organisation.

But then the question is, when the tenure of top management is short term, would thinking at strategic level in such an organization be long term, or would the organization be too busy in day to day firefighting activities.

3. We have very often seen that for certain organisations, strategy becomes the function of an available resource. These resources may have been available to the organisation by mere chance, ease of availability, and/or monetary power. When strategy becomes a function of such randomly available resources, then it shall always be deemed short term, simply because these were never inherent strengths of the organisation. While we strongly advocate strategy being a function of inherent strengths, organisations need

to differentiate between an inherent strength and an available resource. For example, in the industry that we represent, i.e. Management Education, there are certain institutes which try to make a brand name for themselves as excelling in a specific area of specialization, such as Finance, not because that was their intention to begin with, or it was their original aim, but rather by default, because these institutes managed to get some quality faculties in the field of Finance. Once these faculties have left the institute, this half baked strategy has no meaning anymore. It would be ideal from the long term perspective and continuity in strategy if institutes initially develop a sound strategy for excelling and making a brand name in a particular area and then work forward towards it with all the resources geared towards this end, rather than working backwards.

It is our firm belief that strategy can ***NEVER OCCUR BY DEFAULT OR CHANCE.*** This is one of the most fundamental myths we wish to clarify.

It is the core organisational strategy which needs to be identified first, and then individual available resources need to be put in place. Once an organisational strategy is in place, the usage of available resources would now be obviously optimized and focused, and not haphazard and scattered.

But what we have often seen in practice is the reverse. What happens in reality is that availability of resources leads to a so called strategy. For example, if an organization has set aside some funds for advertising, it would now use them to hire a brand endorser, simply because funds are available.

Some brands which have derived advantages from clear, specific and long term strategy formulation are ***Toyota, 3M, Wal-Mart, Singapore Airlines, Reader's Digest and Disney.***

Toyota is renowned world wide as the leader in its industry for its manufacturing excellence.

3M is immediately identified with leading edge innovation.

Wal-Mart is known for its strategy of providing the customer with value for money.

Singapore Airlines is one of the first airlines one thinks of when it comes to quality service.

Reader's Digest comes first to mind for reading material for the family.

Disney is the leader when it comes to clean, wholesome, family entertainment

In the Indian context, an excellent example could be the ***Tata Group,*** which is ***known, recognized, and stands*** for ***trust*** and ***reliability*** and has reaped the benefits of customer goodwill associated with this continued, century long strategy.

The reason for discussing and clarifying the issue of strategy in this book at this stage shall be abundantly clear from the next chapter onwards.

Chapter 3

RETENTION VERSUS ATTRACTION

Which strategy gets you the big bucks?

Forsake not the old friend, for the new is not comparable unto him. A new friend is as new wine; when it is old thou shalt drink it with pleasure.

- Ecclesiastes, IX. 10

Brains Trust definition of the term - Customer Attraction

"The set of organizational activities which are undertaken with the primary objective of inducing a current non-user or non-buyer of your brand of product or service to experience and purchase your brand of product or service."

Brains Trust definition of the term - Customer Retention

"The set of organizational activities which are undertaken with the primary objective of ensuring that current users and buyers of your brand of product or service continue to prefer and remain users and buyers of your brand of product or service."

Peter Drucker, the undisputed guru of the world of management thought, was very clear on the fact that the most important focal point of any business in any industry had to be customer retention. Everything else could follow this one activity.

This chapter is our contribution to propose four possible long term strategies that an organisation could adopt with respect to customers. It explains the four long term possible strategies that any organization in any industry could broadly focus upon, and clearly demonstrates which one of these strategies, if adopted, will push an organization into the big league, and generate an unending stream of revenue and profitability in the process.

A point to be noted is that these four strategies are not mutually exclusive. Just as in any other recipe, the perfect blend of ingredients is vital to get the final dish tasting just right. For example, if you're making a biryani, you can't put in more garnish than rice, but the garnish is still essential. Similarly, here one needs to get the correct combination of the proposed strategies. There is no mathematical formula for this combination. Logic and fine tuning would decide the correct combination. But there is no doubt that for clarity of focus and unity of resource allocation to exist in any organisation, ***one strategy should take precedence over the others,*** and whichever one is chosen, that strategy becomes the dominant strategy for that organization.

Consider the following model we have developed at Brains Trust Management Consultancy.

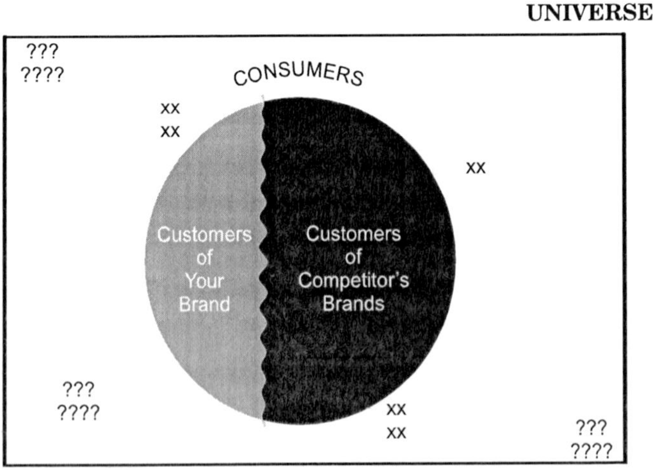

UNIVERSE

???
????

CONSUMERS

XX
XX

XX

Customers of Your Brand

Customers of Competitor's Brands

???
????

XX
XX

???
????

Brains Trust Customer Consumer Model

The contents of the rectangle indicate the universe. By universe, we mean all individuals or institutions who could be current buyers / users or possible and potential buyers / users for this product category. Hence it is made up of people who may or may not be buyers or users of a particular product category for whatever reason.

The circle within the rectangle indicates all those who currently buy or use, or are enjoying or experiencing the services or products of that category. Hence the circle is made up of all consumers of this product category.

This circle can be divided into users / buyers, or non-users / non-buyers, for a particular brand. The part of the circle which is made up of the buyers or users of a particular brand represent the *customers* of that brand.

The remainder in the circle would be consumers of that product category but not customers for that brand.

The set of people outside the circle represent current non buyers or non users of the category. They could again be categorized in two ways. One is a set of people who are in close proximity to the circle. (These are indicated by the 'X' sign in the model.) This means that they have a perceived need for that product category or could be converted as buyers or users in a considerably easier manner. The others are a set of people far away from the circle who may not need, know or value that product category. (This set of people are indicated by the '?' symbol.)

To get a clear idea about these four segments, let's take the example of book stores. For a book store such as Crossword, the customers are the ones who buy from it or visit it and experience its ambience and service. The other side of the circle represents people who visit and buy from other competing book stores such as Strand, Landmark, etc. but not Crossword. The ones outside the circle but close to it are a set of people who read but have never visited bookstores or bought books, and the set farthest away from the circle are those people who can't read or don't prefer reading at all.

Another example. Take the product category of LCD projectors. Buyers and users of the Philips brand of LCD are customers to Philips and consumers of the LCD category on the whole. Buyers and users of brands other than Philips are also consumers of the LCD product category, but are customers to their respective brands. In the current scenario, corporate houses and business schools make up a very large chunk of the consumers of the LCD category and thus they represent a major portion of the circle. Engineering colleges and other undergraduate colleges may yet not be buying LCD projectors but may have a strong perceived need for the same. These then represent the set of people in the rectangle outside the circle, but in close proximity to the circle. Primary and secondary schools would constitute a set of people who really may not be even thinking of an LCD projector as of now, but could in the distant future, and thus they represent the set far away from the circle., (denoted by the '?'.)

Now the question is, what strategy should an organization adopt or primarily focus its resources on, considering the fact that we have these four distinct sets of entities, namely:

1. The buyer or user or experiencer of your brand - ***The Customer.***
2. The buyer or user or experiencer not of your brand, but of your competitor's brand - ***The Competitor's Customer.***
3. Those that apparently have a clearly visible need, but are not consumers for the industry currently - ***The Immediate Potential Consumer.***
4. Those that don't have an immediate need for the product or service, but could have a need in the future - ***The Distant Potential Consumer.***

The logic of our theory and the reason for differentiating between the terms Customer and Consumer follows:

Our ***Brains Trust Customer Consumer Model*** (BTCCM) is designed to clarify decision making in strategy identification for an organization when it is faced with the aforesaid four sets of entities.

1. The first set of people is made up of people who buy, use or experience a particular brand, say Brand X. Hence from the point of view of Brand X, these are its customers, and the strategy here ought to be ***retention***.

2. The second set of people are the ones who buy, use or experience the product category of any other competing brand, but not Brand X. These are consumers but not customers for brand X. Hence the strategy here for Brand X towards this set would be ***conversion.***

3. The third set is made up of people who have a perceived need for the product category but are not yet buying or using or experiencing the product category. The task here for Brand X is not only to make them buy or use that product category, but ultimately buy or use Brand X. Hence the strategy for Brand X here would be ***development.***

4. The fourth set is made up of people who may not be currently aware or have a perceived need for that product category, but who would find it genuinely beneficial once they understand and adopt it. Hence the task here for Brand X would be to educate, create awareness and demonstrate benefits. This strategy would be called ***creation***.

As we saw earlier, the term strategy indicates direction. When an organisation's resources are limited (and no organisation can ever possess unlimited resources), which direction should these resources focus on in an either/or situation. That is the essence of strategy. Hypothetically, if an organisation has unlimited resources, it could focus on all four categories and thus on all four strategies simultaneously. But as in real life, where resources are limited, when one has to choose between providing resources towards servicing and thus retaining an existing customer, or attracting and converting a new one, which one would an organisation follow.

Identifying Your Organisational Strategy

With the background to strategy clarified, and one of the four strategies identified as a dominant strategy, decision making or direction taking becomes much easier. If, as is the case with most organizations, you do not have sufficient resources to perform all four strategies, then the one strategy you choose to primarily drive your resources towards becomes your organizational strategy.

All four possible strategies can and will be adopted and followed by every organization simultaneously, but the strategy that is given priority in terms of organizational resources and management focus will be labeled as ***the*** organizational strategy.

1. **RETENTION**

Retention is the strategy that deals with ensuring that your existing customers stay with you and most importantly generate repeat business. The key task here is to continually provide immaculate customer service with each experience of the customer being at least as good, if not better than the previous one. This means taking pride in customer service and defect free products which ensures customer pride in associating with the brand. The most important deliverable of this strategy is creating advocates and evangelists out of existing customers. This will occur when defects and errors in the service delivery chain are focused on, kept to the minimum, and ideally eliminated. Thus focusing on these needs to be the one of the thrusts or focal areas of implementing a strategy of customer retention. (The technical meaning of the words defect and error is not that there may be anything inherently bad in the product or service, but that it is not as per customer requirement or fit for the customer to use.)

This strategy of ***retention***, if executed and implemented flawlessly, ***primarily results in a repeat, loyal client base which assures regular steady revenue, and also results in word of mouth advertising, which as we elaborate later, is the best form of advertising.*** In the ultimate analysis, isn't every single activity in business conducted with the ultimate intention and objective to increase sales and profitability?

And if retention as a strategy is a more beneficial and cost effective way of enhancing profitability, shouldn't it be the logical focus of activity and channelisation of resources for an organisation.

2. **CONVERSION**

Conversion as a strategy makes attempts to create customers out of those consumers who are already users of the product category and revenue generators for the industry but not your brand. The main task here is to put forth the advantages and USPs of your brand and ***the key deliverables from adopting this strategy would be an increased***

market share in terms of purchase, usage and exposure to the brand.

3. **DEVELOPMENT**

Development is a strategic attempt to create new buyers for the industry at large, leading them to the organisation's brand in particular. The attempt here is to focus on all those sets of people who may have a perceived need for the product category but would not be buyers or users currently. The main task here is to develop the perceived need which is at the surface to an actual need. The brand needs to put forth and ***educate*** on the advantage of using that particular product category and then lead to the USP of the specific brand. ***The key deliverable here is increasing the market size for that product or service in terms of buyers or users or experiencers,*** with the ultimate objective of enhanced market share, goodwill, revenue and profitability.

4. **CREATION**

Creation as a strategy tries to build awareness for the product category in that section of the mass which may not know about the product category and / or does not currently find it relevant for use. This reminds us of the anecdote where a shoe salesman is sent to an undeveloped island and reports back saying, "No potential, no one here has heard of shoes, all are walking barefoot." Another salesman is sent there and reports - "Great potential, no one currently wears shoes here, have introduced to them the concept of footwear and the benefits of wearing shoes and have made sales to all." ***The main task while following this strategy is to create awareness of the product category at large.*** The key deliverables would be if certain individuals were not aware of the existence and therefore the benefits of the category for their purpose, they now become aware of the same.

Now the poser.

Which of these four possible strategies would be the best for an existing organization to adopt as its ***dominant strategy?*** We have ourselves been surprised when we got mixed responses to this question from practitioners. Our stand is very clearly that it should be ***Retention.*** You may agree or disagree.

In case you disagree, the following is the explanation from us at Brains Trust to validate ***Retention*** as the optimum strategy for an existing organisation in an existing industry, (which is where a majority of organisations lie.)

1. Amongst the four strategies, retention is the only strategy that assures revenue generation for your investment.
2. All research across time and place has proved that the cost and time involved in retaining an existing customer is far lesser than that put into attracting a new customer. (Most research shows it to be five times less.) A penny saved is a penny earned.
3. According to the universally applicable 80:20 principle, eighty percent of your revenue is generated from twenty percent of your regular, repeat, retained clientele, and the balance twenty percent of revenue is generated from eighty percent of floating customer base.
4. So from point **2** and **3** above, we gather that it is five times cheaper to retain customers than to attract new customers, as well as five times more profitable to do so. Therefore five multiplied by five makes it twenty five times more beneficial for the organization to focus on retention. This figure need not be taken literally, but definitely indicates the exponential benefits to be gained from adopting retention as a strategy.
5. Retention is the only strategy that creates a customer base for an organisation with the help of existing customers through word of mouth publicity.
6. Currently, many industries still operate under the umbrella of protection, and thus operate under a sense of complacency when it comes to customer retention. The managements in these industries feel that customer retention is bound to happen as a result of the umbrella of protection that they enjoy. For example, in the cellular industry, the management of an organization may be under the comfortable notion that they would be able to retain a huge hunk of their customers by default, even if the services they offered were not up to customer standards. This is because the organization operates in an industry which has the advantage and umbrella of no number convertibility. Once a customer takes his connection, he has distributed his number to his acquaintances. Now even if he receives poor service, he would find it very difficult

to move to another service provider, and would be retained by default. ***But all this is now changing.*** Number convertibility among service providers, (a customer can change his service provider yet retain his number), is a norm in Western countries, and is going to be a part of the cellular industry in India very soon. Now customer retention through excellent service will have to be focused on, the sense of complacency and only rushing after attracting new customers will have to take a back seat. Similar is the case in many other industries.

7. We believe that retention is the only next logical activity in the gamut of strategy. That is, once you have a customer, the next logical activity would be to retain that customer. Creating a customer and then moving on to acquire another without satisfying the first one is simply not a logical or profitable activity.

8. The higher the level of competition in the industry, retention as a strategy is the only one you can count on for an assured customer base.

9. A majority of individuals your organization intends to approach to attract as new customers are already having their own service providers with whose products and services they may already be satisfied. The only ones whom you can assuredly count on for revenue generation are your own satisfied and hence retained customers.

10. By not focusing on retention activities, the organization constantly shrinks and alienates the customer base it can do business with.

11. More opportunities for cross-selling exist when dealing with retained customers, as they are already assured of the quality of product and service provided by your organization as a whole.

12. Existing customers give free valuable feedback and ideas for improvement and innovation. This is a fundamental essential for continuous development for the organisation.

13. Research demonstrates that with the passage of time, most well treated customers generate increasing amounts of revenue for an organisation.

14. An often ignored benefit of customer retention is employee retention. There are two reasons for this. One, there is less pressure on sales and business development staff to achieve unrealistic targets of attracting new customers to make up for the customers which are being lost, and not retained. Second, the organizational staff will be more comfortable and less stressed when dealing with satisfied, retained customers with whom they already share a healthy relationship.

15. It is difficult and expensive to get back a lost customer.

A fish that frees itself from a hook, will swim away, never to return.

- Chinese saying

It makes more all round sense to pay attention to and retain the existing customer in the first place. Isn't his money as good as a new customer's money?

16. Attracting new customers to become first time buyers has become a very expensive proposition today. Unless the customer is retained and does repeat business with the brand over a period of time, it doesn't make sense spending huge amounts on advertising and other promotional activities, and then just getting the benefit of a one time sale.

Thus, assured customers, goodwill, assured advocates, assured revenue and low costs are the main pillars of adopting retention as a primary strategy and maximizing your organisation's resource focus thereon.

Look after customers as an investment in the future.

- Claes Fornell

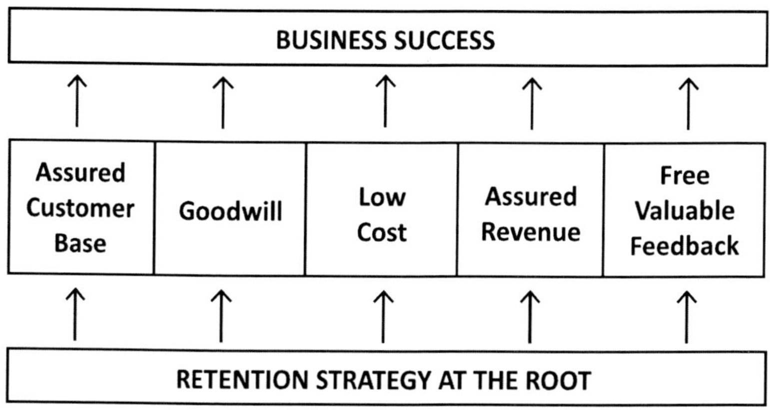

The following is an example to understand the importance even a roadside bookseller we know gives to the factor of customer retention over physical assets such as his stall.

When his roadside bookstall was demolished by the municipality, the owner confided that he was not worried about the shop. As he said, "You can get a shop on rent anywhere." What he was worried about was the loss of regular customers he had built up over a period of time by providing them with good books of their choice at a reasonable price. This man understood the importance of customer retention over physical assets.

We learnt the following brilliant lesson of focusing the maximum on your oldest and earliest customers from the same man. He has many regular customers who are interested in various categories of books. They request him to contact them whenever he gets some books in their area of interest. His policy is to always inform his oldest customers first, let them come and take the pick of the bunch, and then inform the others. He says that even though the older customers may pay him a little less than what his more recent customers may have paid, he has no regrets. He says that he is confident that over a period of time this policy of his and the loyalty it has generated has amply repaid him for any loss of short term profit.

I find as I grow older that I love those most whom I loved first.

- Thomas Jefferson

Yet it is observed that most organizations today focus their resources on the strategy of attraction rather than focusing on retention.

The following is typical of a recurring scenario. Take an existing mobile service customer who has been loyal to his service provider since the past five years. Passing by a mobile gallery, he sees a new scheme advertised by his service provider which is far more attractive to him than the one he is currently on. He visits the gallery, proudly states that he has been a customer of this organization for five years and would now like to convert to the new scheme. Imagine the slap on his face when he is bluntly told, "Sorry, this scheme is only to attract new customers, you as an existing customer are not eligible for it." (The implication being - You are already with us, we don't need to do things to please you. Why should we take extra efforts over you by providing you with goodies. These are only to trap and snare new customers by creating a good first impression.)

OR, take the Private Sector Banks which advertise - "If you have a loan existing with any other bank, you can convert it to our bank. As an incentive we will waive off the first three months interest." But have they even waived off a month's interest for an existing customer as a token of goodwill? No such gesture is deemed necessary. 'Why make extra efforts to keep him happy,' is the warped logic. All relationship experts and advisers advise the husband and wife to not get lethargic about their relationship after marriage but to make the same if not more efforts as time passes to keep the relationship going. In business and with customers, familiarity should definitely not breed contempt. Forget doing extra for existing customers, brands are known to do less for their existing customers than they do for new and potential clients.

Focusing on customer retention is sage advice. Yet in the lure for short term market gain, we find large organizations doing the absolute opposite. This is because resources in any organization are limited, and rather than shower them on existing customers first and reap the benefits, existing customers are taken for granted and these resources are showered on first timers, with the aim of increasing the customer base.

Retention thus according us should be ***the heart of all strategic focus,*** and is the driving force behind this book. We do not say that the other three strategies should be ignored and not given attention at all. But the balance has to be skewed very heavily towards retention as far as resources and senior management focus go, especially for an existing firm which already has a customer base.

For an existing firm, retention as a primary or dominant strategy holds the key to continued business success.

The failure to focus on retention, thus leading to lack of repeat business and word of mouth recommendations is the single largest cause for brands going out of business.

This is the primary reason why the annual list of Fortune 500 organisations sees so many drop-outs every year.

There is place in the world for any business that takes care of its customers.

\- Harvey MacKay

Our message is not one of, ***"Don't Focus on Attraction,"*** but rather that the main or primary focus of an organization has to be on Retention. Once an organisation has systems in place and has excess resources available to satisfy existing customers, only then should the focus be on ***attracting*** new customers. Unfortunately when customers complain about poor service, organizations proudly respond, ***we have so many customers, we can't service and cater to all***.

If resources in an organisation were infinite, (a happy but utopian dream), we could definitely focus as much on attracting new customers and all other strategies as well as we do on retaining existing customers. But when resources are limited, as every organisation well knows, and when prioritisation is key, then the limited resources have to be put to optimum use, where they can secure maximum benefit. ***This*** optimum use, as our model explains, will be achieved through the focus on retention.

Don't bite off more than you can chew.

Cut your coat according to cloth.

Don't drink all the water in the ocean, it will lead to diarrhea.

The above proverbs have stood the sensible test of time.

Consider the scenario in a management institute, from where most of the decision makers into the corporate world graduate. Every year, a reputed management institute gets at least five times the number of applications from potential students than it has seats to fill. Imagine if in its short sighted mindset to maximise short term revenue, the management institute admitted every applicant who had the ability to pay his fees. The revenue for the institute would swell five fold. But then chaos would reign supreme. Quality faculty would not be available to all. Classrooms would fall short. Placements would be a problem. Most students (customers), would not get the value they expected. Negative word of mouth about the institute would spread. Over the years the institute would lose its reputation. Applications would drop to a trickle. The brand equity would be diluted. All because the focus was short term maximisation without bothering to analyse whether existing infrastructure, staff and resources were capable of delivering a quality experience to all aspirants.

A similar scenario is being replicated in many corporate houses.

Haven't we heard of multiple brands going into oblivion taking this route? ***And these very same B- School graduates, who flowered and blossomed under this wise policy of the B - Schools to limit their customer base to the extent they could cater to, get into decision making positions in corporate life and do the exact opposite to what their colleges did, by expanding their customer base to limits where it is not possible to serve them attentively.***

The most important point one can carry away from the ***Brains Trust Customer Consumer Model*** is that one's current and retained customers are one's ***cash cows.*** This is because they not only are the ***only*** sources of revenue for any organisation, but also because if they are served well, they keep generating leads and referrals. This is actually free advertising which is done passionately on the organisation's behalf by customers who are glad to be associated with the organisation. ***But no one will recommend a product or service provider with whom they've had even a single bad experience.***

We have stressed the importance of customer retention and the value it generates to business. But organisations rarely focus on this. Attraction seems to be a very attractive option for organisations today. This psyche is also depicted in the way organisations function at all levels.

It can be demonstrated with the aid of the following example.

Consider an organisation which has two employees, one of whom is brilliant, a fantastic go getter. The other is comparatively dull, who has been selected due to influence of some sort. Now they both have to be placed. There is a vacancy in the sales department, and another vacancy in the after-sales-service function. It does not require a fortune teller to predict which of the two would be placed in the sales function by most organisations. This is unfortunately an all too common scenario. Organisations tend to put their best and brightest people in the sales function. The logic being that attracting new clientele is the priority activity. After sales service is given step motherly treatment for obvious reasons. It is even looked at as a cost rather than an investment. It is viewed at as a non-core activity, and therefore often outsourced.

One reason organizations tend to focus on attraction is that it is apparently more exciting. The organisation feels ***"Something is being done."***

But ***activity should never be mistaken for productivity.*** Running aimlessly around a tree definitely qualifies as activity. But is it productive? You decide.

Above all, we wish to avoid having a dissatisfied customer. We consider our customers as part of our organization, and we want them to feel free to make any criticism they see fit in regard to our merchandise or service. Sell practical, tested merchandise at reasonable profit, treat your customers like human beings – and they will always come back.

- L L Bean

All these above reasons and examples prove that attraction should precede retention only in the dictionary.

It is our strong contention that if an organisation clearly understood the difference between Customer and Consumer, the true meaning of the word Strategy, and the importance of a long term goal, then Retention as a strategy would be the default option for that organisation.

All this not only holds true for retail business, but also for B 2 B businesses, where retention becomes even more important, as in B 2 B business models, each existing customer represents a comparatively larger slice of the revenue pie.

Many good things are lost in life by INDIFFERENCE than were ever lost by active hostility.

- Robert Gordon Menzies

A survey conducted which reveals the reasons that organizations tend to lose their existing customers will give food for thought.

Why Do Companies Lose Customers

Death	**One percent**
Customer moves to another town	**Three percent**
Competitors have won him over	**Five percent**
Lower price elsewhere	**Nine percent**
Unsatisfactory handling of complaints	**Fourteen percent**
Lack of interest on part of the supplier	**Sixty Eight percent**

(Source of above survey - Swedish Post Office - 1990's)

Isn't this a high price to pay for indifference and lethargy?

Fully eighty seven percent is avoidable loss.

Again the eighty twenty principle at work.

(Death of customer, customer moving to another town, and customer finding lower prices elsewhere are the only three reasons which are unavoidable reasons for losing the customer, and these total only thirteen percent.)

The reason for this eighty seven percent loss can best be summed up in the following quote from a shrewd business analyst:

"It seems to me that most companies are much better at getting new customers and selling to them than they are at retaining their old customers."

And the other EIGHTY SEVEN percent customers which are lost is TOTALLY AVOIDABLE if the tenets we have put forth in Part Two of this book are sincerely followed.

Instead of dreaming up **Sales Slogans** for attracting new clientele such as:

SOME WILL

SOME WON'T

SO WHAT

WHO'S NEXT

Why not channelise the organisational energies into Retention activities by encouraging the operational and sales staff to think in terms of communicating with the customer in terms of:

WHAT WOULD YOU LIKE

SURE, WE'LL DO THAT

YOU'RE THE BOSS/KING (Customer)

WHAT NEXT CAN WE DO FOR YOU

Unfortunately, very few organizations focus on motivating staff by motivating them to serve rather than to sell.

- Cyrus M. Gonda, Kalim Khan

The selling will then take care of itself. It would be so much more productive and beneficial for everyone concerned.

Let us examine the rationale why retention and not attraction should be the default option for any existing organization in the next chapter.

THE HOLE IN THE BUCKET

Plug the leak before the bucket's empty

Only when the well runs dry do we know the value of water.

- Ancient Indian proverb

There's this typical mathematical teaser which says that there is a water tank with a capacity to store a hundred litres. Currently, this tank is full of water. It is being drained due to a hole at the bottom of the tank at a rate of four litres every minute, and simultaneously being filled up through another tap at the rate of two litres per minute. How much time would elapse before the water tank is empty?

While traditionally the focus is on the mathematical solution of this teaser, let us pause for a moment and understand some ***wonderful marketing lessons*** this teaser can teach us. Could you think of some?

Lessons from this basic mathematical concept

1. If there is a leak in the bucket, then ***outflow is inevitable.***
2. A small leak, if not given the attention it deserves, will inevitably ***lead to a larger leak.***
3. When the rate of outflow through the leak in the bucket outpaces the rate of inflow from the tap, ***at some point, sooner or later, the bucket will get empty.***

4. Increasing the rate of inflow is difficult and sometimes almost impossible, as the limited water available, (customers), may also be diverted to other buckets, (competitors.) This is a major reason why organizations look to cut costs, as it is much more difficult to increase sales rather than cut costs. It is also more of an ***uncontrollable factor*** as it does not exactly lie in your hands whether the inflow could constantly be increased or even maintained at the same pace.

5. But the plugging of the leak and therefore the outflow is a factor ***mostly within the organisation's control and therefore an internal factor.*** This is what any sensible, forward thinking organisation would focus its energies on. (To refresh the memory, refer to the survey results towards the end of the previous chapter.)

Most organisations today focus on the tap that's doing the filling (attracting new customers), but ignore the hole at the bottom that's draining away the existing content (retaining existing customers.) Most of the focus and attention is on the tap that's filling the tank, little attention is paid to stopping the outflow.

The following are the mistaken assumptions, reasons and explanations that organisations use and provide for focusing their attention on enhancing inflow rather than plugging the outflow:

1. The primary reason for this being the case is that ***inflow can be easily calculated and shown at the end of each accounting period but outflow can be disguised, hidden, or not even taken into account.***

2. Similar to the familiar analogy of the iceberg, ***ninety percent of the outflow is invisible or unrecorded, and therefore ignored*** by organisations.

3. Performance Appraisals for sales persons are normally done on the basis of how many more clientele they have added to their list rather than on the basis of ones they have lost or the ones they have retained. Naturally then, the focus would be on attraction.

4. Another incorrect assumption is that outflow is inevitable and therefore not worth controlling. Some amount of outflow is definitely inevitable, (but most of the outflow can definitely be

controlled and avoided.) Unfortunately, through this attitude of clubbing all outflow in the same boat, ***the baby of controllable outflow is thrown out with the unavoidable bathwater of uncontrollable outflow.***

5. As mentioned later in the tenet "Circle of Influence", a customer by himself may not be a repeat buyer and therefore considered important enough to make attempts to prevent him from leaving the organisation. But he may be responsible for many other customers being added to, or others leaving the organisation due to his positive or negative recommendations. Since this is difficult to calculate, this aspect is often ignored. Logically, all the additions and deletions in an organisation's customer base that occur due to word of mouth of a particular customer rightly need to be attributed to that customer. This is rarely if ever done. If this attitude is developed, existing customers will be treated with healthy respect. Even the technical formula for calculating the ***lifetime value of a customer*** ensures that referrals attained through a customer are attributed to his credit.

6. Surveys show that more than ninety five percent of customers who are dissatisfied with an organisation don't complain. They just spread the negative word to all ears within hearing distance, and never come back themselves. So if an organization is not proactive about its customer feedback, it will not even be aware that outflow is occurring, till it is too late to salvage.

7. To conduct Corporate Training Programmes, many times an external faculty is preferred, not because they have superior content as compared to the organisation's own internal trainers, but for the fact that employees participating in these programmes tend to pay more attention to what an outsider has to say. The in-house organisational trainer's words are taken with a pinch of salt. As the Hindi saying goes - ***Ghar ki murgi daal barabar.*** A similar error occurs at the organisation's end by ignoring the benefits an existing customer can provide, and running after the elusive bird in the bush rather than servicing the one already in hand. It is rightly said, ***Familiarity breeds contempt.***

8. It is considered more glamorous and beneficial by many organisations to have contributed to adding new customers to the pie rather than preventing existing ones from leaving. ***But on the balance sheet, both have the same impact.***

9. ***A Penny Saved is a Penny Earned.*** This can also be transposed in marketing parlance to indicate, ***a customer retained is a customer earned.***

10. Consider most organisations you have dealt with as a customer. ***Do you feel the organisations were more attentive towards you when they wanted to convert you into a buyer, or when you were already a buyer and wanted a complaint or an issue resolved.***

11. We always feel excited while meeting a new person or starting a new project. Then complacency and inertia set in. Take your New Year resolutions, with what enthusiasm are they initiated, and how soon they fizzle out in most cases. Or a person joining a gymnasium. For the first three days or a week, energy pours out. But then the fallout starts. Very few actually continue with the same enthusiasm which they began with. Multiple other instances will give similar endings. Even in marriage, there is something called the ***Seven Year Itch,*** at which point of time after a marriage, the partners start actively looking at other options. Similarly, once a customer is yours, (or so you think), you tend to lose interest and ignore such a customer. That could be your biggest error in marketing and in business.

Consider the fact that most Business Magazine surveys which award winners in each industry category as Best Bank, Best Insurance Company, and so on, ***rarely take into account the levels of service*** provided to existing customers as a parameter. If you refer to most of these surveys, you will find that the parameters considered for giving the awards are always - ***Size of customer base, New Clients added, Number of branches, and so on; parameters which only identify and focus on attraction. The focus is never on Customers lost, Customer complaints, Customer delight, and other parameters which take into account retention through service and satisfaction.*** Existing customer feedback is rarely a parameter considered in such surveys, but it should be a vital one.

Also consider this. If clients who have disassociated dealing with you lie behind you, clients you hope may be yours in future lie ahead of you, and clients you currently have are a part of you, then you would do well to reflect on the following lines penned by the great sage and philosopher, ***Ralph Waldo Emerson:***

"What lies behind us and what lies ahead of us are small matters compared to what lies within us."

What lies within you are your existing customers. ***Remember, a bird in hand is worth at least two in the bush.***

Unfortunately for much of industry today, the focus is only on the additional customers, the focus is NOT on the vital element of how many existing customers are being lost, which are already an integral and profitable and revenue generating part of the organisation.

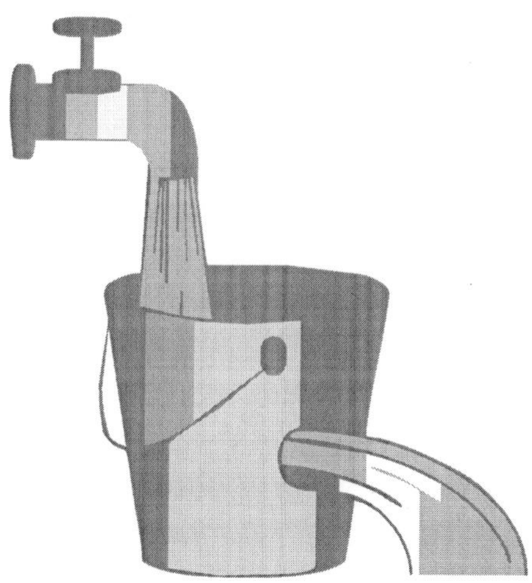

Only a fool would open the tap and let water flow out without taking steps to first plug the leak. Isn't this basic common sense?

Focusing on attraction without keeping a corresponding focus on retention is akin to a supposedly unending flow from a tap pouring into a bucket which has a hole at the bottom. Till water from the tap at the top continues to flow, there may appear to be no problem. But when inflow stops or slows down, you are unable to get fresh inflow. This is when your miseries begin, and they get compounded when it becomes difficult to plug the leak, (because it may be too late), and thus even retain the reduced existing mass. This is why so many organisations in times of recession say ***NOW WE NEED TO FOCUS ON IMPROVING relationships with existing customers. Till lean times began, this was never given priority.***

For those of you who are familiar with the **Dohas** or poetry of **Sant Kabir,** you would find the following Doha a perfect analogy. In fact the whole of our Brains Trust Customer Consumer Model can be explained beautifully through the following lines:

Dukh mein sumiran sub kare,

Sukh mein kare na koi.

Jo sukh mein sumiran kare,

To dukh kahe ko hoi

The above quatrain indicates that we remember the Almighty only in times of despair, sorrow and need. It is a typical human trait to forget the Lord when the sailing is smooth and all is well. The quatrain makes a wonderful attempt to preach that if we ordinary souls were to constantly remember and focus on God even when times were good, then bad times would never come our way.

Sheer brilliance. Four centuries ago.

The time to repair the roof is when the Sun is shining.

- John F Kennedy

The same holds true for business houses and their approach to their customers. When times are good, business is booming, and more customers approach you than you can effectively handle. A feeling of complacency sets in. We tend to forget, that ***this too shall pass.***

Taking Kabir's doha, if we substitute ***Customer*** for ***God,*** (after all don't we say Customer Is God), then the ***entire quatrain is a brilliant lesson for all businesses, large and small.***

If we build, strengthen and solidify our relationships with our customers during good times, paying them the attention that they rightly and richly deserve, they will reciprocate and stick with us when business is in a slump.

We know of one multinational organisation which was almost a monopoly in its field a couple of decades ago. It used to be in the business of manufacturing and marketing a certain component for use in cars, fans, machinery, etc. The organisation's sales people used to behave more like rationing officers, making customers wait endlessly outside their cabin while they decided which customers should get the few crumbs available. (Demand for this component was much higher than supply.) In a few short years, the situation reversed. Chinese substitutes flooded the market. Local competition also arrived. Now the organisation woke from its slumber. Instead of the customers waiting outside the sales peoples cabins, it was the turn of the sales people to run after the customers, who now had multiple choices. This running after approach still didn't work, as the customers were now tired of the arrogant attitude of the organisation when times had been good. It's not that the customers had wanted to deal with the organization at any stage and suffer this bad treatment, but at some point in time the customers had no option or alternative. Now that they ***had*** choices, none of the customers wanted to touch this organisation with a barge pole. The organization's customer bucket was soon empty.

The moment the ***attraction tap*** stops flowing, the problem arising from the lack of focus on plugging the ***retention leak*** (a problem which always existed, but was not obvious), now becomes blatantly visible.

And we all know that no earthly tap has an unending flow. It would be folly to think otherwise.

When out of the four strategies enumerated earlier in the Brains Trust Model, if the focus is on retention, the probability of the other three strategies (including attraction), occurring as a byproduct happening is very high because of Word of Mouth. But if your primary focus is on the other three strategies, they may or may not fructify, but retention will definitely not happen.

The next chapter gives us some idea of the distortion in managerial focus prevailing today, with regards to attraction and retention.

THE SCENARIO TODAY

Urgent reforms needed

Do not fear going forward slowly. Fear only to stand still.

- Chinese Proverb

No one in a management position today would publicly deny the importance of the customer being at the centre of all business decisions. Yet an in-depth look at some statements made by senior corporate functionaries over the past few years indicates that the reality may be a little different.

Before going further, we would like to clarify that this chapter is not meant as a criticism, but as a reality check. This chapter consists of comments we have heard, made over the years by corporate personnel, most in public forums, and some elsewhere. Who said them is not important. Neither is the organization they represent. What is important is that they provide an insight into the sub-conscious mindset prevalent among corporate decision makers today. The learnings from these could be huge, provided we treat them as learnings and opportunities for improvement. As the English author and philosopher, G.K. Chesterton said so aptly - ***The greatest patriot is the greatest critic.***

We have a genuine desire to see Indian industry attain and retain the pinnacle of business success and excellence. Hence this chapter depicting the current scenario assumes prime importance.

The interpretation of the following statements reveals the overwhelming current attitude towards mindless expansion, lack of priority given to customer service, higher focus on short term results, and therefore lack of focus on customer retention.

1. ***"If seven out of ten customers are happy, we are doing fine. Everyone can't be satisfied."***

   This was a comment passed by the CEO of a cellular company when an individual known to him complained to him about the poor levels of service prevalent in his organisation.

   We live today in an age of Six Sigma (which is a level of quality where only three errors are tolerated per million transactions or interactions.) And if this is the attitude prevalent at the top level, (how can we satisfy everyone), imagine what happens by the time this attitude percolates to the bottom of the hierarchy.

   Even if there is a ten percent increase in tolerance for errors and defects at every level we drop lower in the hierarchy, the front end service provider at the operational level who actually faces the customer will be happy with a twenty percent level of customer satisfaction. An attitude of mediocrity will percolate throughout the organisation, and it would have initiated at the top. Just for the purpose of information, the organization where the CEO made this particular comment has been taken over thrice in the past seven years. The organisation also needs a huge advertising budget and some film stars as its brand endorsers.

   The kind of attitude which leads people to make such statements also stems from the mistaken belief that most customers being victims of inertia, would not shift their service provider even if the service they receive falls short of expectations.

2. ***"Today, relationships have become important, so we are instructing our sales personnel to build relationships. In this bad financial market, customer retention should get priority."***

   Comment made by a senior executive of a Non-Banking Finance Corporation after the sub-prime crisis led to loss of investor confidence. The implied meaning is, in a boom market, maintaining relationships with existing clientele was not considered important by the management. Now that attracting new clientele has become difficult, the focus by default is on retention. If this had been the organisation's policy from the beginning, they would not have been in this mess today, and wouldn't have had been in this precarious situation. (Remember Kabir's Doha.)

3. ***"Let me say that none of us service providers would be happy with the concept of number convertibility being introduced."***

   This was a comment passed by the head of a telecom giant at the launch of an IPO for the purpose of generating funds for the expansion of his organisation. After all the queries from the audience members, (potential investors for the IPO), about various financial parameters had been answered satisfactorily by the head, one potential investor from the audience brought up the question about the possible introduction of number convertibility in the country and the preparedness of this organisation for the same. The above statement given as answer is extremely telling. It's a clear admission that service levels of the organisation are not up to the mark.

   And the same holds true across all providers across the industry. Else, if even a single service provider would have been proud about their service and hence confident about their customer's levels of satisfaction, they would have gladly welcomed number convertibility. Because of their superior customer satisfaction levels, they would be aware that they would not lose their existing customer base, and any new customers that came in would be an add-on. The only time an organisation would not welcome number convertibility in the industry would be when they were well aware that their service levels left much to be desired and that they would lose a huge chunk of existing customers from the leaking bucket which they had not effectively plugged. The admission is, "We know it, yet we would not focus on it, our priority is attracting new clientele." If they knew their service was good, they would have been confident of retaining their existing client base and would have welcomed number convertibility. The comment clearly indicates that all players in the industry are currently at a low level of service. The consumer has no option but to go to one of these service providers if he is in need of that service. So all existing telecom service providers should not mistakenly believe that they have a huge customer base because their customers are satisfied with their services and hence are sticking on. ***The reality is, customers need cellular services, and for lack of a superior option, they have to stay with their current service provider.*** In the land of the blind, the one eyed man is king. ***All it needs is one player in that industry to raise the service bar and reap exponential benefits.*** (Needless to say, this would obviously be at the cost of the existing players.)

4. ***"I instruct my staff to give the bare minimum level of service the customer is willing to accept. Anything more would be a waste. I'm not here to pamper the customer."***

   This quote comes from the V.P. of a leading insurance firm which recently had to be bailed out by the U.S. Government. This statement was made during a panel discussion on marketing when the issue of customer service as a differentiator came up. The V.P. justified his statement and his stand saying that since better service has a cost attached to it, why should we as an organisation give more service than is necessary for the customer to be just about or barely satisfied? *"Why Spoil And Pamper The Customer"*, was the further justification. Obviously this gentleman had never heard of *Phil Cosby's Classic Work - Quality Is Free,* where the author clearly demonstrates with facts and figures that the extra cost of improved quality is more than absorbed and taken care of by the enhanced benefits that superior service quality provides. *"If I can get the customer to remain with me at x level of service, why should I give him x plus one"*, is the unfortunate interpretation of this statement. The answer is, *"At level x, the organisation's relationship with the customer is shaky, easily broken. At level x plus one, the relationship would be strong and possibility of customer retention and positive word of mouth publicity is much higher."* It is sadly apparent that most organizations don't offer excellence simply because they lack faith in their people and their processes.

5. ***"Our confectionery products can never be as good as the Irani bakery on the corner."***

   This was stated by the CEO of a confectionery giant which spends millions annually on advertising. In spite of state of the art technology, using the best possible ingredients, (as they themselves claim), having all possible brand endorsers dancing to promote the biscuits on prime time TV, the statement is an open admission that the vital ingredient of ***Love*** and ***Customer Orientation*** which the tiny Irani bakeries seem capable of infusing, are lacking in the multinational's biscuits. That's why we strongly believe that a passionate workforce led by a passionate leader is one of the most vital ingredients necessary for business success.

6. ***"Today we are very clear our focus is targets, volumes and growth. If in the process Customer Service suffers to some extent, it is okay by us."***

   This blatant admission of the customer being sidelined was made at a B School seminar by the Regional Manager, Marketing, of a leading private sector bank, a few years ago, when the finance markets were booming. Unfortunately this bank has won Best Bank Award of The Year awarded by certain business publications, which itself is another sham, as although the methodology of awarding is explained in the magazine, Nowhere do the parameters of customer delight, element of service, number of complaints, or customer feedback and opinion come in the picture. Only parameters such as deposit base, number of branches, breadth of product offerings, number of ATM machines, - everything to do with numbers, not quality, is considered. Which is precisely why organizations such as Satyam are awarded the Golden Peacock Award for Corporate Excellence. Most of these awards rely only on the numbers.

   Today this bank is facing tough times and has been in the news for all the wrong reasons.

   Contrast this with an example from that organization which is the epitome of quality, Toyota. Toyota in 2006 was roughly the same size as Ford at that time, and recalled less than half the vehicles that Ford did in that year for defects. Yet while Ford was happy with the number of defects, which it considered a very acceptable figure, the *Toyota Company President Watanabe was so disturbed, upset and troubled by Toyota's imperfection figure, (less than half that of Ford), that he bowed publicly in apology.*

This is precisely the attitude towards quality that a leader needs to have.

7. ***"At last we have shooed away our customers from the branch and made them use the ATM."***

This statement was made by the Head - Marketing, of a leading multinational bank at a seminar on marketing.

Banks have made their calculations and identified that it costs the bank more to interact with a customer at the teller's counter, rather than the customer going to the ATM machine. With this in mind, the marketing department of this bank, (so did some other banks), created an environment which would literally force the customer to go to the ATM to withdraw cash rather than visit the cashier, by levying a certain charge each time the customer approached the cashier for a transaction. Once a majority of customers had been coerced into transacting through the ATM and kept away from the bank premises, the head of Marketing of this bank heaved a sigh of relief and made the above statement. From the banks point of view, this may be convenient, but is it convenient for the customer? That is what is ignored and organizations pay the price in the long run.

In USA a few years ago, Citibank adopted a similar policy. Its competitors, who were not as large, took this as an ideal opportunity to approach the disgruntled customers, telling them, *"We smaller banks may not be too large, but we let you deal with us the way YOU want, keeping in mind YOUR convenience."* The customers flocked to these smaller but more customer savvy and marketing oriented banks in droves. Citibank in USA realised its folly, backtracked on its policy and tried to recapture the lost sheep, but by then it was too late. Their former customers were delighted with the caring approach of the smaller banks and saw no reason to shift.

Imagine, a Head of Marketing at a multinational bank thinking in terms of ***"At last we have managed to shoo away our customers."***

8. ***"How can we guarantee that?"***

A friend of ours runs a mid-size organisation where approximately a hundred staff are employed. He kept the salary accounts of his staff with a leading private sector bank, where the minimum balance required in an account was Rupees Five Hundred. One fine day, the bank increased the minimum balance amount to Rupees Two Thousand Five Hundred. Again within a short span, they hiked it to Rupees Five Thousand, and then almost immediately to Rupees Ten Thousand. Naturally the employees who held their salary accounts there did not want to block up ten thousand rupees in a savings account, and convinced their employer to shift the salary accounts to another bank, which had a more modest minimum balance policy. Sometime later, our friend was approached by a salesman representing the original bank where the salary accounts had been previously held. The salesman said that the bank had once again revised its policy to the older one and now once again only required Rupees Five Hundred as a minimum balance. Would he like to shift the salary accounts back to this bank again? Our friend agreed as he had always been otherwise satisfied with the services of the bank, but he had only one query. *Would the policy of minimum balance now remain stable at Rupees Five Hundred or would it change again shortly?* If so, our friend felt there was no sense in shifting and going through all the formalities of shifting salary accounts for a short period. Instead of reassuring our friend about the stability of the policy, the response he from the bank representative was, *"How can we guarantee that? It can change anytime."* Our friend politely declined the offer to shift banks. The issue over here is, an organisation cannot radically keep changing policies which impact and affect customers, just for its own convenience. A customer would primarily want stability and consistency in policy and not gross confusion. Here, the customer's interests appeared not to have been taken into consideration at all, while formulating customer related policies.

9. ***"Why should we focus on the Bakra? He is already with us."***

A friend informed us of an informal chat he once had with the Marketing Head of a leading White Goods firm, dealing in washing machines, refrigerators, and the like. The issue being discussed was one of After Sales Service, and the comparative lack of attention paid to this area by the organisation, as compared to the aggression and thrust it showed in its sales activities. This is when the above comment was made by the Marketing Head of the organisation. The Marketing Head also added, "When it comes to white goods, what is the frequency of repeat purchase in any case that I should focus so much on after sales service and customer retention?", thus completely ignoring the vital component of word of mouth publicity and reccomendations.

Why do some organisations try to fleece the customer at the first opportunity they get? Probably because they are aware that their service is so pathetic, that the customer is never going to return anyway.

10. ***"We have such a large customer base. Some are BOUND to be unhappy."***

Some of your customers, (your most valuable assets), are ***bound*** to be unhappy? Unbelievable that such language should come from a senior corporate functionary. But this was the precise remark made by the V.P. - Marketing of an FMCG firm, when an issue of increased customer complaints and decreasing satisfaction levels came up after a survey. And this comment and subsequent attitude is common in multiple sectors where the belief is that the loss of some customers doesn't really matter if the base denominator is huge.

A point for organiations with such a large customer base to ponder. Should organizations which are blessed with such a huge customer base, (obviously built through effort), now start to compromise on quality and customer experiences? Rather, they should introspect and ask themselves that if they had compromised on quality and service when they first started off, would they have ever reached this stage at which they can display this unwarranted arrogance?

Organizations with such an attitude are chopping down their own foundations by cutting corners where it matters.

11. ***"We outsource non-core functions so that we can focus on our core activities."***

    (And this organization is talking of outsourcing its after sales service, which it feels is a non-core activity. That tells you what this organisation thinks of customer retention.)

    While an H.R. executive was discussing training needs in an organisation with his H. R. Head, the H.R. Head was happy to remark that he did not need to focus on Customer Service Training for his staff as the entire After Sales Service function had been outsourced to an agency, as the function was not considered a *Core Function* by the organisation. The tragedy is that organisations focusing only on conventional accounting practices believe that *There Is No Money To Be Made In After Sales Service,* as hardly any revenue is generated from there. It's obvious that in such an environment, the only core activity is getting more sales. *Without after sales service of a very high quality being provided, the organisation's customer tap soon dries up.*

12. ***"There are at least ten new books being released every week. How can I expect my staff to be aware of them when I myself am not?"***

    When we mentioned to the manager of a leading bookstore about his staff being unable to help us with locating a book which had been newly released, forget help us locate it, they hadn't even heard about it. Ultimately when we ourselves located it on the shelf, this is the casual comment he made. Could a pharmaceutical company manager excuse his staff for not being aware about a newly launched medicine, stating this as an excuse? Could a school child get away with this answer in his exams, saying he has too many issues to memorise? Organisations should at least ensure that their staff gear up in product knowledge to assist the customer who has come in with the intention to buy.

13. ***"Please take the credit card. Don't use it if you don't want to. Tear it up after a few months. At least I will have met my targets."***

    A sales executive of a leading bank approached us with this request to avail of a credit card from him. The issue here is, the sales executive would hardly have resorted to this mindless method of attracting customers if he had not been under extreme pressure of targets to do so. The only thing that apparently he had been told was not to bother about whether a customer actually needed the card and would make use of it, but just ram it down his throat and meet monthly targets at all costs. If we pause for a moment, we will realise that not only does this not benefit the customer, (in fact it gives him a very negative perspective of the bank's functioning), but it does not benefit the bank either. After all, the administrative expense of printing a card, dispatching it to him, and other expenses involved would amount to quite a sum, and no revenue could ever be generated from such a customer. (Note, although no revenue is generated from this individual, we still term him as a customer, as he has experienced the brand.) No wonder banks have stopped providing Rexene jackets with credit cards since they've realised it would be a waste as far as most such spurious customers are concerned. Once again we see the focus is only on expanding the customer base, and quite a hollow base at that, by focusing on attraction rather than retention.

14. ***"It is back to classical marketing and stepping into customers shoes."***

    Statement made by a leading marketing person at a seminar on marketing, held after the global economic slowdown. The remark, in short, indicates that when the customer has deserted you, and you desperately miss the revenue he used to generate, you need to empathise and step in his shoes and get him back. How come this language is never heard when the going is good and organisations have an opportunity to capitalise on the goodwill rather than behave complacent and let the goodwill drain away. ***Remember Kabir's doha?*** It all comes back to that.

15. ***"In a downturn, it is crucial to maintain existing brands and communicate with customers."***

    Comment made by another speaker, a leading advertising personality, at the same seminar. We admire the arrogance in this comment. In a downturn, it is crucial to communicate with customers. Therefore, the implication is, in good times, this communication can be ignored. No wonder companies face downturns and financial bad times if this is how they distance themselves from customers in good times. *This is like the attitude of a well fed cat, which ignores its master when its stomach is full, but rushes to him purring hypocritically when it is hungry. And though it has many other virtues, rarely is a cat considered a faithful and dependable animal.*

No wonder customers have lost faith in brands if this is the way in which they see-saw.

And the key takeaways from the panel discussion where leading marketing and advertising people were present to discuss what steps to were to be taken in difficult times were summed up as:

a. Maintain existing brands by talking more with customers.

b. Focus on understanding customers and leveraging consumer insight.

c. Invest in brands with a long term perspective.

If these were takeaways and action plans from the seminar and participants who were professional marketers needed to be reminded about the same, it implies that these issues were currently forgotten and not being done. And if you recall the fable of the fun loving, irresponsible and short sighted grasshopper, and the hard working, foresighted and industrious ant, it is very clear which insect the current lot of marketers emulate.

16. ***"Forget luxuries like extended training. We want you guys to hit the ground running."***

This was a comment made by the regional head of a private sector insurance firm to his new batch of management trainee recruits. Just eight hours of training were provided to this batch of future managers for explaining to them twenty four different types of insurance policies. The trainees were then told, *"Don't worry if you've not understood the policies in detail. You can go and learn feet on street." In other words, use the customer as your guinea pig and go ahead and make your mistakes at his expense.*

Sending untrained recruits into the front line is sending them to their graves.

- Confucius

Too many organizations today have turned myopic and either skip or substantially shorten the duration of induction and training they provide to new employees in their eagerness to get these new recruits productive as soon as possible.

17. ***"Be patient. Our billing system is new. We are having teething problems."***

    This is a statement made by the billing department of a leading mobile service provider to many, many customers for a period of at least six months after they commenced operations. Customers faced multiple problems in billing on multiple counts, and when they expressed their concern to representatives of this organization, this was the standard response. In the hurry to commence operations and attract new customers immediately, quality and customer experience take a back seat.

    Perfect your systems before letting the customer experience them.

    Once again remember -

Your Customers are human beings to be treated with care, not guinea pigs to be experimented upon.

- Cyrus M Gonda, Kalim Khan

In a similar context, we would love to refer to the thought process of ***J.R.R. Tolkien,*** the author of the famed triology, ***Lord of the Rings.*** Tolkien was in the process of writing the story. It was a vast, involved and complicated tale. He was about half way through writing the story, and realized that if he continued writing the same level of quality to complete the story as he had done so far, it would take about a couple of years more to do so. He was sorely tempted to cut it short, push it out into the market, let it sell a few copies, and earn the money he was desperately in need of at that time. But he didn't do so. He ***believed*** in his story and in his own ability to do a high quality job, and took his time to complete the story, maintaining consistency of quality and detail. All those who have read the Lord of the Rings are glad that he did so. So was Tolkien himself. If he had cut the book short and pushed it out hurriedly into the market, it would never have got him the kind of financial success that it actually did.

18. ***"Till you meet your sales targets for the day, you can't go home."***

    Believe it or not, this is the real situation in one of the call centres which conducts telemarketing for a leading private insurance brand, where one of our students used to work for a short period of time. In that organization, the staff operate in two shifts, morning and afternoon. The staff have been given a *daily sales target* with a certain minimum amount of premium to be sold everyday. If a staff on duty in the morning shift cannot complete his daily target by the time his shift ends, he has to compulsorily *wait back extra hours in the evening shift without pay till he achieves his sales quota for the day.*

    Can you imagine the quality of professional advice provided to customers in such a scenario? The poor salesman will be desperate to sell any insurance package to any customer by convincing, confusing and even downright lying about the terms and conditions. And we all have interacted with such sales representatives. In such a scenario, customer retention and positive word of mouth could never ever occur.

19. ***"How can the CEO meet every customer who has a genuine complaint? There are so many of them."***

    This was the comment made by the Regional Marketing Manager of a leading Private Sector Bank to a close friend of ours, who is a senior officer with the Indian Navy. This officer, who is a customer of the bank, had major service issues which were not being acknowledged and resolved by the bank staff he interacted with. In frustration, he asked to see the top man to appraise him of the poor service being given by his bank to customers. This is the reply that he received. Shocking. After all, the most important person in any organization is the customer. and what ought to be of more concern to senior management than customer complaints not being resolved by organizational staff. And if the warped logic being used is that the ***CEO won't have time to meet customers with complaints as there are so many of them,*** we feel it is even more reason for the CEO to spare time to know why so many complaints are pouring in and why so many customers are dissatisfied with the services provided by the organization. In fact, in such a scenario, logically this ought to be his first priority. Unfortunately, its not on his list of priorities at all.

These nineteen statements we have selected from a vast repertoire are just the tip of the iceberg. They are just a small representative sample. But they speak volumes about the unwritten but established faulty norms that industry on a whole is practicing today in the garb of marketing.

Why these comments passed by top level executives of leading organizations need to be viewed with utmost seriousness is that it is the attitude at the top which percolates to every pore at the middle and bottom rungs, and affects each and every customer interaction, and ultimately the customer retention rate.

Attitude, and therefore attention devoted to customer convenience, requests and needs at the front line operational level are merely enhanced mirror images of the philosophy prevalent at the apex level of management. ***If the philosophy at the top level is truly one of Customer First, there will be a magnificient manifestation of this attitude at the operational level.***

Conversely, if top management is paying mere ***lip service to the philosophy of Customer First, a perverse parody of inefficiency and lethargy at the operational level will be the order of the day.***

A recent survey conducted among a vast number of CEO's and Marketing Heads of leading organisations asked them to rank in order of importance their business priorities. The sad results of this survey in percentage term of response are as follows:

The top three concerns of the CEO's in order of priority were :

1. Top line growth
2. Speed, flexibility, adaptability
3. Customer loyalty

The top three concerns of the Marketing Heads were:

1. Managing branding guidelines
2. Counselling divisions (whatever that may mean)
3. Sharing best practices

These responses indicate that CEO's on an average at least felt that customer loyalty was third on list of their priorities. ***For the Marketing Heads, Customer Loyalty, Customer Retention and Service Quality didn't feature in the top three list at all.***

To balance the comments discussed in this chapter, and by extension, attitudes, we do have and personally know many excellent individuals at the helm of affairs in Corporate India.

Unfortunately, the statements we have highlighted in this chapter are not exceptions, but reflect a wide spread, short term, attraction focused, (and not ***retention focused***), attitude. This is what we intended to highlight through this chapter.

Only if we face the problem, can we go ahead with the task of rectifying it.

The next chapter and the tenets that follow it is our attempt to get back on track to the True Art of Marketing.

MARKETING RENAISSANCE

Usher an era of prosperity into your organization

Every renaissance comes to the world with a cry, the cry of the human spirit to be free

- Anne Sullivan Macy

The word ***Renaissance,*** is a French word meaning ***Rebirth.*** It has its roots in the Latin ***Re***, (again), and ***Nascere,*** (be born). The renaissance was a period of great development and progress in Europe. Tremendous gains were seen in this period in the areas of literature, philosophy, music, art, and even in politics and the sciences. The period encompassed a ***revival of true learning based on classical sources.***

The renaissance began in Italy as a search for the glories of the past.

It was a cultural tidal wave that profoundly and positively impacted life in Europe, and consequently, the entire world. In fact, it has been identified as the most productive period in recent history.

It is pertinent to note that worldwide, most progress has come during periods of history where the focus of society was never on aggression or warfare.

What we need in organizations today in the approach towards the customer is not a revolution, nor restructuring, nor re-engineering, but a renaissance. Renaissance is a beautiful word. The other words such as revolution, re-engineering and restructuring are relatively ugly by comparison. Revolution, restructuring and re-engineering create ***change,*** (and not necessarily ***progress***), through some form of destruction. Renaissance does not do that. Renaissance is a rebirth, and rebirth never causes destruction. The renaissance period has been likened to the change that occurs when a veil is lifted from a man's eye, allowing him to see clearly.

When the Veil is Lifted the Vision is Clear

When one's focus is on the proper process, it is obvious that the desired result will follow.

Consider students in college who focus on obtaining marks without gaining the requisite knowledge, thus concentrating on short cuts, guide books and twenty one question sets. Similarly, organizations concentrating with myopic vision on the immediate weekly, monthly and quarterly bottom line will focus on aggressive tactics and unrealistic targets to achieve short term objectives, bypassing the long term objectives of greater error free product and service, constant proactive feedback from customers, and providing sufficient training, incentives and infrastructure to staff. If these areas are concentrated upon, automatically a healthy bottom line will emerge and sustain.

The trees that are slow to grow,
bear the best fruit.

- Moliere

Similarly, terms such as ***USP, Branding, Brand Endorser, Moments-of-Truth, Public Relations,*** which all had a certain meaning when they originated, have diluted in and diverged from their true meaning over a period of time. Thus they have lost the effectiveness and subsequent benefits which their understanding and application was originally meant to provide.

We examine each of these terms and many more in the second part of this book, as separate ***tenets,*** where the original meaning and definition of these terms will be our area of focus.

Terms which are at the forefront of marketing jargon today - terms such as ***aggression, target, aim,*** need to be deleted from the lexicon of professional marketers. They do far more harm than good, and have been responsible for the degeneration of marketing as a discipline. (We have even heard a senior marketing professional defining ***marketing*** as throwing a flock of corn to attract the geese, and ***selling*** as targeting and shooting the geese (customers), one by one, once they have been attracted.)

Just as an example, let's examine the word ***AGGRESSIVE*** - a favourite word with modern marketing practitioners. Below are a couple of typical comments indulged by them frequently.

"We want our salespeople and marketing people to be more AGGRESSIVE with our customers."

"We are looking for AGGRESSIVE individuals to join our sales team."

We are not aware whether these marketing professionals have taken the effort to refer to the word ***Aggressive*** in a good dictionary. We did undertake the exercise, and the following are the results.

Some of the synonyms to the word ***Aggressive*** we found, are:

- **Violent**
- **Hostile**
- **Destructive**
- **Belligerent**
- **Antagonistic**
- **Insistent**
- **Hard-line**
- **Uncompromising**
- **Pushy**

- **Ready to attack**
- **Oppose**

WOW

Takes your breath away, doesn't it? These are the qualities which marketers insist their sales people display. No wonder customers are increasingly repulsed when approached by sales people who subconsciously display these types of behaviour, under the garb of being ***aggressive.***

Some of the other words beloved by the marketing profession are hardly any better. Let's take some other words, ***Target*** and ***Aim.***

The only thing left after ***targeting*** and ***aiming,*** is to shoot the customer.

These are all terms associated with warfare. We even have books titled ***Marketing Warfare,*** with tanks, guns and military personnel decorating the cover.

The period of the renaissance was not connected with progress in the field of aggression and military might.

There is no victory in winning a hundred battles.
There is victory in subduing the other without fighting at all.

- Sun Zi

Warfare and aggressive behaviour always create bad and negative vibrations. Aggression as a quality, which so many marketing people look for and appreciate in their sales force, actually creates negative and unhealthy vibrations which the potential customer can immediately detect and sense.

The term ***Warfare*** carries undercurrents of the urge and lust of battle.

The outcome of any warfare, battle or aggression can NEVER be a Win-Win. In any war or battle, one side HAS to lose. And as the only two sides involved in the field of marketing are the product and service provider on one hand, and on the other hand the customer, one of them HAS to lose. Whichever one loses is immaterial. There can never be a long term relationship which does not have the concept of

Win-Win at its heart and core. And if there is no long term relationship, THERE CAN BE NO RETENTION, ONLY SHORT TERM ATTRACTION.

And even if this warfare is directed towards one's competitors, the intention being to crush them through aggressive behaviour, ***the outcome would be a stagnated industry with no motivation to innovate or improve existing products and services.***

Firstly, because most of the organization's valuable energies and resources would have been directed towards competitors, leaving little finance and energy for improving systems, quality of products and services and research and development.

Secondly, because customers can sense they are being ignored in this entire business of one-upmanship among competing organisations.

And ***thirdly,*** because in the absence of competition, (which is the ultimate objective of marketing warfare), no brand with an aggressive and therefore short term attitude would bother much about focusing on product and service improvement. The brands which are successful today did not become so by directing negative energies and wasting resources towards competitors, but by directing them positively towards customers.

In Marketing Warfare, the focus is on the COMPETITOR.

In Marketing Renaissance, the focus is on the CUSTOMER.

- Cyrus M Gonda, Kalim Khan

Today, the best organizations worldwide are not competing, but collaborating with competitors to benefit and better serve the customer and improve overall industry standards.

For example, in the pharmaceutical industry, where competition apparently is at peak levels, the safety managers of leading pharmaceutical organizations regularly meet to discuss developments they have come up with to improve safety standards in their organizations, and share these developments with safety managers of competing organizations. How does this help - you may ask. The answer is that it is impossible to constantly reinvent the wheel. Sensible individuals would rather share basic knowledge with competitors which will help to raise the overall industry standards and repute, and then individually go ahead to develop better products and provide better services to customers.

A Rising Tide Raises all Ships

We love the word ***co-opetition,*** which indicates ***picking the best from the two terms - co-operation and competition,*** which is what ***leads to healthy competition and ultimately Win-Win.***

When scarce organizational resources are rightly channelised to benefit the customer, the outputs and benefits are controllable and always in the organization's favour.

But when these scarce organizational resources are incorrectly channelised to hinder the competitor, the output and benefits may backfire.

Multiple researches across time and place clearly shows that displaying acts of kindness towards others, rather than aggression, works well for humans, giving them a longer, healthier, happier life, with more people looking at them positively and wanting to interact with them. What works for humans stands to reason works for organizations. Aren't organizations run by human beings? And aren't organizations also considered entities? And don't they cater to human needs? And aggressive behaviour can never be equated with being kind.

So by following the path of ***the renaissance,*** an organisation would be channelising its limited energies and resources into rising ***above*** what its competitors have to offer, so as to reach the level of customer's expectations, which by their very nature, keep rising higher and higher. Any organisation can do it. The organisation which wishes to follow this strategy just needs to look for the right path and follow it.

The process of identifying that path to the customer's heart, the process of going that extra mile for the customer, is the path at the heart of the Marketing Renaissance.

It is the Path to the Land of Win-Win

And it's a path on which there will be little traffic to disturb you. As someone rightly said: ***"There are no traffic jams along the extra mile."***

It's like this. You and your competitor are both currently on level five of a ten point scale on the customer's rating of satisfaction. You have limited resources with which to compete. Let us say the units of resource you possess are five. You can either use these limited resources to push your competitor down to zero, or you could rather focus on the customer and use the five units to raise yourself to level ten, not wasting your precious resources on pushing your competitor down. By doing this, you will be raising the overall standards of the industry. And remember, as we said before, ***a rising tide raises all ships.*** The path to win-win is through channelising your resources into positive efforts which benefit your organisation as well as your customer. Negative channelisation and use of organizational resources bring no added benefit to the customer.

The words and terms we constantly use reveal our subconscious intentions, and when the audience, (customers), is within hearing distance, they form their opinions of the organisation based on the language the organization through its representatives at various levels, uses. Words like ***target, aim, aggression, push strategy,*** would never endear an organisation to its customers. Customers may tolerate such an organisation in the absence of better alternatives, but would never feel a sense of belongingness and loyalty towards it, which is vital for customer retention. The moment better alternatives are available, such an organization would collapse.

The term, ***Marketing Renaissance,*** therefore needs to be embraced by all true marketers with open minds and open hearts. The way in which organisations have been currently viewing their customers needs to be given a serious rethink. The way in which terms such as Brand, USP, Public Relations, are being debauched and perverted needs to be reversed.

In short, the discipline of marketing needs to be reborn to reclaim its past glory. And THAT is the essence of the Marketing Renaissance.

The second part of this book will deal with the terms which need to be given priority by all marketing professionals.

PROLOGUE TO PART TWO

In Part One, we have touched upon the **WHAT** and the **WHY** of customer retention.

In short, the thrust of Part One was on establishing the importance of customer retention, the primary role of retention in organizational success, and all the advantages retention brings to an organisation which focuses on this vital area. The advantages include reduced cost, increased sales, enhanced customer loyalty, positive word of mouth, and reduction in complaints, among others.

In Part Two, we demonstrate through thirteen tenets, **HOW** higher levels of customer retention can be achieved by **ANY** organization, irrespective of the scarce physical resources at its command.

Knowledge of the **WHAT**, the **WHY** and the **HOW** of customer retention, along with implementation of this knowledge is our personal, comprehensive, guaranteed recipe for business success.

We have identified certain core areas or disciplines, which if followed implicitly, enable any organisation to achieve high levels of customer retention. These ideas and disciplines are not all new. But they have got distorted over time. As the sub-title of this book goes, **REMASTER THE LOST ART OF MARKETING,** it is our earnest attempt to restore the basic fundamentals of marketing in the business world.

These tenets we will talk about do exist and are demonstrated in some form or the other, in bits and pieces and fragments, by most organisations today. They are even regularly talked about at seminars and conferences. But that's where the story ends. The tenets talked about today are distorted versions of the original as you shall see. So everyone talks of Public Relations, but the concept of genuine Public Relations is rarely understood. The same goes with the terms Marketing, USP, Branding, and many others, which are distorted beyond belief.

We believe the starting point to remastering the lost art of marketing is in first calling things by their right names. What's in a name? Everything. We can't distort existing disciplines to suit our purpose and continue to label them with the old terminology.

As the ancient Chinese saying goes – "***The beginning of wisdom is to call things by their right names.***"

If we don't get basic terminologies right, we fall prey to misconceptions.

And, misconceptions will ruin good intentions.

We feel that the current trend in thinking at apex levels of management in many organizations is focused primarily towards attraction, rather than retention. Through our tenets, we will demonstrate why we feel this is the current situation, and why it should be rectified. Part One of the book has laid out the current situation into proper perspective.

Part Two will proceed to demonstrate as to how what is termed as an ideal, (and therefore according to many, unachievable in reality), can actually be achieved by any organization which follows our tenets in entirety.

The message of our tenets is equally valid in good times and bad. In boom economies and rough. In developing economies and developed. Our message is not only a good time message or a bad time message.

If an organization can put these tenets to work, if an organization can honestly say it scores considerably high on all of them from the customer's perspective, it's a recipe for success. And the beauty is that none of these tenets cost a lot to implement. In fact most of them show you how to save money. (For example, the tenet on Advertising and the tenet on Brand endorser.)

Our Brains Trust Customer Retention consultancy model and programme is structured around these tenets to provide your organization with a scorecard through quantified research to show where your organisation stands on this vital parameter.

The beauty of the model is that there is no special equipment, technology or additional investment required to implement these tenets.

ETHICS – THE FOUNDATION STONE TO MARKETING SUCCESS

With Ethics at the core Organizational Revenues will Soar

Today, ethics in marketing and in business is no longer an option. It is mandatory. It is a must.

Why do we put this tenet first? Not for alphabetical reasons. But simply because without ethics in place first, the other tenets would make no sense.

Ethics is the oil in the wheel of marketing

So what exactly do we mean by ethics in marketing? Simply put, it means treating the customer as you would like to be treated if you were in his place.

Any individual who is familiar with the spiritual texts of his religion, irrespective of whichever religion he follows, would have no difficulty in understanding the difference between right and wrong. There are no grey areas, ***repeat, NO GREY AREAS,*** when it comes to ***ethical behaviour with a customer, who is the ONLY source of an organisation's bread, butter, jam, and cheese.***

Providing the customer with complete and correct relevant information, fair pricing, ensuring a quality product and service, full disclosure of even inconvenient truths, understanding his unique needs and requirements and doing your best to meet them, being attentive to his needs and queries even after he has paid the bill, and much more - All these are signals of strong marketing ethics at work.

Although organizations complain that customers are getting more unreasonable and difficult to please and satisfy, we have observed over a period of time that a species termed as the ***Unreasonable Customer*** is very rarely found in reality. It's largely a mythical beast. A figment of the imagination.

Upset customers? Yes. Many abound. Unreasonable customer? A very rare species.

As far as we have observed, every *upset customer* we have encountered has had *a valid underlying reason* for being upset. Maybe his expectations were higher than others. Maybe his temperament was hotter than most.

But there will be in most cases, a genuine reason for his apparently unreasonable behaviour.

Let's ask *YOU* as a reader a simple question.

Of all the occasions that *you* have ever been upset as a customer, in how many of these occasions do you feel you have been *unreasonable or unjustified?*

Most customers would answer - *Very rarely, if ever.*

There is a *world of a difference* between someone who is termed as an *Unreasonable Customer,* and a *Customer who is upset for a valid reason.* When customers get upset with an organisation, it is usually for a genuine, valid reason. No one walks into a McDonalds and gets upset because he wasn't given five-star levels of service at the table. No guest attends a Jain reception and expects a chicken dish to be served.

Customers approach organisations which they believe will serve the particular need that they have at that point of time, in the most desirable manner possible. And they approach the organisation with certain expectations, which the organisations themselves have built up, mostly through some advertising message or the other.

It is only when those expectations are not met do we get to see an upset customer. And if organisations *clarified* all aspects of their product, service, and the entire transaction, going into depth to communicate and clarify the minutest detail on which the customer may have ambiguity, *then unreasonable expectations from the customer's end would never be a problem.*

This is an area where the following of marketing ethics would lead to a ***win-win*** situation for all concerned. But most organisations believed :

"Why tell the customer everything? He may not make a purchase if he has all the information."

Or, the classic excuse provided by organisations for not providing sufficient relevant information about the product or service to potential customers :

"He may get confused."

Wow. It's the duty of the organisation to proactively explain all aspects of the purchase that may affect the customer clearly to him so that no confusion occurs.

Unfortunately, in corporate life, how many have the time to explain all these elements to the customer in depth. ***Or the inclination to do so?*** The misplaced priority is to rush to the next sale without completing the current one to the customer's complete satisfaction.

Ethics is quite an inconvenient word in marketing today. It appears to get in the way of short term profits.

That's the current general opinion at this moment of time.

Yes, practicing ethics may appear inconvenient. But so is the practice of many other essential apparently inconvenient truisms. For example, it is also inconvenient to chew your food thoroughly before swallowing it. But all these truisms have stood the test of time and provide immense benefits to those who have faith in them and follow them always.

Arthur Andersen as an organization felt ethics to be inconvenient.

So did Enron.

So did Worldcom.

And Tyco.

And Satyam.

And many other organizations did so as well.

In fact, 'ethics' was considered such a redundant term, the relic of another age, that in Business Schools in USA where it was offered as an optional subject, the faculty who taught it could consider himself fortunate if a couple of students opted to attend ethics lectures.

But then arrived the ethical scandals of the year 2000.

Fortune 500 companies tumbled by the wayside.

A similar freefall has started in the Indian IT sector in 2008, with Satyam leading the pack. The fault lay not in the stars or destinies of these organisations, but in the policies of the organisations themselves. Ethical considerations towards customers and shareholders had been put aside for rapid short term profit escalation. The organizational cupboards overflowed with skeletons, till finally the skeletons tumbled out in a Tsunami fashion.

Leading organisations simply ceased to exist. One common factor could be attributed as a root cause to all these corporate tragedies. The organisations in question had lost their ethical way.

They had taken the wrong turn at the crossroads of Ethics.

All of a sudden, the very same MBA classrooms where Ethics lectures had gone almost empty and unattended, were now overflowing with students. Seating space being saturated, the students literally stood at the door to absorb the inputs being provided in this ***now*** vital area of business.

That's where the problem with ethics lies. Ethics is an area where organisations tend to be ***reactive,*** rather than ***proactive.*** Wells tend to be dug after the organisation catches the ethical fire. By then, in most cases, it's just too late.

Exaggeration, tall claims, putting untrained staff in the customer frontline, falling back on technicalities as excuses (the all time favourite - ***system or technical failure***), using poor quality raw material, the ever present ***"Conditions Apply",*** over promising and under delivering - all these are ethical lacunae committed by many organisations in business today. And these affect customers and customer perceptions about the organisation negatively.

Why then, are such things resorted to?

They are resorted to under the false impression that such self destructive activities strengthen the bottom line.

But nothing could be further from the truth.

Legality Versus Ethics, which Lies at a Higher Level?

Many organisations claim and perceive that as long as they are legally in the right, ethics don't matter. We pity such organisations. The following quote beautifully explains why shrewd reason would always be subservient to honest truth.

I have one request. May I never use my reason against truth.

- Hasidic Rabbi prayer

In marketing and in business, resorting to legality to justify unethical behaviour can only work up to a certain extent. Beyond that extent lies the vast ocean of ethics.

We recall an interview a senior advertising personality had given to a magazine a few years ago, in which he proudly stated, ***"For me, there is no difference between legality and ethics. If the law permits it, I don't let my conscience act as a barrier."***

Do you feel the difference matters? We feel it matters. And it matters big time.

So too, felt ***Abraham Lincoln.***

There is a wonderful anecdote concerning Lincoln, who was a lawyer before he became President of the United States.

Once, while handling a case, he listened to a prospective client's statement, then abruptly rose up and said, "Well, you have got a good case in technical law, but a pretty bad one in ethics, equity and justice. You'll have to get some other lawyer to win it for you. I couldn't do it. All the time standing while talking to the jury, I'd be thinking, ***'Lincoln, you're a liar.'*** And I believe I should forget myself and say it out loud."

Not recognizing this difference between legality and ethics has its impact on the bottom line of an organisation in a damaging way.

As a wise man once said - *"An advertising copywriter without values and ethics is nothing but a stenographer."*

A clear conscience is the greatest armour.

- Chinese proverb

Consider the following scenario. An organisation spends great effort in legally protecting itself against returned goods even if the customer's grievance is genuine, by having a very carefully worded "Exchange and Return Policy", which clearly favours the organisation and not the customer.

The organisation smugly shields itself behind a legal barrier and tells the customer, ***"Legally we are in the right."***

Fine. Legally you may be in the right. The customer may not be able to legally redress his rights. But can he resort to other activities? He can. He can *stop buying* from you completely if he feels he's been unfairly treated. *(This increases the size of the hole in your bucket.)* He is also free to go ahead and speak of the negative experience he has been subjected to with all means at his disposal, and thus influence maybe hundreds of others from ever dealing with you again. *(This widens the hole in the bucket still further.)*

Loss of confidence, goodwill, damage to reputation, people thinking ten times before deciding whether to deal with you or not. Is this worth it? Think it over. If you feel it is, go ahead.

But the attitude your organisation displays towards this vital but apparently trivial issue can mean the difference between business success and failure.

Failing to recognize the difference between ethics and legality can mean the difference between success and failure for an organisation.

- Cyrus M Gonda, Kalim Khan

Recently there was a front page article in a leading newspaper, which highlighted how a film had been advertised, by claiming that any viewer who did not like the movie for any reason would be refunded the amount he had paid for his movie ticket. A disgruntled viewer, (Customer), of this movie ***Ek – The Power of One,*** who said that the movie did not appeal to him at all, that it was far too violent, didn't have a good storyline, had characters who were unappealing; was harangued and made to run from pillar to post by the production house which had released the movie and which had advertised the commitment of a refund. The viewer was made to call up the office and personally visit it umpteen times, where he was made to wait long hours. Ultimately someone from the office curtly told him that the whole world had liked the movie, and should they make another movie specifically for his taste? He was asked to give a written complaint explaining the reasons why he didn't like the movie, and the production house would review the letter to see if his reasons were valid. Then he was called to the office and given a cheque for Rs. Fifty Five, (the price of the movie ticket.) The viewer was highly upset that the production house wanted publicity and wished to demonstrate to the world that the movie was so brilliant, and that they conveyed that everyone would enjoy it. But the moment a genuine complaint was received, the production house of the movie which must have spent millions to get the movie produced, was so stingy, that to refund Rupees Fifty Five which they themselves had committed, they hemmed and hawed and gave the refund with very bad grace, suffering a lot of negative publicity in the bargain.

The idea of refunding the ticket price to any viewer who did not enjoy the movie was wonderful. But why not carry it forward to its ethically logical conclusion by actually delivering on the commitment?

To counter this, take the example of ***L.L. Bean,*** an American icon in mail order purchase. L.L. Bean, who was the pioneer of the chain, himself had the hobby of fishing. He realized that when he went fishing, the gear and clothing available in sporting goods shops were not up to the toughness that was required and which he desired. He got into the business of producing quality equipment and gear for outdoor activities. He was so confident of the tough material he used to produce shoes, that he gave an unconditional guarantee for the same. "Anytime within ***TEN YEARS*** of purchase of these shoes if you feel that the quality has let you down, you are free to enter the L.L. Bean store and get them exchanged for a new pair. No questions asked." And the policy was followed in practice.

THAT'S CONFIDENCE IN YOUR PRODUCT.

When you have that confidence in your brand, it transfers itself to your employees and your customers. A warm glow then surrounds the entire organisation, almost like a spiritual aura.

We do have some organisations realizing the value of this tenet today. The retail chain, ***Tata Westside,*** follows it as a philosophy, and it works wonders. We met someone who told us that he was so impressed by the return policy of Tata Westside he personally experienced, that the next time he wanted to purchase a television for his household, he thought of no other place than ***Croma,*** the electronics store. What's the connection? Nothing, apart from the fact that ***Croma is also a Tata brand.*** This customer realized that he wasn't simply dealing with Westside as an organisation. He was dealing with the ***HOUSE OF TATA***. He put his faith in the mother brand. If the television he purchased gave him a problem, (as any electronic product could), he now was comfortable with the knowledge that the parent brand, Tata, would do everything to ensure he didn't have to run from pillar to post to get his complaint redressed. That's the power of genuine branding. And that comes from healthy, positive Moments of Truth experienced by the brand's customers. As we shall see in the ***tenets*** on ***Brand*** and ***Moments of Truth,*** the only way to build a brand with the strength of steel, is by approaching the objective through the path of ethics.

I have seen people drown and burn,
but I have never seen anyone harmed by doing good.

- Confucius

Ethical Auditing

We earlier mentioned an organisation named Arthur Andersen. It used to be the largest Audit Firm in the world. The 'Big Daddy' among the Audit Firms. How did it get to be so big? Well, that's a good story. And a true one.

Arthur Andersen, the founder of the firm, was one of thousands of other CPAs (equivalent to the Chartered Accountant in India), in the 1930's. Just one CPA among many others. There was nothing unique about the services he provided or the knowledge of auditing and accounting he possessed.

Yet, his firm grew for one reason, and one reason alone.

Arthur Andersen clearly understood who his customer was.

And he serviced him ethically, even though in the short term it may have been inconvenient for him to do so.

Who *is* the customer for an audit firm? It's not only the man who pays the bill and the organisation whose accounts are being certified. *The actual customer for an audit firm is the POTENTIAL INVESTOR who bases his decision to invest in the firm based on the audited accounts.*

(Remember the chapter on Customer versus Consumer? The customer could be any individual who uses and experiences the product or service, he need not be the buyer. *According to the traditional definition of the term customer, these potential investors would not be classified as customers, as they don't pay or buy from the auditor. That's the limitation of the traditional definition of the term CUSTOMER. That's why these important people, the potential investors, are ignored if one follows the traditional definition of the term customer. The potential investors don't pay the auditor his fees.)*

While most other Audit Firms at that time were sacrificing their ethics and certifying balance sheets which were not true and correct, simply so they could get short term business, ***ARTHUR ANDERSEN REFUSED TO DO SO.***

The man and the organisation that he led were crystal clear on that point. He had very clearly identified his customer not only as the man who paid the bill, but more importantly as the men (potential investors), who would read the accounts statements he had certified, and then make their investment decisions based on these.

He wanted these potential investors to get the true and correct financial picture.

If he lost some business because clients wanted him to certify incorrect account statements, then that was perfectly fine by him.

His competitors laughed at his apparent foolishness and lack of "Business Sense."

But soon, something strange started to happen.

The potential investors, (the true ***customers,*** although not the paying ones), started to realize that if Arthur Andersen had certified the accounts of a firm, they were genuine. Arthur Andersen did not certify accounts which were to put it at best, inaccurate; and to put it bluntly, fraudulent. If he felt there were grey area in the accounting statements of his client, and if the client was not prepared to compromise and clarify them, Arthur Andersen could well do without such clients.

His fame grew. So did his reputation.

Now investors started to put their faith in organisations where the accounts had been certified by Arthur Andersen. Investors started investing in such organisations. Organisations started to realise that if they wanted investors to put money in their firm, getting the accounts certified by Arthur Andersen would be the best bet.

Arthur Andersen's certification was like an iron clad stamp of authority.

Arthur Andersen's business thus grew and grew.

He had the last laugh.

All because he stuck to his principles, even though it initially meant some loss of business. ***He put his true customers first.***

In Arthur Andersen's words, "My own mother told me in Norweigian, ' THINK STRAIGHT- TALK STRAIGHT.' No finer heritage could possibly be passed on from one generation to another. It has been as a firm rock to which I could anchor in a storm. Never has it failed me. This challenge will never fail anyone in a time of trial and temptation."

Now comes the sorry part of the tale. Arthur Andersen, the man, passed on (as all men do), and the organisation which bore his name was now managed by new hands and with new minds. Minds which soon deviated from the principles and ethics which had made the organisation the largest and most trusted audit firm in the world.

Minds which put the true customer, (the potential investor), in second or even third place.

The organisation now began certifying accounts without verifying their accuracy, as long as the client was willing to pay an inflated bill. Enron was one of their clients.

All possible financial manipulation that could be conceived was present in the accounts statements of Enron. Yet the Arthur Andersen representatives saw no wrong. ***Blinded by greed, they ignored the interests of the investors (the true customers), who they were supposed to keep uppermost.***

Such deception and manipulation could not last forever. Enron collapsed overnight like a pack of cheap cards. Arthur Andersen too, ceased to exist. It was ordered by Government decree to wind up operations and cease functioning as an entity forever, for having participated in the deluding of investors (customers), who had put their faith in it.

The Moral of the Story?

Arthur Andersen initially grew to be a giant in its industry simply because its founder followed a high set of ethics towards his customers. Arthur Andersen's rise to greatness and the Number One position it enjoyed in the audit industry could be attributed towards the path of ethics it adopted in respect to serving its customers.

The organisation's sudden fall, by direct contrast, can be similarly attributed to the deviation from the path of ethics towards customers that its future bosses chose to take.

As Arthur Andersen proved, strengthening and securing a reputation for being ethical is a very strong Unique Selling Proposition. Customers pay a higher price to such organisations for their products and services, peaceful in the knowledge that quality and delivery will be as per commitment.

One for the Road

One more incident, for the road, fittingly from an automobile giant. In the 1970's, an American automobile company, developed and sold a model of car which they later realized had an inherent defect. Ideally the cars should have been recalled and the defect rectified. Hundreds of thousands of that model of car had by now been sold. The management of the company played smart, (or thought they did.) They did some calculations. They calculated the amount it would cost them per car to recall it, rectify the defect and send it back to the customer. Then they multiplied this amount per car by the total number of cars they would have to do this for. Let's call this figure as **X**.

Then they did some more mathematics. They tried to calculate the number of cars in which this defect could lead to a probably fatal accident for the occupants, (customers), and they multiplied the compensation they would have to pay per fatality by the number of probable fatalities. Let's call this figure as **Y.** The figure **X** was considerably greater than figure **Y**, and this made the management's job easy (or so they thought.) Based on these numbers alone, the management took a decision that it would be more convenient and cost effective ***NOT*** to recall the cars. They preferred to let the estimated number of fatal accidents occur, pay compensation for the same, and spend a lesser amount overall. This is precisely what they did.

Then the predicted accidents started to occur. Compensation was paid out, and it was later unearthed that the management of the company had full knowledge of the defect and thus were aware of the fatal danger it could potentially pose to customers. But they had chosen to not recall the cars merely because of the calculations involved. There was a huge public outcry. ***The reputation of the organisation took a tremendous beating, and the goodwill and consequently the sales they lost over the next decade and more, far outweighed the amount they would have had to spend if they had done the right thing and recalled the cars in the first place.***

When a man's fight begins with himself, he is worth something.

- Robert Browning

Browning indicated that it is convenient and simple for any man or organisation to take the path of least resistance. The path which gives him immediate gain. But when the man begins to question himself for taking the easy way out, when he *begins to fight with himself,* as Browning so aptly puts it; that's when his eyes open to the folly of following this easy path, which ultimately drops him off a cliff without warning. It is at this point, when the man decides to take the right path, even though it does not give him short term gain, is he *worth something.*

Yes, Honesty does have a small price attached to it.
But it's worth paying that small price,
else you will soon pay a larger price for ignoring it.

- Cyrus M Gonda, Kalim Khan

Every industry and each leading organisation has had its share of defects. Nokia, Sony, Toyota - have all had their share of product failures.

But what puts these brands in the top drawer of faith and trust as far as the customer is concerned, is that when these brands became aware of defects in their products, they proactively took measures to recall the defective products and took suitable action to rectify or replace the defects. Such actions go a long way in restoring customer faith and enhance the customer's association with the brand. ***Does the brand stand behind its defects and honestly rectify or replace them when things go wrong?*** That's what gives customers confidence in the brand.

A Brand will be strong

When it improves on it's wrong

- Cyrus M Gonda, Kalim Khan

The customer is not so irrational to unrealistically expect that products never can and never should fail. They can. ***But what the brand does AFTER the failure becomes known to it, differentiates between an ethical top class brand and an unethical also ran.***

Values are the signposts on the path of Ethics.

- Cyrus M Gonda, Kalim Khan

The ethics we follow are based on the values we hold dear.

There are over the surface values which we display for public consumption.

And then there are underlying values which form the rock solid foundation for our deepest decisions.

What goes UNDER the Hood Matters most in the Long Run

There are many more examples similar to the ones above which we could provide, but these ought to suffice. They send out a most clear, unambiguous message to all organisations, that all success in business and marketing comes from putting the customer's interest first and foremost.

The examples we have focused on relate primarily to ethical practices of organisations which concern the customer, his interests, and the service and attention he receives.

There is definitely a need for ethical practices in ***all*** aspects of an organisation's functioning, but since the starting point of any organisation's activities should be the customer, if an organisation is ethical in its dealings with its customers, it stands to reason that ethics would be a way of life with the organisation in all its dealings.

As an example, we would like to cite the example of an organisation, ***CDSL,*** the ***Central Depository Services Limited.*** This organisation clears all its supplier's bills within the maximum period of a week. If a particular supplier's bill is not cleared within a week for any reason, the CEO of CDSL, Mr. V. Raut, has to be informed by his accounts department immediately, and the CEO would want to know the reason why the bill has not been cleared. And once the cheque reaches the supplier, if he doesn't deposit it in his account for whatever reason, (he may forget to do so), a CDSL employee will remind them that their cheque has not been deposited.

In a day and age where even cash rich organisations try every trick in the book to delay payments to their suppliers, here is the ethical CDSL, which goes out of its way to pay its creditors as soon as possible. This ethical policy on their part sends across a great message to all stakeholders that dealing with this organisation is going to be smooth in all respects.

Such policies and practices send down a very strong signal from the CEO to all staff in the organisation that ethical practices in this organisation shall be a way of life.

Another organization we appreciate in this regard is ***Godrej.*** Among the many training programmes we regulary conduct for them is a programme on selling skills for their sales managers and sales team. The Human Resource department which organizes this training ensures that at the heart of our customized training module, we as the trainers communicate and reiterate the ethical organizational values of ***Godrej*** at the forefront of the training programme, as they wish their front end sales persons to imbibe and display this philosophy to the outside world. They would prefer their sales person to not make a sale, rather than push a product on to a customer who doesn't have a need for it. This is why Godrej as an organization is still thriving and expanding after a hundred years of being in existence.

At Brains Trust, it is our strong belief that Ethical Behaviour is the route to marketing success. We also strongly believe that the concept of ***Ethical Behaviour*** can be understood and expressed through a ***formula*** which we have devised for this purpose.

Brains Trust formula for Ethical Behaviour

An organisation or an individual continues to remain ethical as long as its:

Capabilities > Desires

(Capabilities are GREATER than Desires)

Unethical behaviour and subsequently unethical activities surface and become prominent when its:

Desires > Capabilities

(Desires EXCEED Capabilities)

What one needs to understand is that ***desires are uncontrollable and continue to multiply.***

Capabilities are qualities, skill sets and competencies, which individuals and organisations need to constantly develop for continuous improvement to occur. An organisation needs to constantly enhance its capabilities. These enhanced capabilities in turn become an organisation's ***USP or offerings.***

Until the point in time when capabilities and capacities are equal to, or exceed desires, unethical practices will never occur.

This is simply because available capabilities shall create outcomes that are capable of meeting desires. So even if desires continue to multiply, (as is natural), the increased and enhanced capabilities which have been developed are more than a match for satisfying these desires.

It is only when desires exceed capability and capacity, (which decide one's income and inflow), that ethical behaviour begins to take a backseat.

Any individual or organsiation where desires are greater than capabilities, capacities, and competencies of deliverables; can and ultimately will fall prey to unethical practices.

We in no way are implying that desires ought to be controlled. It is essential to be ambitious in order to grow and expand. That in itself is desirable.

But in line with increased desires, increased and enhanced capabilities and competencies need to be the focus of any organisation's activity base, so that both sides of the equation are balanced or are in sync with each other.

This is why, ***continuous improvement*** for organisations is absolutely a must. Hence, any organisation which practices the Japanese philosophy of ***Kaizen,*** (continuous improvement), in its entity and essence is bound to be ethical in the right sense of the word.

When the above become a way of life, then the organisation's aims and interests will be achieved as well.

The entire tenet on Ethics was brilliantly practiced and demonstrated by the late ***Mr. Shanbag*** of ***Strand Book Store,*** the grand old man of the Indian book trade. When we once met him, he opened his briefcase, in which the maxim, ***"The Customer Comes First",*** was prominently stuck on the inside of the top of the briefcase, visible each time he used to open his briefcase. "That's great," we told him.

He asked us if we understood what it meant. We said we did. That for him, the customer always came first and was uppermost in mind.

He told us that was only half the message. Just one part of it. The complete picture he told us would emerge if we looked beyond the obvious.

He continued to explain what he meant. "Yes, for me the customer does come first. Uppermost. The reason for all my actions. But since I put the customer first, **THE CUSTOMER ALSO IN TURN PUTS ME FIRST.** Everytime my customer thinks of buying a book, **HE COMES FIRST TO ME.** It's a two way street." So it's not only ethical to keep your customer first and uppermost, it's highly profitable as well.

Ethics is not a luxury. It is a vital need. Its presence may not be noticed, but it's absence is life threatening to any organisation.

In a nutshell, here is why we put Ethics at the top spot as far as our tenets are concerned.

1. First and foremost, we have seen time and again, through example after example, of organisation after organisation, in age after age,

that it is the ***only*** way of doing business which makes long term business sense.

2. Let's understand the basic fact that financial benefits to business houses accrue only through repeat business. Repeat business is a function of trust. And trust is a product of faith. Faith for a customer transpires only when he has solid reasons to believe through experiences which consolidate his belief that the organisation he deals with is ethical in all aspects of behaviour which concern him. ***Ethical outcomes are not a function of an organisaton's financial strength, but rather it is the other way around that holds true. That is, organisations which display ethical behaviour are bound to achieve financial strength.***

3. The more that ethics take an organisational backseat, inevitably the more will systems in all their aspects and discipline for that organisation be ignored. And if an organisation lacks systems in its functioning, it simply cannot be a long term financial success.

4. The first teachings we learn as infants pertain to ethics, which come from the spiritual texts of the religions to which we belong. Thus it is fitting that the tenet of Ethics, which is the direct outcome of the wisdom of these first teachings we obtain in life, ought to take pride of place, logically, as well as emotionally.

Unfortunately, Ethics today has become more of a REACTIVE OUTCRY rather than a PROACTIVE CONSIDERATION, uttered only when scandals and disaster strike organisations and the economies they function in. Seminars and conferences on ethics are purely farcical displays when done reactively in response to scandals. Ethical organisations would never need such false window displays. Their actions would always speak louder than words.

- Cyrus M Gonda, Kalim Khan

Today, most organisations try to run with the customer before he is ready to even walk with them. The attempt on the part of the organizations is to try to create an environment of hype and delight before succeeding in winning the customer's faith. We strongly advocate that it is ***faith*** which should come first and supersede Customer Delight. Wouldn't it be ***delightful*** to ***acquire*** Customer Delight as a ***by-product*** of Customer Faith, rather than ***lose*** faith in a hurried and half-baked attempt to demonstrate false Customer Delight?

Any part of the manufacturing or service process which does not meet the required and projected levels of quality in all it's aspects, thus negatively affecting the customer experience, whether the customer is aware of the deficiency and lacunae at the instant of purchase or consumption or not aware at that time, is an ethical lacunae which ultimately affects the marketing of that brand adversely. For example, we have seen recent examples of pharmaceutical giants falling by the wayside as they falsified data while testing new molecules. This came to light much after the tablets had been developed, manufactured and consumed by trusting patients. These patients, (customers), lost faith. So did shareholders. The loss of future revenue as a result was a foregone conclusion.

Following ethical practices, and consequently attaining a rock solid reputation, while crucial to the success of all firms, acquires even more importance for firms which fall under the service industry. This includes accounting firms, software organisations, insurance companies, telecom giants, banks, airlines, hotels, and many more.

As Brian Sommer, the former Accenture partner put it, ***"There are only two things a service firm has, its people and its reputation."***

With the tenet of ethics firmly entrenched as an unshakable entity, let us now proceed to the remaining tenets to understand how the customer relationship can be still further cemented.

We would like to conclude this tenet by defining Ethics from a marketing, (i.e. the customer's), perspective –

E - xceptionally

T - rustworthy &

H - onest

I - n

C - ustomer

S - ervice

Remember always - ***Basics through Ethics.***

MARKETING PHILOSOPHY AND NOT SELLING PHILOSOPHY

Revenue abundance Through selling redundance

Marketing and Selling

Two apparently linked terms.

Yes, as far as ***physical function*** goes, they are closely inter-related.

But as far as philosophy, approach, attitude and mindset go, the two are as different as chalk and cheese. No two words could be further apart in meaning. Because as we will demonstrate, ***IF YOU GENUINELY MARKET, YOU DONT NEED TO SELL.***

For top management which is responsible for formulating a ***strategic perspective*** for the organisation, it is the ***philosophy*** behind the two terms which should be kept uppermost in mind. That's where the true interpretation of the two terms lies.

A multinational organisation, spending tons on advertising, promotional events and integrated marketing communication exercises, may still be following the selling philosophy in spite of having a marketing department and having a marketing budget of millions.

But on the other hand, a tiny organization, with no budget for self promotional activities and no separate marketing department, may be in top gear, operating in the genuine marketing mode.

As the saying goes, it's all in the mind. It all depends on the philosophy of top management as to which path or philosophy out of the two is the chosen one for the entire organisation. (Remember the chapter on strategy?)

A word of clarification before the chapter commences in earnest. Please don't get us wrong as to the difference between the two terms. There is nothing wrong with the ***function*** of selling. In fact there is everything right with it. Selling is the ***only*** function in the organisation which generates revenue, and all sales people should be justifiably proud about their chosen profession.

Our argument is not against the ***function of selling,*** which is a noble profession. What we are against is an organization following the ***selling philosophy,*** which is something totally different from the function of selling.

It is ironic that great and memorable selling activity can best be done by following a marketing philosophy, and not a selling philosophy.

- Cyrus M Gonda, Kalim Khan

So when we are discussing the difference between selling and marketing in this tenet, we are not looking at the functional difference, but the difference in philosophy between the two terms.

Let's begin to understand what the difference between the terms, ***"Selling philosophy"*** and ***"Marketing Philosophy"*** is all about.

In simple terms, the ***selling philosophy*** or mindset can be said to prevail in an organization if the organization consciously or subconsciously, continues to put its own interests at the forefront and gears its processes and functioning to suit self convenience, thus making the selling mindset obvious to customers through its unwillingness and reluctance to be flexible and customize organisational offerings, even though it may be easily possible for it to do so.

Correspondingly, a ***marketing philosophy*** can be said to prevail in an organization if it consciously and constantly puts the needs and interests of customers uppermost, and gears organizational processes around customer convenience and requirements, even if that means making life a little difficult or inconvenient for the organization in the short run.

The Chinese Marketing Philosophy

Let's begin with a simple question. What's your opinion regarding the quality of Chinese made products?

A possible string of adjectives as answers could include; bad, poor quality, substandard, low grade, unreliable, etc. But that is just not true.

Another question. When buying a Hot Water Geyser, what parameter would you keep uppermost in your mind? Heating capacity? Low power consumption? No, the first thing you would look for is safety and reliability.

A piece of information. The majority of hot water geysers sold in India (and in several other countries as well) today, are manufactured in China. If their quality and dependability was not up to the mark, this would definitely not be the case.

Another bit of information. One of the major reasons that the American economy has been in the doldrums for the past decade is that it has been flooded with Chinese products. Now the American consumer (notice we didn't say customer), has traditionally been a very quality conscious individual. For him, low cost has not been as important a parameter while making a purchase decision as quality has been. Thus the fact that Chinese products have flooded the American market and are doing so well, is a function of their acceptable quality, even by high American standards.

Recently, a newspaper report mentioned Warren Buffet and Bill Gates as saying that they preferred wearing the suits manufactured by a Chinese suit-maker, as they found them to be superior in quality to any suits manufactured elsewhere.

A friend of ours narrated an incident which occurred when he visited the U.S. many years ago and wanted to purchase a carry bag. He saw a bag of a well known American brand for $ 150. In the same store, he also saw a pair of bags, Chinese made, identical to the single American bag, and both the Chinese bags together as a pair were priced at $ 150. (So he could literally get two for the price of one,) He debated which option to pick up, decided to go for the two Chinese bags, has been using both of them for years, traveled all over the world with them, and they still are as rugged as the day he bought them. Looking back, he feels that the American brand which cost twice the price may have been made in the same factory as the Chinese bags. He would only have been paying double for the label. Now obviously if you were offered ten Chinese bags for $ 150, they would ***by nature*** have to be of poor quality. Ten American manufactured bags for $ 150 could be no better.

The point is, we have to compare horses with horses. Granted there are Chinese products which are poor in quality, but in any country, when you pay peanuts you get monkeys.

We give this background so we can now demonstrate how good the Chinese are at following the genuine marketing philosophy, keeping the customer uppermost in mind. Let's take a look at the ***Chinese way of marketing.***

Let's assume for example that you're in the business of making a simple product like a ceiling fan. If you follow the ***selling philosophy,*** you will keep on making the same types of fans that you're used to making and are comfortable in manufacturing, and push them out into the market, supported by a blitzkrieg advertising campaign, hoping that people will buy them.

But if you're following the ***marketing philosophy,*** you will not produce a single fan till you go out into the market, speak with potential customers, ask them their likes, dislikes, tastes, preferences, requirements, and give them as many options and varieties that you can in keeping with their preferences.

In the selling philosophy, the organizations are less bothered about their customer's satisfaction, they are more bothered about the immediate sale. That's why, when an organisation follows the selling philosophy, the customers are in turn not bothered about or loyal to such an organisation.

Let's carry forward with our example of the fan. We all know what an

inverter is. It's an instrument which provides the power to keep your fan and other electrical gadgets going when the electricity supply fails. An inverter in India costs around ten thousand rupees, (around two hundred dollars), and every year one needs to change or recharge the battery of the inverter, which costs another two thousand rupees approximately.

IN CHINA, THEY ARE MANUFACTURING FANS WITH BUILT IN INVERTERS AT ALMOST NO EXTRA COST WHICH KEEP THE FANS MOVING EVEN WHEN THE POWER SUPPLY FAILS.

What would you call this?

This is the ***TRUE MARKETING PHILOSOPHY*** at work. The Chinese have understood an important, genuine need of their customer and addressed it by centering their product and entire organizational systems around the ***customer's*** convenience.

Another example from China. Take the most common vehicle on the road today, the bicycle. In India, if one goes to purchase a bicycle, the options available in terms of size would be - small, medium and large. In terms of colour options, one may be offered red, green or blue. But in China, if a person goes to purchase a cycle, he will not even be shown the cycles first. He will be invited into a room, the service providers will measure his height, weight, his leg length and the arch of his foot. All these details about him will be entered into a computer programme, which will determine the ideal cycle frame, shape and size for his body size, shape and type.

Then they will take the customer into another room, where he will be shown a range of colours, seat types, handles, carriers and other accessories. The customer can select his preferences on these parameters, and the same will incorporated in and attached to the ideal frame which has been specifically designed for his body type. In forty eight hours time, the customer's custom made cycle is ready for him at hardly any extra cost.

Again, what would you call this? This is the true ***MARKETING*** philosophy at work.

Or take your fire cracker industry. Again the Chinese have put true marketing philosophy at work. What would be the main problem with a fire cracker from the customer's point of view? Fire crackers are dangerous, unstable and may blow up in one's face while being lit. The Chinese manufacturers have understood this very well, and are now starting to produce fire crackers with ***REMOTE CONTROLS*** which can be burst from a distance with no possibility of harm to the customer. What do you call this? You got it right. ***MARKETING***.

All these examples don't appear to be marketing related in the conventional stance of the word as we understand it today. There are no film stars or sportspersons involved as brand endorsers. There is no visible high power expensive advertising. There are no paid press releases, nor what goes on under the name of Integrated Marketing Communication.

What ***does*** exist in the Chinese philosophy is a true, genuine understanding of, and concern for the customer and his needs, and centering the organizational processes and systems around these needs, requirements and conveniences. ***THAT'S MARKETING PHILOSOPHY AT WORK.***

If the genuine marketing philosophy is constantly at work throughout the length and breadth of your organization, then your costs and efforts to sell your products and services need be minimal, or even non-existent.

- Cyrus M Gonda, Kalim Khan

As the saying goes, if your customers need mousetraps, then build a better mousetrap with features which are more convenient and user friendly for your customers, and the world will beat a path to your door.

Unfortunately, some people normally tend to only latch on to one parameter of Chinese goods - that they're cheap, and they're not even aware of, or tend to ignore all these other genuine marketing efforts the Chinese put in.

The wonder of it all is the Chinese have rarely advertised their products. Rarely do we recall a Chinese brand name or logo or even an advertisement inducing us to purchase Chinese goods. It's simply the magic of ***Brand China*** at work.

Check out most of the dollar shops (buy anything for Rupees 49 or 99), in your locality and you'll find they're flooded with Chinese goods. And these shops do roaring business. We recently picked up a good quality magnifying glass, with a nice rubber handle and a directional compass attached to the handle, for rupees fifty. We also picked up a nice tool set with about twenty handy tools in a rexene carry case for rupees fifty. Visit your nearby malls and you'll find potato peelers, fruit scoops, attractive toys, innovative kitchen tools and equipment, puzzles, pencil boxes, colourful wall hanging rods for towels, decorative articles, ***ALL CHINESE MANUFACTURED.***

And it is not only in the manufacturing sector that the Chinese demonstrate the true marketing philosophy at work. The same holds true for the Chinese approach to services, where customer orientation, eye for detail, and commitment hold sway.

An example from the pen of the author of ***One Land, One Billion Minds,*** when he recalls his visit to China.

He mentions about his train journey from Shanghai to Beijing on a magnetic levitation train, which travels at over four hundred kilometers an hour. The cubicle in which the author traveled had four berths, and there was a tiny toothpaste tube with toothbrushes for each of the four passengers. There was a pair of bathroom slippers for each of the four passengers too. But the icing on the cake was that each of the four slippers was of a different colour, ***so that each passenger could differentiate and identify his own slippers. As the author says, it was a simple gesture, but delightful in its simplicity***. Literally putting oneself in the customer's shoes, (or in this case, in the customer's bathroom slippers), and understanding what would be things of importance to him. ***That's true marketing.***

We are ***NOT*** the advertising agency for the Chinese. All we're trying to say is that the Chinese have got the concept of ***MARKETING*** as a ***PHILOSOPHY*** bang on. We strongly feel that genuine efforts at marketing need to be appreciated and used as benchmarks to be followed. The Chinese don't ***NEED TO SELL OR ADVERTISE OR PUSH their products.*** Customers are waiting to pick up what the Chinese have to offer as soon as their products reach the shelf. ***SUCH HAPPY SITUATIONS TRANSPIRE***

WHEN THE MANUFACTURER AND SERVICE PROVIDER HAVE KEPT THE CUSTOMERS UPPERMOST IN HIS MIND. As someone once said, IT'S THE MOST WORTHLESS PRODUCTS THAT NEED TO BE ADVERTISED THE MAXIMUM, OVER AND OVER AGAIN. But provide a product or service that someone genuinely needs, just announce it, and people flock towards such suppliers and service providers.

Again, we are not against advertising as a discipline, as it's necessary to create awareness and inform consumers about new developments and features in the product or service. But if a hundred year old brand such as an aerated cola needs to constantly advertise merely to keep people aware of its existence, then somebody in that brand has not done their job well, or it's just a product that doesn't fill a genuine need in the first place.

The textbook definition of ***advertising*** itself states, ***"A medium to create awareness and provide information about product or service price, features and availability."*** What percentage of advertisements today provide these basics? The focus rather is more on moronic entertainment and high level exaggeration. (More on this in Tenet Three.)

Buzzzzzzz Marketing

In fact nowadays, the trend has shifted away from paid advertising and moved towards ***BUZZ MARKETING. Buzz*** represents the sound the bee makes as it gravitates from flower to flower. The logic behind ***buzz marketing*** is that the organization gears up to provide such a fantastic experience to the customer, that he becomes its fan, and spreads the good word about the organisation from his heart from person to person that he meets, the same way that a bee goes ***BUZZING*** from flower to flower, carrying the productive pollen along with it.

Making Life Easy for your Customer

We used to lecture at a series of training programmes for Chartered Accountants on enhancing communication and general management skills. In one particular programme, there were about seventy Chartered Accountants in the training room. We decided to conduct a simple exercise. We called two of these Chartered Accountants forward and showed them a sample mobile bill of a particular cellular service provider. We told both of them to go through it and understand what each of the headers and entries in the bill meant to them. Columns and headers in the bill such as current balance, amount carried forward, rounded off, carried back, value added services (which include items such as SMS's), and multiple other columns. We then asked them to explain what each of the entries and columns and headers meant. Being Chartered Accountants, and experts in finance, the two of them could not agree on what all the column headers and entries did mean. They were confused. Our job was done. They were not to blame. The error lay with the way in which the bills have been designed in such a confusing format that the vast majority of users would never understand every entry on them. But ***IF*** the bills could be designed in a simple and easy to understand format for the most illiterate of customers (which the mobile companies also target), ***THAT*** would be considered as ***true marketing philosophy at work.*** And we don't think that that's such a difficult task for the cellular providers.

A similar, real life example from the birth place of marketing activities, the United States, comes to us from the book - ***Beyond Quality.*** It goes as follows.

One fine day, the President of ***Fidelity Bank,*** Rosemarie Greco, stopped to fill up petrol at a petrol pump in Philadelphia. She paid by credit card. The owner of the pump saw her name and designation on her credit card, and took the opportunity to tell her that he was applying for a loan at Fidelity Bank, but didn't clearly understand the terms and conditions for the loan. When he explained the terms and conditions of the loan which confused him, ***she as President of the bank confessed that she didn't understand them either.*** She went to her office, spoke to her loan officer concerned, got the petrol pump owner on a conference call, and went over the terms and conditions line by line with him, assisted by the loan officer.

All this brings us to the next important issue. ***WHOSE JOB IS MARKETING?***

Marketing as a philosophy cannot be left to the Marketing department alone, but it is ***EVERYBODY'S JOB.*** It is truly a holistic activity. True marketing needs to be indulged in by each and every member of the organisation. Whoever in the organization has made life easier and more convenient for the customer has participated in the Marketing philosophy. Everyone in the organization needs to know the product and service offering thoroughly and acquaint themselves with diverse customer needs so that they can be creative in their own work areas and create improved systems within their job responsibility to enhance customer experiences. Everyone in the organisation needs to be made aware of the concept of quality from the customer's perspective.

If there is one secret to success, it lies in the ability to get the other person's point of view and see things from his angle as well as your own.

- Henry Ford

Each individual staff member representing the organization can and should make the customer feel comfortable, welcome, and feel glad he dealt with the organization, whether these staff are in direct contact with the customer or not. For example, the individual or team which devised the format of the mobile bill should not do so in isolation, but ideally after a lot of customer interaction and feedback.

Research need not only be conducted in areas which lead to immediate sales enhancement.

Research in areas of customer comfort and delight ought to be an organizational and marketing priority. So should the inculcation of this welcoming marketing philosophy among all members of the organisation. ***The minutest element can make a customer decide which service provider to select for satisfying his needs.***

Marketing Begins with a Smile

There is this marvelous example provided in the book, ***The Power of Nice*** which referred to the Account Director of a large advertising agency. There was a client which this particular agency, as well as a competing agency, were keen to secure. The decision maker from the client's end visited the offices of both the agencies, and then made his decision to go with the first agency. The Account Director of this agency was delighted. After he got a little comfortable with the client, he asked the client as to what made his decision swing in their favour. Was it the quality of work they had done in the past, the proven ability of their creative people, or any other such USP.

The client mentioned that as far as these things were concerned, the two agencies were almost at par. Which is why he said it was such a difficult job deciding between the two agencies in the first place. But when he visited the office of this particular agency which he ultimately selected, he was given such a cheerful greeting and a broad genuine smile by the doorman at the gate, that he made up his mind on the spot. He felt that any organisation in which the doorman, standing the entire day in the heat outside the gate, could still manage to give such a cheery, enthusiastic greeting to visitors, was definitely an organisation which treated its people well. ***In such a healthy environment, quality work was bound to be produced.***

Would you Call the Doorman a Great Marketer?

Most definitely. After all, it's entirely due to his effort, attitude and behaviour that the agency managed to secure a highly sought after client.

Similarly at the ***Shopper's Stop outlet in Bandra, Mumbai,*** we have observed our very own Smiley Face, the lift attendant ***Mr. Sadanand Parab.*** He has been with the Shopper's Stop chain for a long time, and we recall his ever smiling face whenever we enter the outlet. He always has a cheery greeting for us. When we visited the mall on a Sunday evening, (the 12th of July, 2009), he was merrily distributing toffees to visitors at the mall and to his co-workers. We asked him what the occasion was, and he said that it was his birthday and he wanted to share it with visitors at the place he worked. A truly great gesture. We wish him a long, happy life ahead and hope the management of Shopper's Stop realize and appreciate how fortunate they are to have the services of their ever smiling ambassador, Mr. Parab.

On the other hand, we have heard our friends telling us of surly attendants at certain institutions who have literally put visiting customers off mood and made them walk away to the competitor.

As we said, ***Marketing is everybody's job.***

And the beauty of the marketing philosophy is, ***THE MORE YOU***

GENUINELY MARKET, THE LESSER YOU ACTUALLY NEED TO GO OUT AND PERSUADE AND SELL. So whether it's the Research and Development team, the Production team, the Finance team, they ***ALL NEED TO BE AT THE HEART AND CORE OF THE MARKETING EFFORT,*** ensuring that products are designed and manufactured, and services are generated and provided at *all times, keeping the end customer constantly uppermost in mind. The customer's convenience comes first, always and everytime. This is what the marketing philosophy or mindset is all about. As you see, you don't need a separate marketing department to do this. And conversely, in spite of having a full fledged "marketing department", your organisation may still be in the selling mode and stuck in the rut of following the outdated sales philosophy when it comes to actual practice.*

Are you Operating in Reverse Gear or Top Gear?

We refer to the ***SELLING PHILOSOPHY*** as ***REVERSE GEAR*** and the ***MARKETING PHILOSPHY*** as ***TOP GEAR,*** because these are the diverse directions that these two ***DIVERSE, OPPOSITE*** philosophies will lead you to.

So, is ***YOUR*** organization as a whole ***GEARED UP*** towards the ***MARKETING PHILOSOPHY?*** This has to be your ***ORGANISATIONAL STRATEGY*** for success. And this is what leads to customer retention and positive word of mouth publicity. It has to be the organisation's underlying and overlying strategy. It has to get priority at all times. This has to become part of every policy, every action, the very DNA of your organization. Your ***OWN*** convenience as an organisation has to come secondary. Once this message is very clearly conveyed from top to bottom in your organization and is understood and absorbed by all concerned, and followed in every customer interaction, ***THERE IS NO OTHER PLACE YOUR ORGANISATION WILL OCCUPY IN YOUR INDUSTRY BUT THE VERY TOP.***

As the ***Ritz-Carlton*** hotel policy goes, whenever a guest says, ***May I make a request,*** the staff have been trained to reply, ***"THE ANSWER IS YES, NOW WHAT IS THE QUESTION."*** Brilliant philosophy. Even before the guest request is made, it is agreed to be undertaken by the hotel staff, provided the request is ***ETHICAL*** and ***LEGAL.*** And the staff is trained to put this philosophy in practice and have been given the resources to carry it through. Do you think any guest who has stayed at a Ritz hotel would ever be happy staying in any other hotel ever again?

The question in your mind may be, "That's all very well for an organisation with the resources such as the ***Ritz-Carlton*** to say, ***The answer is yes, now what is the question,*** I just run a small shop. What can I do to differentiate?"

Our answer is, it's not the physical resource that prevents you from differentiating in a positive way. What typically holds organisations back is that they ***DO NOT ADOPT THE MARKETING PHILOSOPHY IN TOTALITY.***

In the chapter on the ***Tenet of USP,*** we provide numerous examples of small businesses which have managed to find a niche and go many extra miles for their customers, thus generating tremendous customer loyalty and customer retention for themselves in the process.

The Ritz is not in the happy position of being able to fulfill unique guest requests and requirements because it has vast resources.

It has been the other way around.

It has vast resources as a result of repeat business and retained guests which is the outcome and result of putting in place this policy of going the extra mile even from the time they were a fledgling organization with scant resources. But what they did have in abundance was a true marketing philosophy, initiated by the founder, Cesar Ritz.

The Ritz marketing philosophy has been soundly put in place by the hotel chain's founder, Cesar Ritz himself. Ritz was a simple peasant with hardly any education. Yet today his name is synonymous with excellence in hospitality.

Ritz formulated four rules for his hotel staff to follow:

- To see all without looking.
- To hear all without listening.
- To be attentive without being servile.
- To anticipate without assuming.

To give but one example of the single minded devotion that ***Cesar Ritz*** gave towards customer orientation, the following makes for delightful reading. Before Ritz opened his Grand Hotel in Paris to the public in 1898, ***he personally slept in a different room of that hotel every night to check and inspect the quality and comfort of each and every mattress.***

With such fanatical attention to detail and customer convenience displayed by the top man, an organization cannot help but succeed in its aim of customer retention.

Identify what ***YOUR*** organisation can do extra to delight your customers. But whatever extras you have identified, ***YOUR*** organisation has to do it. Not an external celebrity mentioning it as a gimmick on your behalf.

Selling Ice to Eskimos Just doesn't Work

We were once participating in a seminar on marketing and were seated in the audience as we were scheduled to be the next speakers on the agenda. It was a mixed audience consisting of working executives, retired individuals, housewives and management students. And the speaker who was on stage before us said a line to justify a point he was making. A line which has been often heard.

He said, - ***"THE BEST SALESMAN IS ONE WHO CAN SELL ICE TO THE ESKIMO."***

Immediately a person from the front row of the audience got up, rushed on stage, grabbed the mike from the speaker, and challenged him, saying, ***"IN THE SHORT TERM, FROM THE COMPANY'S POINT OF VIEW, THE BEST SALESMAN MAY BE THE PERSON WHO CAN SELL ICE TO THE ESKIMO. MY QUESTION IS, DOES THE ESKIMO NEED THE ICE?"***

BRILLIANT.

This is a very, very valid question and one which needs to be asked with repeated regularity by any organization which follows the ***GENUINE MARKETING PHILOSOPHY.***

If you can avoid falling into the trap this statement encourages you to, it will do wonders for your credibility and ultimately your sales, your market share and your profitably. ***Following the philosophy in the***

Eskimo statement relegates one into the category of the conman. A cheat. A hit and run artist.

IN THE SAME STUPID WAY, MANY RECRUITERS CONDUCTING INTERVIEWS FOR SALES PERSONNEL ASK JOB APPLICANTS THE STUPID QUESTION, "SELL THIS COMB TO A BALD MAN", OR, "SELL THIS PEN TO AN ILLETERATE PERSON."

Nonsense. The title of the book, ***"How to sell anything to anybody",*** has done the ***maximum damage to the sales profession.*** Such things just can't be done successfully over any period of time. It destroys the salesperson's and the organisation's credibility.

Such techniques don't develop selling skills, they build cheating skills.

Gift of the Gab is NOT a Marketing Skill

Let's assume that you have a slick tongue and manage to convince an Eskimo to buy some ice. (In short, convince someone to buy something he doesn't need.) Five minutes after you have made the sale and left him, and he has had time to think, he realizes he's been ***cheated.*** There's no other word for it, however much you try to sugarcoat it.

This can only lead to a ***WIN-LOSE*** situation, (the salesperson wins, the customer loses), which ultimately will lead to a ***lose-lose*** scenario. (Refer the later tenet on ***Moments of Truth,*** which will elaborate on this.)

Why do we say ultimately lose-lose?

Because neither will the cheated customer ever buy ***this*** product from you ever again, nor will he buy ***any other*** product that your brand or organization represents ever again, nor will he ***ever recommend you to anyone ever again.*** In fact he will go out of his way to spoil your name wherever possible. Isn't this a large price to pay for gaining one sale?

Does this mean that you are not supposed sell anything to an Eskimo? Not at all. But sell him something he needs.

Does this mean that you should not sell ice to anyone? Yes, of course you can. But sell ice to people who need it.

This means that if you follow genuine marketing principles, you eliminate the need to sell.

The only reason why a salesman would attempt to sell a refrigerator to an Eskimo or a comb to a bald man is to meet his ***OWN SHORT-TERM SALES TARGETS.***

In short, to achieve his ***OWN*** objective rather than understanding and satisfying the customer's need.

Our simple message for any marketer is - Identify genuine customer needs, whether overt or subconscious. Don't get into ***CREATING*** needs such as pet rocks, which were a rage in America in the 1960's as a fad. This ***hollow creation of needs*** is precisely why soft drink firms spend fortunes on their advertising messages, drilling them into the brains of consumers over and over again. And even then these firms are still losing ground to healthful alternatives such as juices, mineral waters and the like. ***You can't create needs which don't genuinely exist and expect such a situation to last forever.***

Average brands create needs. Great brands don't stoop to creating needs. Great brands identify and cater to needs which already exist but may not have been fulfilled.

- Cyrus M Gonda, Kalim Khan

So the statement about selling ice to the Eskimo should be altered to read - ***"The superior marketing person is the one who identifies what the Eskimo needs and provides it to him, or identifies who needs ice and provides it to him, thus generating retained customers, assured revenue, goodwill, positive word of mouth publicity, credibility, high market share and enhanced profitability."***

Once again we reiterate – Don't get carried away by that conman title, ***"How to sell anything to anybody."***

It's a loser's game plan. It just can't be done. It's a foolish short term approach which lacks depth and vision. The only thing such an approach can do for your marketing career and for your organization, apart from gaining a few immediate sales, is to destroy your long term professional credibility forever.

A wonderful lesson was taught to one of us by a shoeshine boy on the street. The pair of shoes the boy was asked to polish was a light shade of brown. The shoeshine boy said, ***"Sorry, Sir, the brown polish I have is of a slightly darker shade. It may darken the colour of your shoes permanently. I wouldn't want to spoil the shade you obviously prefer, since you've chosen to wear that shade."***

Fantastic. The next time, we wore black shoes and specifically went to his stall, although there were other shoeshine boys around. He is now our regular shoeshine boy, and now stocks all shades of polish, catering to all his customers.

This shoeshine boy realized that it is all right to lose a sale, but not to lose a customer. He had the genuine marketing philosophy at heart.

A Stair can Show you Care

One of the best truly customer oriented persons we have ever had the good fortune to meet is a restaurateur by the name of Vinod Kamath. He runs a restaurant called ***'Bamboo Shoot.'*** It is located at Khar in Mumbai. The food is fantastic. But the personalized attention Vinod provides to each guest is even more fantastic. The reason his guests continue to return is the fantastic customer orientation they experience which for Vinod has become a philosophy of life. We will not get into the intricacies of the many extras he provides his regular guests, but the following two examples will sum up the essence of his marketing philosophy. His restaurant is located on the ground floor of a building. There are six to seven other shops and restaurants located in the same building on either side of his restaurant. The footpath outside that building is at quite a height from the road, and it is inconvenient for the elderly to step up onto the footpath from the road if they intend to visit any of the shops there. In front of his restaurant, Vinod has put a small metal ladder which has two steps and a side bannister to hold on to. Not only people visiting his restaurant, but also all customers visiting the neighbouring shops gratefully use the small staircase he has thoughtfully provided. Vinod didn't ***need*** to go this extra mile. In fact, the shops next to him haven't done so. He has done this because he ***cares*** and desires to give ***convenience*** to his customers, and helps others in the bargain as well. This is the essence of the marketing philosophy.

Vinod also goes out of his way to provide his guests with the dishes and tastes they crave for. If as a regular guest you mention to him about a fantastic new dish you tried in another restaurant, he will visit that restaurant, try out that dish and prepare an improved version of it for that guest the next time he comes over.

No wonder Vinod's customers return again and again and again, and get their friends along with them.

The Marketing Philosophy Explained in Six Easy Steps

Following the genuine marketing philosophy is actually very simple. The following steps, if adopted by your organization, will ensure that the marketing philosophy is the one that your organization practices at all times.

- First, identify your strengths and capabilities as an organisation.
- Match your identified strengths with areas of genuine customer need.
- Provide quality products and services in these areas of customer need.
- Build your product and devise your service as carefully and as lovingly as though your own children were going to use it.
- Sell your product or service at a reasonable price at which you make a reasonable profit, and your customer also gets value for money.
- Provide after sales support, stand behind your product or service, provide a solid guarantee. Constantly take customer feedback, improve and innovate.

That's it.

That's the entire marketing philosophy in a nutshell.

Whether you're in the business of making rat-traps or rockets, ***there is no other step involved.*** Everything else worth learning about in marketing are just examples to stretch and justify the above six points.

As we mentioned in the introduction to this book, ***Dale Carnegie*** explained when he wrote his classic work, ***How to win friends and influence people*** **–** 'The entire message of the book I could, and have, delivered in half a page. The rest of the one hundred and forty nine pages in the book merely consist of examples and anecdotes to reinforce the points I have stated in that half a page.'

Make it Easy for your Customer to Spend his Money

Organisations today cry foul that business is down, that customers don't use the purchasing power they have at their disposal. ***It is not that customers don't want to purchase. The problem, rather, is that most organizations, especially in the retail sector, are making it damn difficult for people to buy what they want.*** A few examples of what we ourselves undergo as customers would justify this.

Let's begin with music stores. As we are music lovers, and lovers of specific genres and artists which are not very commonly available in India (although many fans of these artists and genres that we love exist in India), we have a hard time trying to find the kind of music we like on the shelves of music stores. There are some particular country music artists such as Willie Nelson and Merle Haggard who are our favourites, who have released over fifty albums each internationally. And these artists are just representative samples of the ones we like to listen to. We can easily provide the names of at least a hundred other artists, very popular even among many Indian fans, whose albums are easily available in other countries and on sites such as Amazon, while almost no music store in India stocks these or is willing to procure them for a customer. All of these albums by these artists are currently available in music stores overseas and even on the Amazon site. Yet when we visit some of the best music stores in the country, we never find these albums on the shelf.

We have personally requested the attendants in these stores to procure these albums for us. The answer has always been a brief, ***"Not possible. Buy what's on the shelf."***

We have even gone to the extent of telling them that we are willing to pay a hundred percent advance for these albums, plus a premium as service charge for their efforts, and we are willing to wait six to eight weeks for delivery.

The answer from their end is still the same. A big fat ***NO***.

The reason?

The retailers feel it's too much of an effort to go out of the way for individual customers. Imagine, in a day and age where competition is increasing by the day - businesses say they have to extend unlimited credit to customers if they want their business, and sales simply are not happening - here are customers willing to give a hundred percent advance, an additional service fee, and willing to wait for delivery. Yet the organizations shun such customers as they don't want to go out of the way to make an extra buck.

And these responses come even from organisations which claim in their slogans that they are the MUSIC STORES OF THE UNIVERSE.

What a laugh.

Here they are unable to get you what's freely available RIGHT HERE ON PLANET EARTH.

This is what we mean when we say that taglines (for example, Music Store of the Universe), ***make no sense unless backed up by delivery.***

The same holds true for books. And shirts, and trousers, and shoes of leading brands.

For example, we recently visited an exclusive showroom of a leading apparel brand in the Oberoi Mall in December 2008, when their new collection of premium shirts, in which they had tied up for a promotional campaign with a recently released movie, had just been launched. We saw a shirt with a very nice design and immediately asked to see it in size 42. All the five shirts they had in that design were size 40. The design and that entire collection had been launched just two days prior with great fanfare, and now they told us there was no way they could get us a piece we wanted in our size. The design had come in extremely limited stock and was sold out. Imagine the expenditure and effort involved to tie up with the movie and then being unable to deliver what the customer wanted, in just a couple of days after launching the collection. It was such a lovely design that we immediately visited all the Shoppers Stop stores which also stock the same brand of shirts in the hope of getting it there, but it was simply not available.

This is the level of effort that customers take to make a purchase, but brands are simply not bothered. ***What loyalty can brands then expect?***

And we wanted to buy two pieces of that design of shirt each for ourselves, at Rupees Fourteen Hundred a piece. That meant Rupees Five Thousand Six Hundred of revenue, (cash down) lost, for the brand. And how often do we all experience this type of thing, when we go with the intention to buy and are disappointed at the non-availability of stock and lack of effort on part of store staff to procure us what we want? What purpose do advertising and promotional activities serve if they only attract but cannot deliver, in most cases?

In a recent training programme we conducted, the question of recessionary market conditions came up. The fact that organizations bemoan the lack of business, and correspondingly the lack of revenue. We asked the thirty nine participants in the training programme how often they had entered a retail outlet, found something in a design they liked, and were told it wasn't available in their size. Every single one of the participants could recall at least five such instances each in the recent past. Each of these individuals could easily have provided at least Rupees Five Thousand worth of business to the brands they frequented, simply if what they wanted had been available. Imagine, lakhs of rupees of potential business lost among the thirty nine participants of this programme alone. Organizations have no right to bemoan lack of business opportunities till they rectify this unhealthy situation.

We also recently visited a large store of a leading white goods chain to purchase a washing machine. More than half the models which their advertisements claimed they stocked, (which had attracted us to visit the store in the first place), were simply not there. The staff attending us was disinterested in responding to even basic queries. The only thing they kept saying about particular models which we enquired about was the price, which we could easily read for ourselves. How one model differentiated from another was a matter on which they completely lacked knowledge. We walked out in disgust.

In all these organizations, it appears as if the management was reluctant to create systems and an environment which would enable a customer to spend his money.

On one hand, things which the customer DOES NOT need or want are pushed and thrust onto him, (sell ice to the Eskimo), and what the customer DOES want is perversely and sadistically withheld from him. (Not in stock. Don't know when it would come.)

It is amazing that many of these organizations have invested heavily in technologies such as SAP, which if used efficiently, would provide answers to most of these queries regarding when articles requested by customers would be available. But corresponding investment in training the staff and investment in improving policies to make them more customer centric are simply not given the importance they deserve by most organizations today.

The Niche is where the Money is

The book, ***THE LONG TAIL,*** cites the clear advantages and benefits of catering to niche markets, where profit margins are much larger, and competition is far lesser. The only drawback of catering to niche markets is the expenditure involved in stocking niche products which could possibly result into dead stock.

But in the examples we just quoted, even this risk does not exist, as customers were willing to pay a full hundred percent advance, and were willing to wait weeks for delivery. No question of dead stock would arise in such a scenario.

We doubt that these requests for specific items and designs and models pass up the chain of command from the store staff to the decision makers at the top of the hierarchy, and that's where the crux of the problem lies.

The fact is, there is more business available than businesses are geared up to handle, if only they put the customers convenience, taste and preference first, and not their own.

This extra effort that organisations in most cases refuse to take is what makes the difference between service mediocrity and service delight.

- Cyrus M Gonda, Kalim Khan

AND IT IS DELIGHT WHICH TRANSLATES INTO DOLLARS.

RAPTURE WHICH WILL TRANSLATE INTO RUPEES.

This is what we mean when we speak of the difference between the Marketing and the Selling philosophies.

The point is, if organisations become flexible and customer centric, and customise their offerings to suit customer needs and requirements, their balance sheets would be in a much healthier state.

On one hand, brands dealing in apparel, accessories, books, music and the like bemoan the lack of business and are spending huge amounts on advertising to attract people to walk into their stores and outlets. On the other hand, when customers ***do*** walk in to these stores with every intention to make a purchase, on many occasions they walk out disappointed, as what they want is not available, nor is any attendant interested in following up on their request. All this despite the fact that many customers are willing to pay a premium for the same.

Zara Shows the Way

Contrast all the above examples of marketing lethargy and indifference with a brilliant international apparel brand called ***Zara.***

In a Zara store, rarely does a customer walk away disappointed. Even if he does, the top management of Zara immediately comes to know about it and the reason for disappointment is rectified. Let's see how Zara does it, where others fail.

In brand Zara, the top management is connected and in constant touch with events and interactions happening on the shop floor in their retail stores. They not only focus on their top level managerial functions, they constantly involve themselves in day to day operations. Makes sense, doesn't it? After all, strategy formulation is of little use if the implementation is shabby or ignored. At Zara, the top management takes constant proactive feedback from store attendants about customer requests and about which designs and sizes are customers trying on and asking for.

Based on this proactive feedback, management responds quickly. The wheels and systems of production and logistics are centred around this feedback and do not operate in isolation.

What The Customer Wants, The Customer Gets

And he gets it as soon as it is possible for Brand Zara to deliver. Customer requests are not ignored, but are treated with the importance they deserve. All this results in the customer getting what he wants when he enters the store, or at least he is able to place a request and get it delivered.

Customers have told us that they rarely walk out empty handed from a Zara store.

In the Indian apparel brand we spoke of where we could not get the shirt of choice in our size, it is obvious that the top management does none of this. It is not responsive to customer taste and preference. Very few pieces of a particular size in a particular design are provided even to premium stores, even though the same range is heavily advertised and promoted. Once a customer does enter the store, he literally feels he has entered a ration shop. The aim appears to be purely to entice the customer to visit the store. (Customer Attraction at work.)

Before you build a better mousetrap,
it helps to know if there are any mice out there.

- Yogi Berra

The difference between being selling oriented or marketing oriented as an organization is all about attitude. True marketing, or understanding and putting your customer first, comes easily if your organisation has the right attitude. But as someone so aptly put it, ***"An easy task becomes difficult when you do it with reluctance."***

The Big Bad Bank

Taking a case of two players in the same industry and how they differently handle similar customer requests would give a detailed insight as to how following the two different philosophies of selling and marketing can affect customer attitudes with regard to organizations.

The following is a real incident which was recently narrated to us, and it concerns the banking sector. Our observation has been that in India, ***nationalised banks*** in general provide a superior level of service and have a genuine understanding of customers needs as compared to ***private banks*** or ***foreign banks.*** This despite the fact that the nationalised banks operate in a comparatively low key manner.

A Finance Manager with a Multinational Fortune 500 organisation based in UK, having operations in India, shared this anecdote with us. In January 2009, the auditors of this multinational organisation wanted the ***Balance Confirmation Statement*** from the four banks in which the MNC had its accounts, so they could commence the audit process. All the three nationalised banks where the MNC held its accounts gave the balance confirmation statements on the day the request was made. No reminders were necessary. The one foreign bank where the MNC held its accounts, (this bank extensively advertises itself as being very customer oriented and helpful), did not submit the statements. The next day as well, after repeated reminders, this bank kept giving the excuse that submitting the statements would take time, as these things get processed in its back office in another city. By the way, the three Indian nationalised banks, having many more branches and a larger customer base, and thus more overloaded with work than this foreign bank, didn't give this as an excuse. On the third day of requesting, after repeated reminders, the foreign bank grudgingly sent across a ***soft copy*** of the required balance confirmation statement. The MNC had to then take a print out of this soft copy, and obviously since it was not on the bank's letterhead, nor did it carry a bank official's signature, it didn't look authentic. It looked as if the MNC had prepared the statement itself. The auditors were very upset, and made their displeasure known to the finance department of the MNC. Within a month's time, the MNC closed its account at the foreign bank, and shifted the funds to another nationalised bank, which deservingly won this huge chunk of business as it followed a true marketing philosophy of understanding the customer's requirements, rather than burdening the customer by giving excuses. ***If processing done at a back office in another city was the cause for customer delay, obviously the bank's processes are not centred around customer needs, but rather around the bank's own convenience.*** At a subsequent meeting which the Finance Manger of the MNC had with a senior manager from this nationalised bank which won the extra business, the representative of the nationalised bank mentioned, ***"We don't focus too much on advertising. We prefer to let our work speak."***

It is a disgrace for a man's words to be greater than his deeds.

- Confucius

When your work speaks for itself, don't interrupt.

- Henry J Kaiser

Talk low, talk slow, and don't say too much.

- John Wayne

You may term the above bank episode as a one off case, but it's not. Such instances are being reported with increasing regularity. ***And the still more important issue is, if this is the service (or lack of it), provided by this bank to a Key Account, imagine the plight of an average retail customer.***

These banks tend to put their own processes and convenience in the forefront, compared with which the customer's needs are treated like those of an unwanted stepchild's.

If low profile nationalised banks which operate under bureaucratic hurdles can be efficient, what prevents all Private and Foreign Banks from being even more efficient, especially since their service charges for every transaction are so high. The reason nationalised banks perform better and are more efficient, can be related to low attrition of staff, who know the processes of their organization and have their customer's needs at their fingertips.

Also it is due to the extreme importance that nationalized banks give to the function of employee induction and training. Private and foreign banks on the other hand, spend huge amounts on advertising, which could be better diverted to systems improvement and enhanced employee training. Despite customers being more demanding and banking becoming more complex, employees who join these Private and Foreign banks find that the number of days of training provided to newly recruited management trainees reduces drastically each year.

Nothing could justify our contention of shortened duration of induction better than the following:

A batch of MBA students who joined a private sector bank as management trainees in 2007, received a fifty day induction in banking processes and functioning. The batch of students who followed them in the same bank as management trainees in the following year, had their induction period reduced to only ten days.

Recently, when one of us authors who has a Public Provident Fund account with the ***State Bank of India,*** Bandra Branch, visited the branch to get the PPF passbook updated, we found that the person who handled the PPF section was not on his seat. An officer in a cubicle at the back of the branch, who saw us waiting, immediately came out, and helped us cheerfully. When he was thanked for going out of his way, he smiled and said, ***"I love helping customers, whether it's my department or not, I can't let a customer wait in my branch if I can help it. It's our organizational culture, I guess."*** It was a really pleasant experience, one that will be warmly remembered, and as a result, the overall image of the organization goes up several notches in the value chain in our eyes.

To illustrate the shifting trend of customers towards nationalised banks, the following would throw light. After the recent Satyam fiasco, the software giant Infosys, noted for its ethical functioning, decided to be even more transparent than it usually is, and was proactive in publicly disclosing where its assets lay. A newspaper article stated that in a short span of time, Infosys had transferred around a thousand crores of rupees from an Indian Private Sector Bank to a Nationalised Bank, namely the State Bank of India. These are very clear indicators as to where the trust of the large depositor lies.

A good definition of Marketing therefore would be the set of all those activities which make the sales function redundant.

Put Yourself in The Customer's Shoes (Literally)

The idea then is for brands to pull up their socks and give customers what they want, provided organisations as professionals feel what the customers want is good and right for them. ***PUT YOURSELF IN YOUR CUSTOMER'S SHOES, OR RATHER IN THEIR FEET.***

Speaking of feet, both us authors wear size ten in shoes. It's not such an unusual size in feet. In our experience, at least one in six men wear size ten shoes. Yet, when we used to visit most Bata showrooms and select a design, and ask for it in size ten, seven times out of ten the response is a "Sorry, not in stock." That's it. No getting in touch with their warehouse or distribution centre to check availability. No asking for our contact details so they could get in touch if and when the shoes arrive. In short, they gave the impression that they couldn't care less whether the customer feels that someone in the store cares.

And this is such a pity, because the Bata brand, started by Tomas Bata in Czechoslovakia about a century ago, was at one time the epitome of goodness and excellence when it came to shoes and service. Our fathers still swear by the Bata quality and durability which they experienced from the brand in previous years.

An addendum. *This* year Brand Bata gave us a very pleasant surprise. Before the monsoon of 2009 commenced, Bata came out with a lovely range of formal and semi formal shoes in synthetic material which is water resistant. Typically, office goers have a problem in the monsoon, the problem being the lack of shoes which have a formal look and ***yet*** are capable of being worn on water logged streets without getting spoilt. The synthetic range of formal shoes which Bata has recently launched has a wide variety of very classy designs, almost incapable of being differentiated in feel and finish from the traditional leather pairs. Brand Bata has identified a genuine need which was long lying unfulfilled. In fact, another huge segment of customers, (animal lovers), now have sworn to wear these shoes throughout the year, come rain or shine. Brand Bata has truly rejuvenated itself and has got back on track of the genuine marketing philosophy.

Nordstrom Takes Your Breath Away

Compare the previous experience (in terms of non-availability of sizes), with the range of sizes one would get at a ***Nordstrom*** store. (Nordstrom is an internationally renowned retail chain.)

Nordstrom literally stocks all sizes of shoes, ***even in increments of half a size.***

So not only would you get a size ten, you could also get ***size nine and a half.***

And, if one of your feet differed slightly in size from the other, as is the case with most of us, ***they would happily provide you with one shoe in size ten, and the other in size nine and a half.*** Unbelievable? Not at Nordstrom, where this is just routine.

All in the day's work in serving the customer to the best of their ability.

THE OVERHEADS AT NORDSTROM ARE HIGH, BUT THEIR PROFITS AS A PERCENTAGE OF THEIR COSTS ARE HIGHER THAN OTHER RETAIL STORES.

Adopt the Marketing philosophy

And watch your customers dance with glee

In fact, the customers of Nordstrom are so delighted with the brand that there is even a story of a regular customer of theirs who got married in one of their stores, as she wanted to be surrounded on her special day by the friendliest and most helpful people she knew. Imagine the volumes of goodwill the brand Nordstrom generates for itself.

Seeing Your Product Through Your Customer's Eyes

We have observed that many pharmaceutical companies print the name of the tablet in extremely small lettering, that too on glossy, shiny paper. This makes it extremely difficult for even a person with keen eyesight to read. And which set of customers consume the maximum tablets? It is the aged and infirm, whose eyesight is relatively weak. Especially when an individual has been prescribed multiple pills to be consumed at different times of the day, mix-ups would be inevitable under such circumstances. This set of customers would highly appreciate the name of the tablet being printed in larger lettering on paper which has a dull, matt finish, making the name more legible and easier to read. If this is done, it would be in keeping with the true marketing philosophy.

Convenience Lies in The Eyes of The Customer

Another transgressor when it comes to customer convenience is the Worldspace music network. It provides a great choice of uninterrupted music, (no commercial breaks and no chatty Radio Jockeys), all of this at quite a reasonable rate. One of us authors has subscribed to this service but has not been using it since the last six months. The reason for this is that the Worldspace network keeps informing subscribers on quite a regular basis that their password for access has been changed. And this password is a twenty digit password, which the subscriber himself has to enter into his Worldspace receiver by following a procedure that is definitely not easy for a non-technology savvy customer to follow. And this factor is not informed to the customer when he takes on his subscription. We personally know quite a few subscribers, who rather than go through the rigorous procedure of changing their password on their receiver, have preferred to let go of the balance subscription period, which they have already paid for. Why the password should be forcibly changed during the middle of a subscriber's paid period is a mystery. Even if it is necessary for some reason, the least that Worldspace could do to ensure customer convenience is to physically send along its representative to the residence of the subscriber to assist the subscriber in changing the password, without the customer having to request them to do so.

Similarly, in almost every industry we find examples where the customer is not initially informed at the time of purchase about some hindering feature of the service which would crop up during usage.

A true marketing oriented organization would ensure a smooth ride for the customer, free of any speed-breakers and irritating road blocks, during the life cycle of usage.

- Cyrus M Gonda, Kalim Khan

Enhance your Market Share and Revenue by following the Marketing Philosophy

It is our firm belief, strengthened through experience, that if a brand improves its product and service offering and provides what competitors do not provide, the benefits to the brand itself would be exponential.

And in most cases, what would be required to provide that extra would not require huge investments or quantum leaps in technology. But what would be required would be the application of the genuine marketing philosophy.

Taking a hypothetical example to see how a brand could exponentially increase its sales even in a competitive environment, let's consider the branded apparel industry.

There are around five leading brands, occupying a major chunk of the market share in the high end apparel industry. The material they use and the styles and designs they provide are nearly the same. In fact most of these brands outsource their stitching to the same set of tailors. Assume a logical situation each of these five brands has about twenty percent of the total market share.

The trouser waist sizes all these brands currently provide are available in even number waist sizes. Thirty, thirty two, thirty four, thirty six, and so on. There is a gap of two inches between each successive size.

(The above line shows how long 2 inches actually is.)

That's quite a difference between two successive sizes. So someone who has an odd numbered waist size either has to purchase a size which is an inch too large, or an inch too small for him.

Imagine if one of these five brands in the industry decides to provide trousers in odd number waist sizes as well as the even ones they already make. This brand will anyway retain its existing twenty percent of the market share, and assuming the odd numbered waist size customers form fifty percent of the total market, will pull away half of each competitor's customers as well.

This proactive and forward thinking brand would now logically have sixty percent of the market share and the other four players would be left with ten percent each. (The customers who have waists in even numbered sizes.)

The same holds true for any industry, where if one player decides to break away from the pack and improve and enhance his policies and offerings towards customers, train their staff better, do substantial customer research, provide genuine innovations which benefit the customer; they will reap the benefits. ***And most innovations don't require earth shaking research.*** They require a proper will and mindset.

As we just saw, no research or technology is necessary to manufacture trousers in odd numbered sizes.

The reason customer oriented innovations are comparatively few and far between is the lethargy and pure arrogance which prompt some brands to say, ***"If no other brand is doing it, why should I go the extra mile."***

The difference this extra mile makes is the difference between the Selling and the Marketing philosophies.

Tenet 3

FAVOUR PUBLIC RELATIONS OVER ADVERTISING

Don't sell
Let others tell

A Humorous Anecdote to Commence this Tenet

On a restaurant menu, ***"Special reduction for senior citizens,"*** was printed in bold. An elderly gentleman entered the restaurant, had his meal, and called for the bill. To his surprise, no discount had been given, though it was obvious he was a senior citizen. He pointed out the commitment of special reduction for senior citizens made on the menu card, and asked why there had been no reduction in his bill as was promised.

"Oh," answered the waiter. ***"The reduction doesn't refer to the bill. It refers to the size of portion served."***

The above may appear to be a joke, but it symbolizes the problem with most advertising today. Much of the advertising on display builds up individual's expectations, only to bring them down below sea level.

We don't intend to say that advertising is a function with no value. What we intend to bring out through this tenet is, how if done properly and in a genuine manner, as some great brands have done, advertising can be a lethal weapon in the brand building armoury. But much of the mindless advertising on display currently has diluted and distorted this worthwhile and noble profession, which, if done properly and professionally, has the potential of positively impacting the potential customer's decision making process to a very large extent.

The ills of modern advertising

Advertising is basically about communication. The word ***communication*** comes from the Latin term ***COMMUNICO,*** meaning ***share.***

Sharing of ideas, features, information about price, availability of the product and service being advertised, and primarily the brand's unique selling points.

The word is ***share.***

Not ***bombard.***

Not ***subdue.***

Not ***overwhelm.***

When advertisements come on television today, we have to rush for the remote control to reduce the volume, which seems to go suddenly berserk.

Communication for the sake of communication can never be truly effective. Loud yells may not be able to grab the attention that a whisper can get, if the whisper is done right.

Unfortunately, most modern advertising has followed the path of the mindless yell, and lost the art of the sensible, well timed, attention grabbing whisper.

- Cyrus M Gonda, Kalim Khan

Advertising as a communication tool has always been at its effective best when it has been integrated with overall organizational strategy, depicting clearly what the brand stands for, how the brand differentiates itself from related brands in a positive way, and demonstrating the unique features and characteristics of the brand to telling effect.

Integrated Marketing Communication is not only about maintaining similarity between the colour and size of the brand logo in various communication channels, but has more to do with sending out a single, strong, clear, holistic brand message.

Unfortunately, most of the advertising we witness nowadays appears to contain highly exaggerated fiction and very less fact. ***Anything*** seems to go in the name of creativity.

A film star is depicted braving blizzards and climbing the top of a tall mountain to procure an aerated drink, which in real life is easily available on every street.

A kid is shown having iodised salt or a protein or iron filled breakfast cereal, and that factor is attributed as the reason for the kid becoming a resounding success in later life.

Another kid is shown as having a fifty paise sweet and this immediately turns this hitherto nerdy kid into a dancing champion.

The consumer is not a moron. She is your wife. Don't insult her intelligence.

\- David Ogilvy

If advertisers assume that viewers of advertisements are starved of entertainment, and that it is the ad maker's duty to provide that entertainment, they are sadly mistaken and out of touch with reality. For purposes of entertainment, the viewers always have Brad Pitt and Charlie Chaplin.

Yes, no doubt an advertisement needs to be appealing to the viewer, but that appeal can never come at the cost of compromising on providing relevant product or service information, which is the ***basic purpose of advertising.*** There are after all, or should be, such things as priorities, even in advertising.

And what commenced as entertainment in advertising, has now relegated to pure buffoonery. The USPs of the product or service being advertised are not clearly identified and are rarely visible. This could probably be because the research conducted to identify genuine product or service USPs by agencies is half baked at best, if at all done in the first place.

Similarly, the capability and resource base of all departments of the brand being advertised to come together and deliver what is committed in the advertisement to customers is rarely considered.

Only if USPs are properly identified will advertising turn more professional and relate less to the fictional Sidney Sheldon and Enid Blyton variety. ***This epidemic of so called 'CREATIVITY' trespassing into the realms of sheer fiction and fantasy has affected most of the advertising fraternity.*** Creativity can be justified when the creative concepts floated so suggestively in advertisements have their full grounding in the ability of the product or service to deliver what is promised, which rarely appears to be the case nowadays.

Else as ***Arnold H Glasgow*** said, ***"Ideas not coupled with action never become bigger than the brain cells they occupied."***

The Media Mess

The general public in general has lost faith even in media driven awards and rankings, (which ultimately are a form of advertising), as it realizes that these rankings can be procured for a price. For example, certain business publications which come up with an annual ranking of Management Institutes on an All India basis, may approach various Management Institutes before this annual exercise of ranking is done. Their message is very clear. If your institute can assure us six full page advertisements in the course of the coming year, (payable in advance, of course), then we can accommodate your college in the top twenty five colleges ranking list on a particular parameter. Various such package deals and schemes are available to suit all pockets. This is why most media have unfortunately lost their sanctity and credibility. ***First rank appears to be up for grabs to the highest bidder.***

And this lack of faith in rankings and advertising claims in general is a major reason why the general public tends to rely more on word of mouth publicity, (i.e. Public Relations), as far as genuineness of information concerning product and service brands are concerned. Once advertisers realized that the general public had lost faith in paid advertisements, then the concept of selling editorial space for a price commenced. So what one reads as an article in a paper or a magazine pertaining to the goodness of a particular product or service could well have been put there by the newspaper or magazine for reasons other than newsworthiness.

I'm not upset that you lied to me, I'm upset that from now on I can't believe you.

- Friedrich Nietzsche

Slogans do not Make a Brand

It is so easy to make up impressive sounding but hollow and empty slogans, that it has become the norm in advertising, and even the brand with the worst quality of product and service in the industry can easily and comfortably, in beautiful language, proclaim that it is the best in class. In most cases, advertisements for one brand can easily be taken as an advertisement for its competitor, or even for an unrelated product category, as there is hardly any substance in the advertisement pertaining to unique features of the brand being promoted.

You can't build a reputation on saying what you're going to do.

- Henry Ford

Special Effects

A personal example which combines elements of all the above would do wonders to illustrate.

A close friend of ours had been for a vacation to a beach resort. One thing that he brought back as a memento of the vacation was sand on his clothes. After returning to Mumbai, he saw the advertisement of a leading detergent brand, marketed by a multinational giant, and endorsed on television by a celebrity. The advertisement depicted a white shirt coloured with food stains, in which ketchup and oil stains were prominent. On a whim, he purchased a packet of this detergent, and soaked his sand stained shirt in a bucket of water with this detergent overnight. The shirt he soaked had no oil or grease or ketchup stains, just simple sand. The next morning, he dutifully put the soaked shirt in the washing machine, expecting it to come out sparkling white, as the celebrity on television had assured the viewers it would. To his disappointment, the shirt emerged from the washing machine with no indication of the sand stains having been removed or even reduced. Naturally he was upset, as the small packet of detergent had quite a price attached to it. With great difficulty, he managed to get in touch with the marketing department of the firm which marketed this product. A snooty sounding lady told him that if he was so concerned that the company should look into his complaint, they would send across someone to collect his shirt and get it to the company laboratory. When the representative would arrive to collect the shirt, she could not say.

After three days, and two more calls from our friend's end to enquire when that somebody would come, somebody came. An individual, not in company uniform, nor even carrying a letter from the company, nor any company identification, arrived at our friend's residence, and simply said, "I've come for the shirt", as if he were the laundry boy.

Our friend handed over the shirt and received no communication from the company for seven days. Then he contacted the lady again. Her reply was, ***"We are working on it. I can't tell you what the status is. We will let you know once our tests are over."*** A few days later, someone from the company arrived with a parcel, which contained:

1. The shirt, (still as sand stained as before.)
2. A small packet of the same ineffectual detergent which our friend had washed the shirt in.
3. A letter from the marketing department stating that ***since the shirt was quite an old one, the stains would not be possible to remove, please accept the quarter kilogram packet of detergent with compliments from our end, thank you very much.***

What a laugh. The shirt in the advertisement was stained much worse than our friend's shirt in real life, yet the shirt in the advertisement had came out of the wash sparkling white. And if the detergent doesn't do its job, what's the sense of sending across a complimentary packet? Tall claims, but woefully short on delivery.

Our friend was so disgruntled, he narrated his experience to all and sundry, including a friend of his, who was from the advertising profession.

This man laughed and said, "Surely you don't believe what you see in most of these detergent advertisements. When the white shirt is shown to you in the ad, there are powerful strobe lights hitting it from all sides to make it sparkle and shine. There are even chemicals added to certain detergents for a specific purpose, that of making the water in which the detergent and clothes are dipped, murky and brown. The idea is, when you soak even a brand new shirt (which has obviously no dirt attached to it), overnight with the detergent in a bucket of water, the chemical releases a brownish tinge into the water. So when you pick up the shirt from the bucket the next morning and see the murky water, you think the dirt has been released from your shirt, and that the detergent is doing its job. ***These are all special effects, and please don't get carried away by them,"*** advised this man to our friend.

This brings us to the crux of the message of this very important tenet.

While spending on advertising and making people aware of your product or service and grabbing eye balls and attention towards your brand is fine, and is an important part of the sales process, ***it can never be done at the cost of losing trust and faith and credibility and reputation by over promising and under delivering.***

Advertisements have to be in sync with reality. They have to have as their basis and core, the unique selling proposition of the brand being highlighted, and can't be creative at the cost of being unrealistic.

The Emperor's New Clothes

We love this story. We have all heard it in our childhood days. Let's go over it once in brief, in case we have forgotten it, and the important lesson it imparts.

Long, long ago, a pair of rogue tailors approached the king of a country, telling him that they had a special type of cloth. The specialty of this cloth being that it could only be seen by people who were good at heart and honest, and the cloth could never be visible to rogues and rascals. Obviously the cloth did not exist, so the king couldn't see it either. But equally obviously, he pretended to see it as he didn't want to stand out as being dishonest and a rogue. So he pretended to appreciate the fine cloth, and agreed to have a suit made out of it at a hefty price. The rogues took the money, returned the next week, and handed over an empty packet to the king, which they claimed contained the suit. The king pretended to appreciate it, took off the clothes he was wearing, and pretended to put on the new one. Obviously he was now naked. The rogues pretended to appreciate how fine he looked in it, and then suggested that he walk around his kingdom clothed in it, so he could immediately identify the good and honest people in his kingdom, as only good and honest people would be able to see the suit. The king felt this was a fine idea, and paraded around the kingdom nude. The citizens had been ordered to gather around, and had been told the reason they were supposed to be there. The citizens also pretended to appreciate the king's fine new dress, as they didn't want to be seen as rascals and rogues. This continued till a small innocent child also watching the parade, loudly asked the question which was on everyone's mind, ***"Why is the king walking around naked?"***

In the same way, many advertisers today approach client organizations, telling them that the advertisements they have created are highly creative and ***SHOULD*** be accepted by the organization. The underlying message being that if, like the Emperor, the organization cannot appreciate the brilliant creativity displayed in the advertisement, they as an organization have no taste, no class.

Today we see many advertisements which have won awards for creativity but the brand they advertised is no longer available on the shelf. The question is - ***are ad agencies in the business of creating creative gurus, or are they in the business of developing customer faith in their client's brands?***

In many board-rooms today, directors of companies give their brief to advertising agencies as saying, ***"WE KNOW THERE IS NOTHING DIFFERENT IN OUR PRODUCT. BUT MAKE SOMETHING DIFFERENT OUT OF IT AT LEAST IN THE ADVERTISEMENT."***

This is so amazing.

Especially when as you will see in the ***tenet of the USP,*** umpteen small firms, even barber shops, grocery stores and auto rickshaws, can genuinely differentiate and provide benefits to customers by developing something positively different in their product or service offering, directors of huge organizations having the resources to spend on television advertising have no excuse for saying ***WE HAVE IN REALITY NOTHING DIFFERENT TO OFFER OUR CUSTOMERS.***

Think it over. Take the effort. Put more time in being on the shop floor rather than concerning yourself only with balance sheets and excel sheets. There is much more to the genuine marketing philosophy than these things.

It would not be an exaggeration to state that the average Marketing Head spends far more time with his advertising agency than on the field and on the shop floor, where the customers are. The reason for this which he may claim is that he lacks time.

As you will see through several positive examples in the ***tenet*** of ***Moments of Truth,*** lack of time can never be accepted as an excuse for non-performance of service and quality commitment.

Lack of will?	-	**Yes**
Lack of attitude?	-	**Yes**
Lack of time?	-	**NEVER**

Worldwide there is a trend among consumers to shift away from organizations which appear to put their customers and also the environment in second place to short term profitability. The shift of consumers is towards more honest, green, customer friendly, personalized, employee friendly, stakeholder rather than shareholder oriented, responsible brands. These are the brands which are benefiting from genuine public relations.

No amount of advertising expenditure can generate the volume and quality of goodwill that accrues through good actions, good products and great service. These are the foundation of genuine public relations.

As an example, take a product category we previously mentioned, such as aerated colas. In spite of spending the maximum on creative advertising, the cola industry is finding it hard to retain sales volumes and customers, as the consumer trend is moving towards healthful liquids such as juices, fruit based drinks, milk based drinks and mineral water of different types. Billions are being spent on advertising these colas, but if you go to a wedding reception and see aerated colas and juices on the same tray, it's the juices that get picked up first, (although they're rarely advertised), and the colas which are left behind on the tray. Try to observe this the next time you're at a reception and you'll see what we mean. The message for marketers is self-explanatory.

The P.R. we see today is not true P.R. – it is merely 'Disguised Advertising'

What today goes under the garb of ***Public Relations*** is a bustling, hyperactive, multi billion dollar industry, where influential individuals are paid vast sums to speak on behalf of someone or something they hardly know and care about even less. What matters to these so called influencers is the colour of the money on the contract.

When the concept of Public Relations originally took off, it didn't cost a dime to get your ***P R*** done. That's because brands didn't ***get*** it done through an outside agency. You (or the organization), did it yourself. It was, (and still is), far too crucial an activity to be left in the hands of outsiders.

You can't pay someone to study on your behalf and write your exams.

You can't pay someone to digest your food for you.

You can't pay someone to pray on your behalf.

Another person would never be as effective in deriving the benefits of these activities as you would by doing them yourself.

Similarly, Public Relations will be at its effective best when done by the organisation or brand itself.

What IS genuine Public Relations?

True and genuine Public Relations is nothing but the ***word of mouth*** that spreads about your ***organisation and brand as a natural consequence of the experiences, good or bad, that the customers and other stakeholders connected with your organization, actually experience. If they experience a good product, or service, they spread the good word, and if their experience was bad, they say bad. And this is how***

the word spreads. That's all there is to the genuine original concept of Public Relations.

Thus the job of Public Relations is to ensure that the maximum possible number of experiences that your customers and other stakeholders have while interacting with your brand are good, healthy and positive. Then the customers and other stakeholders take over and spread the word on your behalf, free of cost.

Let's understand the difference between Advertising and Public Relations

The two terms, ***ADVERTISING*** and ***PUBLIC RELATIONS,*** the way they have been distorted today, appear to be closely linked and inter-connected. In reality, they ***complement*** each other. Or rather, ***advertising*** complements ***public relations.*** (True and genuine Public Relations, that is, not the pirated, corrupted version of 'Public Relations' we see masquerading in place of the genuine article today.)

The basic ***definition of Advertising*** was, is, and continues to remain as ***Creating awareness and providing information about product price, features, availability and other similar parameters.*** Today, Advertising has regressed into pure unadulterated masala entertainment. There is very little co-ordination between the advertising department and other departments of an organisation such as the production, distribution and supply chain. For example, so often we see a new product or brand or flavour advertised on massive hoardings which must have cost fortunes to rent. Our interest is aroused, we get excited, visit the store or outlet where that newly advertised product is said to be available, and the dealer says – ***Sorry, haven't heard of it.*** We go the second time a few days later and he says the same thing. Rarely do we bother to ask a third time. All that advertising is ultimately wasted because of the huge disconnect which so often exists between advertising and other departments of the organization.

Which came first, the chicken or the egg?

This classic brain teaser till date has no answer. But when it comes to Advertising and Public Relations, the solution is a no brainer.

ADVERTISING is merely the ICING, the add-on.

PUBLIC RELATIONS is the WHOLE CAKE, the substance, the heart, the soul, the core.

One can definitely consume and enjoy the cake without the icing, but without the cake, the icing just makes you throw up.

- Cyrus M. Gonda, Kalim Khan

Ask an MBA graduate today which of the two is more important as a function of marketing, and chances are high that he would say that it's Advertising which is far more important than Public Relations.

This is incorrect thinking, and it happens because the true meaning of Public Relations as a discipline has been grossly distorted by vested interests over a period of time.

The six major differences between Advertising and Public Relations

Let's see what this term ***Public Relations*** is actually and genuinely all about, and let's ***compare*** it with its complementary discipline, ***Advertising.***

1. The basic definition of ***Advertising*** maintains that it's a ***Paid Form of Publicity.***

   And the basic definition of ***Public Relations*** is that it is ***Unpaid Publicity.***

   That's it. ***Unpaid.*** No money changing hands. You can't call it ***P R*** if it's paid for. The moment you pay someone to do ***P R*** on your behalf, it ceases to remain ***P R*** and becomes disguised advertising.

   This means that all the firms out in the market place labeling themselves as P R firms are actually Advertising Agencies in disguise. By the very definition of Public Relations, (unpaid publicity), a paid P R firm simply cannot exist. (Remember, Advertising is paid for, P R is unpaid publicity. ***UNPAID.*** The ***P R*** firms aren't in the business of charity, are they? They may be effective in getting press coverage, but they charge a bomb. ***And once they charge a fee for it, it CAN'T be called P R.)***

The way that most Public Relations agencies functions today is that they first and foremost develop relations with the press. Then they formulate and offer various package deals to clients for inserting paid press coverage. This is not what ***P R*** was originally about at all.

As we mentioned, the basic definition of ***P R*** is that it is ***unpaid publicity,*** and one ***can't alter or tamper with basic definitions.***

Two plus two will remain four, whether at noon or midnight, in the Eastern Hemisphere or the Western. Whether today, tomorrow or five hundred years hence.

Two plus two will remain four.

Basic definitions can't change.

P R began as Unpaid Publicity, and that's when it's at its most effective best. And that's what we're introducing to you once again. (Remember the subtitle of this book, ***Remaster the LOST art of Marketing.)***

2. The *second* area of differentiation between *P R* and *advertising* is that ***advertising*** is *FIRST PARTY ENDORSEMENT* and *P R* is *THIRD PARTY ENORSE-MENT.*

   What does all this jargon mean? Simple.

   First Party Endorsement means someone talking about himself.

   Third Party Endorsement means *someone else talking about you on your behalf.* And even if someone *does* talk on your behalf because he's paid to do it, it's not Public Relations (Because as we saw, *P R* can't be paid for.) Therefore Advertising will *always* be positive. (You're not going to pay somebody to speak bad about you, are you?)

   But genuine ***P R*** could be positive ***OR*** negative, depending upon the experience the person who is speaking about you has had with your organization. If he has had a good experience, he speaks good, if bad, he says so.

Praise is only worthwhile when it comes from someone else.

- Zhuang Zi (Chinese Philosopher)

3. Now this ***third*** difference is a very important difference. And it stems from the second difference. ***Because*** Advertising is ***first party endorsement,*** (someone speaking about himself), it is ***far less believable and credible, as it will always whitewash the brand and project it in good light.*** In fact various surveys have shown that over a period of time, the ***belief factor*** that viewers and audiences have in advertising has gone down drastically. And at the same time, the ***cost*** of advertising has increased by leaps and bounds.

To be persuasive, we must be believable; to be believable, we must be credible; to be credible, we must be truthful.

- Edward R Murrow

Genuine ***P R*** by its very nature is ***much*** more believable than advertising, because it doesn't only give a one sided scenario. ***Genuine P R always speaks the truth.*** And that's what customers want today. ***Authenticity.*** Not exaggeration and distorted versions.

A simple example to clarify this point.

Imagine it's your birthday and you're looking out for a good restaurant to go to for dinner. Its evening time, and you're flipping through the newspaper, and your eyes fall on a ***full page advertisement*** (which must have cost the restaurant hundreds of thousands of rupees to insert), advertising a nice new Thai restaurant that's opened up in your locality. The advertisement mentions attractive features such as ***valet parking,*** and a ***Chef who's come down from Thailand, and a live band, and portions of food that are very filling and prices that are very reasonable.*** You're very pleased as this looks to be just the sort of place you're looking for to celebrate your birthday. You're about to leave home for the restaurant, when your friend drops in to wish you a Happy Birthday. You're irritated because you feel that such a nice restaurant as this new Thai place would get packed up fast, and you would lose out on a table. Your friend asks you where you'd be going for dinner. You tell him about this nice new restaurant and show him the advertisement. He sees the advertisement and tells you that he saw the same advertisement in yesterday's paper, and although it wasn't his birthday it seemed like such an attractive place, that he rushed there for his dinner, and now he advises you never to go there in your life.

Your friend tells you that there was –

- *No valet parking facility operational at the restaurant and his car got towed away.*
- *The Chef hasn't got his visa so he's still stuck in Thailand.*
- *The singer's throat was bad and so there was no live band.*
- *The portions of food were suitable for someone on a crash diet.*
- *And to top it all, the prices were in no way reasonable.*

This is what your friend tells you. Now would you still want to rush to that place or would you look for another restaurant to celebrate your birthday? The answer doesn't require Einstein levels of thinking. But, if you realize, the restaurant has spent a huge sum putting an advertisement in the newspaper, and your friend provided you with this information for free.

Why do you believe your friend and not the restaurant which has advertised itself as a fantastic place to visit? The answer is obvious. *The restaurant has a vested interest in providing a glowing, positive image of itself. Your friend has no such bias.* If the experience your friend had at the restaurant was a positive one, then he would have had no hesitation in recommending the place to you. That would have reinforced your decision to go visit there.

When there is a discrepancy between the ADVERTISEMENT and the WORD OF MOUTH, it is always word of mouth which prevails.

- Cyrus M Gonda, Kalim Khan

Which is precisely why we previously mentioned that Advertising is merely the icing, P R is the whole cake.

Well done is better than well said.

- Benjamin Franklin

And it is not only word of mouth from a friend which shapes your opinion about a brand, and ultimately your purchase decision. It could well be word of mouth coming from an acquaintance, someone you overhear while walking on the street or while waiting in a bus queue, a blogger, someone who's written a letter to a newspaper - the sources are endless. That's what we meant when we said that Advertising is merely the ***icing,*** it's the ***add-on.*** If it's in sync with the word of mouth - great. If not, then that's just too bad for the brand.

The perceived problem with the concept of genuine Public Relations and word of mouth publicity however, is that it apparently works too slowly for some people. They don't want to wait while all this word of mouth spreads. But is it really slow? ***We are convinced that word of mouth spreads like wildfire.***

Research has shown that when a customer gets a great experience from a service provider, on an average he tells two other people about it, and when he receives a bad experience, on an average he tells twelve others. And he doesn't wait to tell others either. He normally does so at the first opportunity he gets. The later ***tenet*** of the ***Circle of Influence*** clarifies this with the help of some wonderful examples.

Genuine ***P R,*** (unpaid word of mouth publicity), like any solid structure which will stand the test of time, needs a good foundation. Deriving the benefits of genuine ***P R*** does take some time. But after that small period of time, as we said, the word spreads like wildfire.

And anything that is worth while, does have a minimum gestation period.

For example, consider that you are getting your house painted.

Would you just directly apply a coat of paint on the existing paint?

Or would you scrape off the existing paint, apply two layers of foundation, and then three layers of fresh paint?

Initially, both these methods would give you a very similar effect and finish on the wall. But in the long run? As they say, time will tell.

In the case of ADVERTISING versus PUBLIC RELATIONS, time will not tell. TIME HAS TOLD.

- Cyrus M Gonda, Kalim Khan

Take your *first mango of the season,* ripe, rosy and red. Chances are high that when you cut it, it may be rotten from the inside, because it would have been artificially ripened before its time.

Or have a look at *how bread is normally baked.* The dough is put in the oven at 200 degrees for about twenty five minutes. Could you bake the bread faster, let's say in five minutes, by zooming up the temperature to a thousand degrees? We doubt it. *All you'd get would be a charred, blackened, lump.*

Or see the trouble a child born in about seven months has to go through, protected in an incubator for a considerable period.

Or *consider education.* A two year full time degree holder will always stand a better chance of securing a good job as compared to a six month diploma holder, all other factors being equal.

Any thing worth while takes its own, natural time. And it would be folly to expect results before their time. So is the case with genuine Public Relations.

4. The ***fourth*** difference. ***The impact of Advertising is generally only short term. The impact of P R sustains over a period of time.***

   Statistics show that *in an urban environment, an average individual is exposed to twenty thousand advertising messages in a single day.* Right from the morning newspaper, with all its full page advertisements and thousands of classifieds, till the time you leave home and are exposed to stationary hoardings, and hoardings on buses, trains, taxi cabs, railway platforms, the flyers handed to you, the pop ups on your screen, the advertisements in the evening paper and magazines, and the advertising messages on radio and television, *twenty thousand advertising messages reaching you everyday.* How many can you recall? You could count the ones you *do* recall on the fingers of your hand.

You can at the most ATTRACT customers through advertising. You can never RETAIN.

- Cyrus M Gonda, Kalim Khan

Genuine ***P R*** messages and word of mouth inputs on the other hand, are remembered for a long, long time. The reason? You've heard of an actual, specific experience someone you know has had, and that's always more personalized, genuine and memorable.

Our favourite example with regards to this point relates to a well known brand of paint, which hired a movie star to endorse the paint in a series of television advertisements. Let's call this paint organization as Company A. There is a rival player in the paint industry which we shall call Company B. Although the film star danced his heart out promoting the paint of Company A, (what the connection between the film star and the paint was, it was never clearly established), a couple of months after the campaign was over, a survey was conducted whereby viewers were asked to recall the advertisement, and the brand of paint involved. Everyone surveyed could immediately and correctly recall the film star involved, but approximately ***EIGHTY*** percent of those surveyed mistakenly mentioned the organization being promoted in the advertisement as the rival organization, Company B.

This sort of thing occurs because while viewers may watch the advertisement, they don't relate to it. They can't recall the organization involved. There is no connection between the film star and the brand of paint that viewers can perceive. Company A spent millions on an advertisement which got benefits for its rival.

Company B actually invested in providing its customers with a great experience. What they did was initiate a ***School of Paint,*** where customers could be educated about the texture and shade of different paints, and Company B also sent across an expert to the residence or office to be painted so that he could advise customers about the most suitable shade and type of paint to use. This genuine concern for providing an excellent experience to its customers gave Company B the leading edge in the industry.

And who makes the decision about which brand of paint to use? It's the painting contractor. Is he going to be impressed by a brand endorser? No way. What he wants is a brand which will give his customer the satisfaction, also leaving the contractor himself with a good margin of profit. ***The film star endorser doesn't remotely enter into this equation at all.***

5. The ***fifth*** difference between the two concepts is that ***advertising*** has a narrow focus, focusing only on the customer, whereas ***P R*** has a broad focus, focusing on providing excellent experiences to ***all*** stakeholders. You may have a great product, and a very innovative advertising campaign, but even if one set of stakeholders is aggrieved or upset with you for some reason, it may cost your organization dear. Nike, an American athletic gear manufacturer, does most of its manufacturing in South East Asian countries where labour is cheap. In fact. labour is so cheap, that employees about a decade ago were working in miserable conditions labeled as sweat shops. It was estimated that the thousands of employees of Nike in these countries did not earn as much all put together, as much as one, single Brand Endorser of Nike back in the USA was paid. The customers of today are increasingly socially aware and environmentally conscious, and when they became aware of this, a majority of them boycotted Nike products, causing Nike severe losses.

   Unfortunately, ***advertising*** only focuses on one set of the stakeholders, that is the customer. On the other hand, the philosophy of genuine ***Public Relations*** ensures that all stakeholders connected with the brand, including employees and suppliers, have a good experience, as any one of them being dissatisfied, such as in the above scenario, can adversely affect the brand, even though the brand's advertising may be of a high quality.

6. The ***sixth*** difference:

   Advertising is something you ***pay*** for.

   P R is something you ***pray*** for.

   Since in order to place an advertisement in a particular medium, all one needs is the requisite money, the job of passing on a desired message to the audience is relatively an easy one. (But it can financially drain an organisation pretty quick. Advertising is not cheap, you know.)

   Public Relations? Word of mouth? The genuine variety? Aha.

   You don't need to ***pay*** and get genuine customers who have had actual experiences with your brand to speak good about you.

   You have to pray that it happens.

   And it ***will*** happen.

   It is ***bound*** to happen.

   Provided your organization has done its job well and has given your customers something good to talk about.

Like every heartfelt and genuine prayer which gets a patient hearing and a positive response from God, the same way the brand's prayer for positive word of mouth publicity will definitely be answered by the customer (God), if the brand deserves it.

- Cyrus M Gonda, Kalim Khan

Advertising by itself can never guarantee positive word of mouth about a brand if the walk doesn't match the talk.

Have you observed that those who have something worth while to say prefer to let others say it, while those who have nothing to say keep saying it themselves.

- Anonymous

Besides the above differences between P R and advertising, there are certain limitations which advertising has, which Public Relations and word of mouth can never suffer from.

The Limitations of Advertising

1. The norms for advertising in USA, UK and many other countries are getting stricter by the day. Some of these restrictions are also visible in the Indian context. One can't advertise alcohol or tobacco products. Advertisements aimed at and targeting children below the age of fifteen are banned. A ban against surrogate advertising is also being considered. The scope of advertising is getting extremely limited.

   But no one prevents any brand in any industry from performing good actions towards customers and other stakeholders. There can never be a ban on that. Genuine Public Relations and word of mouth can only increase in scope.

2. The drawback in a brand speaking about itself, is that ***if the walk falls short of the talk,*** the brand may well regret it.

   Publilius Syrus, the great statesman, once mentioned, ***"I have often regretted my speech. Never my silence."***

   This is exactly the reason why Edward Deming, the acknowledged father of Japan's quality revolution, was very explicit and vocal when he advised organizations to eliminate Mission and Vision statements. His reasoning was crystal clear - ***If you are good, others will talk about you. But by yourself committing something that you may be unable to deliver in totality, you get a bad name.***

It is ironic that the unpaid salesman (the delighted customer), will be far more enthusiastic, credible, effective and genuinely convincing than most salesmen on an organisation's payroll. This is because the paid salesman approaches a prospect through the mind, the delighted customer who is now the missionary and advocate of the brand approaches others from his heart. But when can the unpaid salesman's services be availed of? When the brand succeeds in consistently delighting him.

- Cyrus M Gonda, Kalim Khan

4. Current research indicates that the number of people having faith in, and believing in the claims of the advertisements they view, is steadily declining. This is because of the increasingly exaggerated claims put forth by many brands in their advertisements. These claims which enhance customer expectations, in most cases simply cannot be delivered in reality by the brand. At the same time, the advertising rates are sky rocketing. So on one hand, the number of people in the audience who are convinced by advertising claims is dropping, and on the other hand, the amount spent to convince this reduced audience is going up. In short, advertisers are getting less bang for their buck. (Genuine ***P R*** does not have this drawback, as genuine ***P R*** is free.)

   And the difference between exaggeration and reality could never be better demonstrated than by examining the brilliant piece of reasoning by that gem among American presidents, Abraham Lincoln. Involved in a dispute to adjudicate a matter of fact, he used his common sense to illustrate the point. "How many legs does a cow have?" asked Lincoln of his disputer. "Four, of course," was the reply. "That's right," agreed Lincoln. ***"Now let's ASSUME you call the cow's tail a leg. Then how many legs would a cow have?"*** "Why, five obviously," was the reply. "That's where I differ with you," said Lincoln. ***"Calling a cow's tail a leg doesn't make it a leg."***

   Similar things are seen so often in advertising today, where anything goes in the name of creative license. This is the moment when the viewers begin to lose faith in the brand in entirety.

5. Another argument used by avid proponents of advertising is, ***"Unless we indulge in regular advertising, how else can we make people aware that we exist."*** They might be interested to know that there exist professionals such as ***doctors, lawyers, architects, dentists, chartered accountants*** and many others, who according to the guidelines applicable to their profession, ***are not permitted to advertise.*** Don't the good ones among them do roaring business? Don't they have clients waiting in line to avail of their excellent services? It only happens through word-of-mouth, passed on by satisfied customers to other potential buyers in need of these services, based on the quality of product and service experienced by the existing customer base.

A Good Product or Service is the Best PR

Positive word of mouth publicity is the direct outcome of providing quality goods and services.

A case in point could be taken from the management education industry, to which we authors belong.

Multiple management institutes exist, and continue to flourish. There are others which have steadily seen their fortunes and their applications for admission decline. Although most institutes do place advertisements at the time of admission season, mere placement of advertisements does not secure quality applicants. And it is quality applicants passing out from an institute which ultimately make the institute's name a force to be reckoned with. Quality applicants would rarely if ever secure admission in an institute on the basis of an advertisement. They would determine their decision based on the word of mouth from alumni and passing out batches as to the quality of education and inputs provided by a particular institute. Institutes which have built and continue to strengthen their reputation for providing quality education are found to advertise lesser and lesser with each successive year, as the positive word of mouth is brilliantly doing its job.

It's only when genuine marketing orientation is at a discount that the focus on advertising is seen to be at a premium.

- Cyrus M Gonda, Kalim Khan

In fact, the better institutes sometimes ask applicants how they came to be aware about the institute, and what induced them to apply. ***Rarely is the answer provided by applicants got to do with being induced by expensive advertising.*** In most cases, the reason given by applicants for joining the institute has a lot to do with free word of mouth positive publicity provided by satisfied and delighted alumni. The applicants mention that they have come to know about, and believe in the goodness of the institute and apply for admission based on the recommendation of a friend or relative who has passed out from that institute, rather than come to have faith in it through an advertisement they have seen.

And advertising rates are zooming higher every year.

The simple and sweet lesson to be learnt?

Focus on quality, delight your existing customers. They will become your greatest advocates. And all for free.

The takeaway from this example is that your organization can and should now chart that for every rupee that your organisation spends on advertising, what is the corresponding direct investment it is making in improving and enhancing customer service and experiences. These direct investments in improving quality and product of services in most cases would give your organisation exponential returns compared to advertising spend.

You can't fool all the people all the time

Who says we can't learn from comic books?

A story from the popular and true to life Archie comic book series makes for delightful and thought provoking reading. Jughead, the food loving character in this series, observes a news article which mentions that his favourite Pasta Canned Food Company is being taken over by a giant conglomerate. The pasta company is said to be founded and currently run by a Chef Boy-oh-Boy, and Jughead feels that a giant conglomerate wouldn't be able to provide the tender loving care and personalized touch to the pasta that Chef Boy-oh-Boy must obviously have been taking. The commercials of Chef Boy-oh-Boy have depicted the Chef as someone who initially grew up as a native in small town Italy, where he toiled for years to make the perfect pasta sauce. Then the commercials move forward and show the Chef being employed in a small local restaurant in Italy, earning barely enough to support his large family and saving the balance till he could collect enough money to one day market the perfect pasta sauce. He eventually succeeds in doing so, migrates to the USA, starts his dream company, and the commercials then depict the Chef as never having forgotten his small town life in Italy, and how he still takes personal care to ensure that every batch of pasta sauce that leaves the factory is perfect in every way. The advertisements end by stating that the same grand old tradition is carried on in every can of Chef Boy-oh-Boy pasta.

As a concerned and loyal customer, owing his allegiance to Chef Boy-oh-Boy, Jughead rushes to the Head Office of the Chef Boy-oh-Boy Pasta Company. A receptionist guides him to the Marketing Head. Jughead appeals to the Marketing Head to direct him to Chef Boy-oh-Boy's cabin, so he can personally appeal to him and convince him not to sell out the brand. The Marketing Head bluntly tells Jughead not to be foolish, and ***that Chef Boy-oh-Boy does not, and never did exist.*** He explains to Jughead that their Advertising Agency ***created*** the entire Chef Boy-oh-Boy ***concept*** years ago, and that the recipe never originated in small town Italy, but in a laboratory in New York. Jughead then questions about the Chef Boy-oh-Boy family depicted in the commercials and on every can of their pasta. The Marketing Head tells him that they're all actors. ***"They're quite corny, but convincing in a peasant kind of way,"*** is what the Marketing Head adds about the 'family'. Needless to say, the disillusioned Jughead leaves the office, commenting that ***he'll take good care never to believe any other advertisement ever again.***

The point is, even if advertisements succeed in creating an incorrect image and impression which persuades people to buy, how long can this façade be maintained? That is the question. As a wise man said, "You can't fool all the people all the time."

Trust only MOVEMENT.
Life happens at the level of EVENTS,
not of WORDS. Trust movement.

- Alfred Adler

We would like to conclude this tenet and this debate by remembering a beautiful article we recently read. It made us do a lot of soul searching. The article began by asking the reader if he could answer the following questions.

1. Name the 5 richest people in the world.
2. Name the last 5 Miss Universe winners.
3. Name the last 10 winners of the Best Actor Oscar.

The article then continued by saying –

Can't do it? Rather difficult, isn't it?

Don't worry. Nobody remembers all that.

Applause dies away.

Trophies gather dust.

Winners are soon forgotten.

The article went on by asking a few further questions to the reader.

1. Name 3 teachers who contributed to your education.
2. Name 3 friends who helped you in your hour of need.
3. Think of a few people who made you feel special.
4. Name 5 people that you like to spend time with.

More manageable, isn't it?

The people who mean something to your life weren't rated "the best", don't have the most money, haven't won the greatest prizes.

They are the ones who care about you, take care of you, those who no matter what, stay close by you.

Isn't it a beautiful article? And so, so true.

How is this article relevant to this tenet?

Simply because, it tells us that the ones who we trust the most, listen to the most, take advice from the most, and would be convinced by the most, aren't celebrities from another world. The people we listen to and trust, are the ones we are close to and spend time with. And these are the ones to whom we would listen more avidly, keenly and attentively when they told us about experiences they had with certain brands.

The message of this tenet can be summed up as - ***'Provide every customer and stakeholder with great experiences, and they will spread the good word on your behalf.'***

UNDERSTAND YOUR CUSTOMER

Get into your customer's mind
Then all the profits you will find

Communication does not begin with being understood, but with understanding others.

- W Steven Brown

We would like to begin this tenet by asking an apparently childishly simple question. Do you know ***WHO*** your customer is? Simple question? Laughably simple? Save your laughter. It's not as easy a question as it appears at first, or even at second glance.

With reference to this question, we are not speaking in context of being aware as to what the person currently standing at your cash counter, physically looks like. That part is the simple part. What we refer to when we ask, ***"Who is your customer?"*** goes much, much deeper than merely skin deep.

Before we proceed, a word of caution. We are not addressing the question ***"Who is your customer"***, from the erroneous perspective of undertaking a ***segmentation exercise.***

The problem with segmentation is that it's a negative concept, narrowing down and eliminating potential customers and all the subsequent possible referrals through them. This will be discussed at length with some stunning, real life examples in the ***tenet*** of the ***Circle of Influence.***

As we said, we're not speaking of physically being aware as to who your customer is. That part is relatively easy for most organizations.

Although even that part is sometimes a matter of confusion. For example, soft drink majors consider their distributor to be their customer, rather than the person who finally gulps the drink. Many leading newspapers operate under the assumption that it is their advertisers who are their customers, as that is where they get the lions share of their revenue. Such newspapers consider the reader to be only a by product. So even this simple question of physically being aware as to who your customer is, is not as simple as it seems to be.

But the more important issues that need to be addressed with serious concern as far as understanding the customer goes, by any organization serious about customer retention, are:

1. **Who** is your customer?
2. **How well** do you know your customer?

You may know the customer as a source of revenue. You may know him as a contributor to your balance sheet.

But how well do you know him as a ***PERSON?*** As an ***INDIVIDUAL?*** Having his own unique likes and dislikes, tastes and preferences, even eccentricities.

How well you know all these elements about your customers is what separates the marketing has-beens and also-rans from the marketing legends.

All else being equal, people will prefer to do business with people who have taken the trouble and effort to know them well.

Doesn't the same hold true in a job interview scenario? Does not the organization, (the ***customer*** in this case), usually prefer to select the applicant who has made efforts to know more about the organization to which he is applying? It depicts the applicant's interest, enthusiasm, and a genuine need to serve the other party in the best way possible.

And although there are two parties involved in any relationship, and logically both sides need to make efforts to extend their hand; in a business relationship, the onus lies on the service provider to make the moves necessary for the business relationship to blossom.

When someone prizes us just as we are,
he or she confirms our existence.

- Eugene Kennedy

As in all relationships, it's the small things that matter the most. What may appear insignificant to the organization from its own perspective, may be the most critical factor as far as a particular customer is concerned. Anyone who is married will realise what we are speaking of.

The more genuine effort one takes to understand the other customer, the more one learns.

The more one learns, the more one earns - from that customer
on whom one has taken efforts to understand.

- Cyrus M Gonda, Kalim Khan

Today, in the absence of product USPs, (as will be elaborated in the ***tenet of USP***), it is the ***service*** USPs which have taken precedence. These service USPs can be developed and strengthened through knowledge of what the customer wants, and therefore how he would like to be spoken to, treated, and how he would like to be served.

The Xerox Corporation shows the way

Take the example of the Xerox corporation.

Their representatives are absolutely thorough, and leave nothing to chance when it comes to the vital marketing issue of understanding their customer.

They don't just ***know*** their customer.

They know him as well as his own mother would know him.

In fact, Xerox (in their parent country), does not permit its sales people to approach a customer until and unless they have obtained information about that customer on at least fifty parameters. And its not just information on parameters pertaining to immediate business needs that they focus on.

In most other organisations, the information that a sales representative tries to collect about his potential customer relates to areas such as the customer's field of business, revenue potential from that customer, percentage increase in business each year, and similar parameters.

But Xerox, like an intelligent chess player, makes its sales force look ten steps ahead.

They focus on areas such as the personal background of the customer.

The names of his wife and children.

The schools or colleges his children attend.

The customer's favourite cuisine.

His favourite vacation spot.

The sport he enjoys.

His hobby.

His favourite newspaper, magazine and television channel.

The societies and clubs he is a member of.

The charitable causes he supports.

And everything else that is possible to conceivably know about him, ***irrespective of whether that parameter pertains to business or not.***

What use is all this, you may well ask

All the use in the world. Think how often you have gelled with a service provider because you shared a common bond in an area which has ***nothing*** to do with the product or service you are dealing with him for. It happens all the time.

Just as an example, a customer hates the game of cricket. (We all have our whims and fancies.) If you meet such a customer for a potential deal and attempt to break the ice by saying, "What a fantastic game of cricket yesterday. Did you see it?" You have turned the guy off. Completely. That's human nature. And we presume your customers all belong to the human race.

Or somebody for some reason just doesn't like the colour blue, and a sales person goes for a meeting with him having put on a blue shirt and tie. The meeting starts off on a bad note.

The possibilities for such mess ups are innumerable if one hasn't done one's homework thoroughly and well.

The world of marketing is a school in the real world where doing one's homework thoroughly in the subject of Understanding the Customer is crucial to business success.

- Cyrus M Gonda, Kalim Khan

In the field of psychology and human behaviour, there is an important concept termed as ***Acquiescence Bias.*** This concept indicates, among other things, that ***Common likes between individuals very often lead to further their relationship.***

There is a huge positive connect that occurs between two individuals as a result of acquiescence bias.

By no way do we mean to suggest that as long as you are aware of the personal likes and dislikes of the customer, you can be complacent about your product knowledge. No way. Acquiring thorough knowledge about the product or service you deal in is step one. But step one is just not enough. After successfully clearing step one, the element of common bonding takes over.

It is possible that the common bonding factor between you and your customer may occur by chance, but it is highly likely that it may not. After all, haphazard events don't occur as often as planned events do. A systematic effort in researching the prospect's background in terms of personal likes and dislikes, tastes and preferences, can reap rich dividends, as it gives you lots of common ground and opening gambits with which to steer the conversation in your favour. Why take the risk of being unprepared, especially when business success depends on the outcome?

Just imagine taking a client out for a business lunch and ordering his favourite dish before he can even mention it. What a positive impact that would create.

On the other hand, absence of such information through lack of research has led to many faux pas and slips of tongue which have done irretrievable personal damage.

Imagine asking a man who has just gone through a painful and costly divorce, "So how's the wife." This is just but one possible slip which could so easily have been avoided.

As Don Peppers and Martha Rogers mention so aptly in '***The One To One Future;'*** in today's connected world, you will have to calculate your success ***one customer at a time.*** They mention that an organization needs to focus its efforts on ***Share of Customer,*** not focus on ***Overall Market Share.***

The ***definition of Market Share*** is, "Selling as much of your product you can to the entire ***consumer*** base of that industry." (The word consumer used correctly once again.)

On the other hand, focusing on ***Share of Customer*** would mean ensuring that each individual customer who buys the product or service ***your*** brand deals in, buys only your brand of product or service each time he has a need, and is truly satisfied using your brand as compared to a competing brand.

And the key to enhancing Share of Customer is to ***know*** and ***understand*** your customer as well as possible, so that you can be proactive in your customized offering, thus making your brand indispensable to your customer. Needless to say, this will also drastically reduce your advertising expenses.

Make yourself indispensable, and you will move up.
Make a show of being indispensable, and you will move out.

- Jules Ormont

If you and your organization wish to attain excellence in knowing and understanding the customer, there is a structured process to be followed. It does ***not*** happen haphazardly.

Geoff Colvin in his masterpiece ***Talent is Overrated,*** gives multiple examples which prove beyond any doubt that if one wishes to gain mastery in any activity, then attention, concentration and focus on the task at hand over a period of time give the best results. Colvin explains how top tennis players look at the server's body and not at the tennis ball to gauge their best response to the opponent's serve. Through practice, these top performers have learnt to spot information that is not so obvious but is vitally important. Colvin gives examples from diverse fields. He explains how musicians are much better than non-musicians at detecting very minute differences in pitch and volume of notes, although both hear the same sounds. Or how expert radiologists, while seeing the same X-rays as junior and apprentice doctors are able to provide better diagnoses. As Colvin says, it is not that the experts have sharper physical eyesight. The difference didn't lie in what they saw, but in what they perceived.

This is exactly what we are trying to say when we speak of taking sustained and structured efforts in the area of understanding the customer till one becomes an expert at it through sheer determination and practice, anticipating the unspoken needs and desires of the customer even before he expresses them.

Cultural Differences

There is this time tested anecdote concerning an American businessman visiting Japan for the purpose of business. The Japanese businessman gently and politely greets the American, who gives a hurried greeting in return. The American hands over his business card which the Japanese respectfully receives with both hands, reads carefully, thoroughly, giving the card the importance it deserves, and then puts it into his card holder. The American is by now in a hurry to get the deal done, and when the Japanese hands over his business card, the American almost without reading it, shoves it into his pocket, ***as if it were a hindrance to the deal at hand.*** The Japanese asks the American if he would care for a cup of tea. The American almost rudely refuses, removes some papers from his briefcase, literally shoving them onto the Japanese. The implication being, let's first get these signed, then we can have all the cups of tea you wish. And as a result, the deal never gets done, as the Japanese has a strong need to understand the person he will be dealing with. The cup of tea would have been an opportunity for him to get closer to the American and understand more about his values, his principles and his driving forces and motivators.

You can make more friends in two months by becoming interested in other people than you can in two years by trying to get other people interested in you.

- Dale Carnegie

Today, corporate etiquette demands that while having a business dinner, one doesn't speak business till the coffee after the meal is served. Then what does one talk of throughout the meal? Topics of general interest, of course. And preferably topics of interest to your customer, rather than to yourself. And you can be thoroughly prepared to speak on topics which would be of interest to your customer, provided you have taken efforts to find out his areas of interest.

Today there is a wealth of information and material available on the culture, habits and way of life of various communities, regions and countries. This knowledge is considered more necessary to the successful outcome of a business deal than any other area today. The customer gets an immediate feeling of warmth when you display knowledge of his personal tastes. ***It also gives him the message that you consider him important enough to have taken this extra effort to get to know him well. It displays respect for him as an individual***.

Once the rapport is established, then the path is clear for you to have a good opportunity for a fair hearing about your product or service from the prospect. He will feel he owes it to you. Your presentation and sales talk is taken more seriously by him. ***In short, the customer reciprocates the respect you have shown him through the effort you have taken to know him well.*** Then, the price of the product or service you are offering becomes a secondary issue. ***TRUST*** has now been established.

To give a simple example of how important it is to be aware of the broad cultural background of the individual you are dealing with, consider the following scenario. You are invited to a wedding reception. In India, if the wedding invitation is scheduled for 7 pm, one goes at 9. If one does go at 7, chances are that even the couple getting wedded won't be present. They wouldn't have yet arrived. In Switzerland, 7 means 7. If in Switzerland one were to go for a 7 o'clock reception at 9, again the couple wouldn't be there, but for a different reason. The function would be over and they would have left.

And this example just considers a broad scenario applicable to a cultural group as a whole. Much more effort needs to be taken to understand the driving forces that open avenues to areas of ***individual*** interest. There is no magic wand for obtaining this. You need to take the time and effort necessary to understand your customer as an individual and the culture he comes from. Believe us, it is possible. And believe us, it pays rich dividends.

Even Emergency Services can perform better when they understand their customer

Somchai Yoosabai, a fireman in Thailand, was called on to rescue a eight year old boy from a third floor window ledge. The boy was huddled to the wall and refused to come into the fireman's arms as he was absolutely terrified. Someone suggested that since the boy was a fan of the comic hero, Spiderman, if Somchai could shed his fireman's uniform and don a Spiderman suit, the boy would lose his fear. A Spiderman suit was quickly organised from a nearby toy store and Somchai donned it and rescued the now comforted child, who was thrilled with the knowledge that his hero had arrived to save him. Brilliant. The fire department truly understood their customer and acted accordingly.

Understanding your Customer Gets you Repeat Business

We are fortunate to be acquainted with an event manager who always manages to secure contracts and events that event managers representing even larger organizations fail to bag. And once he gets a client to do an event with him, in most cases the client is retained with him for life. His customer retention rate is simply fantastic.

This event manager uses the same venues as his competitors do, and similar suppliers as other event companies, so obviously his tangible offerings could hardly differ from those offered by competitors. Then where does he stand out? He scores because he ***invests the time and effort to understand his customer, not as a source of revenue, but rather as an individual, having unique likes, dislikes, tastes and preferences.***

For example, he recently handled a dinner event for a corporate client at which approximately five hundred guests attended. The menu contained a good variety of dishes. One of the dishes was a simple variety of ***daal,*** (a typical Indian dish, of which there are many varieties), which was on the menu for a very good reason. The event manager had developed a good rapport with the personal secretary of the CEO of the organization which was hosting the dinner. During the course of conversations the event manager had with the secretary, he found out that the favourite dish of the CEO was this particular ***daal***. The event manager ensured that this ***daal*** was on the dinner menu.

The function proceeded well, and all the guests were happy.

But the CEO, (who was the person who would ultimately sign the event manager's bill and also ensure repeat business in the future), was thrilled beyond belief. Never at any banquet had he seen this ***daal*** on the menu. The dish was a favourite of his since his childhood days. Needless to say, he wanted to personally thank the event manager responsible for devising the menu. And he thanked him by providing him repeat business in future as well.

Today there are many books occupying prime space on the business section in book stores which discuss diverse cultural differences between regions and nationalities. And if you don't take advantage of this information which is yours to use, and hence miss an opportunity to connect at a personal level with your customer, there are other savvy marketers just waiting to take advantage. It could well be considered a show of indifference from the organisation's end if its representative displays ignorance about the client's culture.

There is the classic case of a cola company displaying a print advertisement in the Gulf countries. The advertisement consisted of a sequence of three visuals.

- The visual on the left showed an apparently tired and exhausted man.
- The centre one depicted him drinking from a bottle of the cola being advertised.
- And the one on the right showed him as refreshed and raring to go.

The message obviously being intended to convey that drinking the cola would energise a tired man.

But what this cola company and it's advertising agency failed to take into account was the fact that in the Gulf countries, the script is Arabic, and people in the Gulf ***read from Right to Left, and NOT from Left to Right.***

You can guess the results.

This is what happens when one spends millions on trying to connect and establish rapport with customers, but fails to take local customs and practices into account.

Adapting to your customer doesn't mean giving up your organisation's values and principles, but culturally tuning your organisation in to your customer's wavelength, with the objective of making him comfortable.

For example, in certain restaurants, the regular waiter may be well aware of individual customer taste and how the customer would like a particular dish to be prepared, and he ensures the order is taken to the customer's choice even without the customer saying so. For example, a lady who is a regular at a particular club, has a preference for a dish, Paneer Chilly. She likes the dish, but ironically without the chilly in the dish. So she wants Paneer Chilly without the chilly. The waiters at this place know this well and bear this in mind and get it to her table without her having to explain her requirements. ***She says this is a major factor in her frequenting this place on a regular basis, and even getting her dinner guests to dine there.***

Children understand this concept well. They know how to gauge the mood of the parent, how to bring up an issue at a right time, after leading the conversation in their favour, thus attaining their objective.

Another example of this tenet in action comes from a particular bookshop we frequent, Ensign Bookstore, located at Bandra in Mumbai. The owner, who is almost always around the store to attend to customers, is a delight to interact with. He takes pride in knowing his regular customers and also their choice in reading material. In fact he will show books which have newly arrived to those customers whose tastes and interests the books match. He knows the customer's choice so well, that it's a matter of pride for him when he says,

"I will not show every book that has recently arrived in the store to every regular customer. I will ensure that from the books I show a specific customer, he would at least buy seven out of ten."

That's a very high conversion rate, only possible when you know your customer almost as well as you know yourself. It also makes the customer attached to the service provider.

When we once asked this bookstore owner to show us any new books which he had procured, he said ***"There is nothing new to suit your taste. My filtering stage is the first. The customer's filtering stage is secondary. I myself will understand his needs first, and I will filter what to show him. WHY SHOULD I UNDERMINE MY OWN CREDIBILITY? I will not show every customer every book that arrives in the store. I know the broad areas he likes and prefers. I'll even show him books which fall on the broad periphery of his tastes. But I will not waste his time and appear to be unduly pushy by shoving every new book onto him to peruse."***

This bookshop owner says that all the big bookstore chains have a facility where they can immediately mail their customers information about newly arrived books as per the customer's choice.

But unfortunately very few bookstore chains use this electronic facility which they already possess and for which they have spent thousands to acquire and install.

This is where the smaller service provider scores, and he scores big time. The personal touch, which requires effort and rapport building, can be cultivated by all businesses, provided they keep this as their priority. But rarely is this excellent practice and philosophy continued, once organizations grow beyond a certain size.

Just as a child slipping into adulthood tends to lose his innate curiosity and wonder in the small but important things that matter, so too, do organizations appear to lose interest in individual customers and their unique needs, once the organisation grows beyond a critical mass.

- Cyrus M Gonda, Kalim Khan

Key Accounts Appear to be Locked Today

Compare and contrast the above positive and enlightened attitude with the lethargic attitude of certain ***Key Account Managers*** with large corporate houses, who ironically need to know their key customers very well.

Irrespective of the industry they operate in, almost all key account managers serve those critical twenty percent of customers of their organization who generate eighty percent of the organization's revenue.

Naturally, these key customers need to be treated with utmost care, concern and a sense of companionship. This can happen only if the key account manager knows each one of these customers he is handling almost as well as he knows himself.

Now, a shocking fact. In one of our training programmes for key account managers of a consumer durable giant, we asked the participants the question, ***"How many Key Accounts do you handle?"***

A typical response we got was, ***"Somewhere around twenty."***

Bad. Key accounts handled will always be a specific figure, else they are not key accounts.

When a Key Account Manager is so vague and not even aware as to the exact number of Key Accounts he is handling, the question of understanding each one of them the way that the Xerox sales people understand them does not even arise. No wonder Key Accounts are being lost by large organizations left, right and centre.

Growth is Good. Reckless Growth is Not Good

We have also observed that the moment an organization increases in size and scale, there is normally an inverse relationship between its scale of operations and the level of understanding and personalisation with its customers. And ironically, it is this increase in organizational scale of operations which is touted as the reason and excuse for the failure of the organization to maintain levels of personalization which existed when the organization was relatively small.

But what is not apparently understood and practiced by these organizations is, that ***as the organization grows in scale and customer***

base, it logically also ought to increase its infrastructure and employee strength. This increased infrastructure and employee base has to be equipped and geared up to continue providing the level of personalization and customization to customers which existed prior to expansion.

In fact even more so.

Because now the enlarged brand, with a larger customer base has a reputation to uphold. But very often the required infrastructure and additional employee strength are simply not added on, althought the increased revenue justifies this investment.

Here we can learn from organizations such as Disney, Nordstrom, and the Ritz group of hotels, which although humongous in size, have not lost touch with the ground on which they and their customers stand.

What we advocate is that the ratio of the quality and quantity of the employee base and infrastructure to number of customers after expansion needs to be at least as much as that existed in the organization prior to expansion, to adequately service the enhanced customer base. This can be achieved through:

1. A superior staff selection process.
2. Providing relevant and adequate training to this properly selected staff.
3. Providing support to operational staff in terms of infrastructure and equipment, customer oriented systems and policies.
4. Sufficient motivation to the staff.
5. And most importantly, the urge from the organisation's end to retain these trained staff, who now are the touch points for the customers, the ones on whom the customers depend and ***identify the brand with.***

There is a certain organization in the USA, where the moment it reaches a staff strength of five hundred employees in a particular location or branch, immediately constructs a new facility for additional employees at least five kilometers away from the existing locations. It does not permit more than five hundred employees to be housed in any one location. This may appear to be an expensive policy in the short run because it apparently appears to duplicate costs, but there is a method to this apparent madness. ***This organization has realized that the larger the employee base is in one location, the more the customer suffers through lack of accountability, lack of attention, and elongated communication chains.***

Why is your product or service purchased?

Understanding the customer also includes an understanding of the purpose for which your customer will be putting to use your brand of product or service.

The following will illustrate.

We are fans of the Dell brand of computers, as we feel they are rugged and reliable machines. Naturally we were excited when Dell recently launched its mini nine inch notebook model. We rushed to the store on day one of it being displayed, with full intention to purchase a piece each on the spot. The functioning and features of the piece were politely and professionally explained to us at a Vijay Sales outlet, but then disappointment set in. Most people who pick up a high end laptop nowadays would at some time or the other be using it to make presentations through an LCD projector. Most other brands of nine inch mini laptops which were launched much before Dell launched its nine inch model, provided this basic facility through a necessary VGA port. But in the Dell nine inch mini model, this feature, a basic need for most users, was not provided for. While we were being given the demonstration, another gentleman came in to look at the same model, and he expressed the same concern. We are not implying that a brand can take care of every feature in every model to suit every taste, but definitely features that competitors are providing as a basic feature and which have become a standard expectation from the product category need to be incorporated. Dell lost three sales on the spot.

Customer service is all about understanding and awareness of needs, problems, fears and aspirations.

- Unknown

An Example from the Pages of History

An excellent example from history about understanding the customer is provided by Michael Farraday, the genius inventor. He evidently understood the ***marketing philosophy,*** (viewing things from the customer's perspective), and also understood his customer perfectly. In short, he knew what made his customers tick.

Farraday wanted the backing of Prime Minister William Gladstone for his invention, ***the first electric motor.*** Gladstone was hardly impressed with the crude bit of machinery, which at that stage was just a piece of wire revolving around a magnet. ***"What use could this be,"*** queried the Prime Minister contemptuously.

Farraday understood his customer perfectly.

He did not elaborate on his own creativity, nor did he spend time explaining the product features, or its potential mighty use.

His brief answer to the Prime Minister was, ***"Sir, it will be of great benefit to our economy. For one day you will be able to tax it."***

Farraday understood Gladstone's world and thus spoke from his perspective. Needless to say, the backing was won.

Loyalty Cards do not by themselves Strengthen Customer Relationships

Understanding your customer has very little to do with showering him with Loyalty Cards simply because he has made a purchase. That's not what the customer primarily wants. As an example, there were two retail outlets offering a similar range of products in close vicinity of each other. Initially, we used to frequent both the stores an equal number of times. We bought goods worth similar amounts from each. One store gave us a Loyalty Card. The second had no such scheme. Yet all the staff in the second store took the effort to know us personally. They greeted us and acknowledged our presence each time we visited. They immediately showed us a newly arrived product which they felt we would like. If they were having a cup of tea, they would offer us a cup as well. They made us feel at home despite having no loyalty card or scheme. They went out of their way to accommodate specific requests that we had.

In the first store where we held a loyalty card, never did any staff member acknowledge our presence or even recognise us as regular customers. We have stopped frequenting that store which gave us the loyalty card, and are firm fans of the second. That is the difference.

The second store clearly understood that customer's needs were on a different level from the routine and mechanical providing of loyalty cards.

Indifference to Customers is a Killer

Not understanding and respecting the customer's need to feel welcome and wanted may keep them away from you permanently. A friend of ours who runs an accessories store in a well known mall, and who is normally extremely attentive and welcoming with each of his regular customers, mentioned that on a particular day he wasn't keeping well, and a regular customer walked in. Our friend wasn't able to greet her or pay her the attention he normally did and to which she was accustomed, because of his poor health on that day. He regrets that she has never returned to his store since then. As he says, ***"The moment the customer senses indifference from your end as a service provider, chances are very high that he or she may move away to another option."***

First seek to Understand rather than to be Understood

This concept was beautifully illustrated in a popular Hindi serial – ***Balika Vadhu.*** In the serial, the eldest son of the house is not having cordial relations with his wife, who is several years younger to him. An aunt, who is a guest at the house, perceives and observes this, and asks the husband what the problem between the two of them is. The husband mentions that he has given his wife everything that he can possibly think of, and yet she is not happy and satisfied. The aunt replies, ***"You may have given her everything YOU have thought of, from YOUR perspective, BUT IS THAT WHAT SHE REALLY WANTS? Have you understood things and requirements from HER perspective?"***

Logically, the next tenet, once you have understood your customer, would be ***maintaining and strengthening relations with him.***

Tenet 5

RELATIONSHIPS ARE AT THE HEART OF MARKETING

Strong customer relationships are essential To ensure long term business potential

We were conducting a training programme on marketing management for the marketing executives of Godrej, when one of the participants narrated this wonderful professional experience he had.

This participant represented the ***Interio*** furniture division of Godrej.

He explained how his division, representing Godrej, were competing with another office furniture manufacturing giant, to secure a substantial order from a bank which needed furniture for the new branches that it was inaugurating. After a lot of presentations and negotiations, the competing organization secured the deal. Which was very fine and fair.

Most other organizations in Godrej's position would have let the matter rest. But not the representatives of the Interio furniture division of Godrej.

The Godrej sales personnel wrote a lovely letter to the bank, thanking the bank officials for the time they had graciously allotted them to present their range of furniture and how great it had been interacting with the bank staff. They wished the bank all success with their new branches. They said that they respected the bank's decision to go with their competitor's range of furniture. They concluded the letter by mentioning that the next time Godrej hoped to come closer to serving the needs of the bank, and they invited the bank staff to feel free and mention any improvements or suggestions they would like to see in the Godrej range of furniture, and if possible, such suggestions would definitely be incorporated.

Based primarily on this lovely letter, (this is what the bank staff themselves confided to the Godrej staff later), relations between the furniture division of Godrej and the bank blossomed, and Godrej secured a huge order from that bank the same year for further new branches that they were coming up with.

The Godrej personnel already recognized the bank as a customer before the bank had even made its first purchase from them. The Godrej sales team had already put into practice our definition of customer from Chapter One of this book.

Although no purchase had been made as yet, the bank staff had an experience with Godrej (when the Godrej representatives made their presentation.) The bank had a touch point with the sales representatives of Godrej, and thus Godrej rightly classified them as customers from day one of their interaction, before the bank had ever made any purchase from, or used or consumed the products of Godrej. Remember the definition of Customer in Chapter One?

Every great business is built on friendship.

- J C Penney

True marketers don't sever relations simply because they didn't secure a deal

Based on your positive and proactive behaviour and continued efforts at maintaining relations, a prospective client, even if he currently purchases goods and services from your competitor, may well decide to deal with your organisation in future.

The worst example of behaviour which cuts and severs relationships comes from the telemarketing industry in general, where the moment the customer mentions he is not interested, in most cases the telemarketers abruptly hang up, without even a goodbye, or a thank you, or a sorry to have disturbed you. A friend of ours mentioned how he once got a telecall for a product he was interested in, and told the marketer to get back the next day as he would like to think the offer over. The caller was sweetness personified. The telecall came the next day to confirm the sale, and our friend said he had thought it over and wasn't interested as of now. The telecaller banged down on him with force without a word. No way is our friend ever going to deal with that brand again.

Organizations have to train, guide and instruct their representatives, that maintaining relations with points of contact in the customer base, even though they may not currently be buyers, is a vital part of their jobs.

A deal has less to do with the monetary aspect of the transaction and more to do with creating lasting relationships.

- Cyrus M Gonda, Kalim Khan

The very word ***Relationship,*** indicates a strong bonding. A cohesion. A gel.

And a bond which is built on trust and faith, which ripens to sweetness through the natural course of time, will prove to be the strongest bond of all.

WISHING to be friends is quick work, but friendship is a slow-ripening fruit.

- Aristotle

Relationships are not built on the foundation of discounts alone

We have observed that money doesn't have that much of a role to play in building long term business relationships. You can't ***buy*** your way into a healthy, long term relationship even in your personal life, can you?

That's why loyalty cards and schemes have a comparatively lesser role to play in developing strong, healthy customer relationships. In fact we were once regular visitors at a shopping chain where we had been given loyalty cards for being regular customers. Whenever we used to shop there, we used to notice something strange. We used to select our merchandise, walk up to the cash counter, where the cashier mechanically used to ask us even without glancing up at our face, ***"Do you have a loyalty card?"*** We used to hand over our card, on which our names were obviously printed, and ***never once in all the purchases we made there did any cashier ever refer to us by our names even after holding the card with our names on it in their hands.***

Such a wonderful opportunity for rapport building lost by the front end staff, time after time after time.

This is mechanical service at its worst.

Just to understand the power of how important a person's name is to him, and how using a person's name while communicating with him would strengthen the relationship, the following true story is wonderful.

The Positive Power of One's Own Name

The story pertains to Andrew Carnegie. Carnegie was once acknowledged as the richest man in the world, a billionaire industrialist and philanthropist, who made his fortune from steel. But he was a self made man, and came from a very modest background. When he was a young boy in his native Scotland, he once managed to catch a rabbit, which soon gave birth to many baby rabbits. He now had many pets, but nothing to feed them with. He then had a brainwave. ***He told his friends in his neighborhood that if they went out and plucked enough grass and herbs to feed the baby rabbits, he would name a baby rabbit after each boy in their honour.*** His job was done. Andrew Carnegie in later life was a great people manager, whose strength in business came from his ability to handle people and maintain strong and lasting relationships. Even at that early age, Carnegie understood the importance that people attached to their own names, and got his rabbits fed for free.

We were watching a programme on television the other day, which depicted luxury hotels of the world. The manager of a luxury hotel in France mentioned with pride how they managed to create a personalized, family type of atmosphere in their hotel by ensuring that rather than refer to a room as Room Number Forty Six, for example, their staff referred to it as Mr. and Mrs. Brown's room. The manager strongly felt that such small but significant touches were what developed healthy guest rapport and ensured that guests came back to the hotel the next time.

When Relations are Good, it Improves the Mood

When your organizational representatives exude a feeling of warmth, it transfers positively to the customer and strengthens the relationship and sweetens the business environment. ***Warmth can secure your organization a monopoly without incurring any extra cost.***

Customers reciprocate to the warmth displayed by your organizational representatives. Warmth spreads like a positive epidemic, and makes the customer feel a part of the organization, and helps him bond and gel with the organization. The line of demarcation between the customer and the organization gradually disappears.

We were recently browsing in an electronic store when we overheard a lady who had just purchased an Olympus camera come up to a salesperson and say, ***"I was about to purchase an expensive model with features I would never have used. I really liked the way you helped and guided me in purchasing this simple piece which meets my needs. I feel so much at home here. After returning from my vacation, I'll come and show you the snaps I took."***

That's the type of relationship and rapport no amount of loyalty cards can ever hope to secure.

We previously mentioned an incident of a regular shopper at the ***Nordstrom*** chain of stores in USA having her marriage ceremony performed inside one of the Nordstrom stores, as she mentioned that **"This is where I feel most at home."**

If you don't genuinely like your customer, chances are they won't buy.

- Thomas J Watson, Jr.

Over the years, we have identified ***three essentials*** which we strongly believe are present in any healthy long term relationship.

The three essential elements are:

1. Love
2. Respect
3. Fear

We will explain ***why*** and in ***what form*** these three elements need to be present for any relationship to be fruitful.

In most relationships, one or two of the above elements may exist.

But it is when all three elements exist simultaneously, that a relationship is at its strongest and best.

1. LOVE

First, let's see why ***Love*** is so essential in any relationship. It is best explained in these beautiful lines by ***Dr. Karl Menninger,*** who said, ***"Love is the basic need of human nature, for without it, life is disrupted emotionally, mentally, spiritually, and physically."***

All customers, being human beings, and having a human nature, would primarily gravitate towards those service providers who infuse a touch of love and personal commitment into their business. It is an organisation's front end representatives, who interact with customers on an ongoing basis, who will be in the best position and have the maximum opportunity to display this element of love to the customer. Your employees, being human beings, can't change their basic nature and turn into loving individuals overnight, but as ***R. Buckminster Fuller,*** one of the most respected thinkers and inventors of the twentieth century noted:

"You can't change people. But if you change the environment the people are in, they will change."

Create that environment where your front end staff, (who are the ones facing the customer), can constantly and in little ways, continue to touch customer's hearts.

And for the cynical minded, it would do good to remember that:

The way to a customer's share of wallet is through his heart.

- Cyrus M Gonda , Kalim Khan

Customers would look forward to interacting with such service providers, and the relationship would never end, provided the flame of love always exists to keep it alive. Love can be displayed in various ways, one of the best expressions of love being ***the amount of time you can devote to understand the other person,*** and then provide what is most essential to the opposite person.

Rings and jewels are not gifts, but apologies for gifts.
The only gift is a portion of thyself.

- Ralph Waldo Emerson

There is a tale of a family with small children who once visited Walt Disney World, and stayed at a resort there. In the daytime, they went out to explore Disney World, and when they returned to their resort room at night, the room had been cleaned and kept ready for them by the housekeeping staff. Nothing unusual about that.

But what ***was*** unusual, was that instead of the fresh cloth towels just being neatly laid out on the bed, ***the housekeeping maid had taken the time and effort to fold the cloth towels into lifelike caricatures of Disney characters - Mickey Mouse, Donald Duck, and so on.***

The children were so delighted that they refused to unfold the towels even to use them to dry themselves off. They called for more towels from the housekeeping department and left these folded as they were.

For the kids, (and in turn for their parents), it was ***wow and delight rolled into one.***

The thing they most fondly remembered about their trip to Disney World was not the awe inspiring sights they saw, or the rides they had. But it was these thoughtfully, lovingly folded towels back in the room, moulded with care by a thoughtful, loving housemaid, who was permitted to work in an environment where she did not have to rush through cleaning and do up twenty rooms before lunchtime. ***Rather, the environment in which she worked, encouraged and gave her sufficient time to put her***

personal touch and her loving signature even in the mundane job of cleaning up a room.

2. RESPECT

The ***second element*** that needs to exist in a healthy relationship is ***Respect.***

Respect is simply defined as the unbiased, perception free, consideration and regard that one displays for the rights, values, beliefs and property of all people. These things are of utmost importance to all people, and when you respect the values and beliefs of the people you deal with, you put them at their ease. The customers you deal with come from diverse backgrounds and cultures, and may find your values, beliefs and ideas, as different and maybe as weird, as you find theirs. But a healthy respect for diversity will ensure unity and commonality of purpose, and will put both parties in the right frame of mind to conduct business, which is why they got together in the first place.

Many times, organizations lose a customer, because the customer feels that the organizational representative he is interacting with, does not show him the respect he deserves. All staff should be explained in depth, repeatedly, that a customer's dignity is most important to him, and should be handled carefully.

Never take a person's dignity. It is worth everything to them, and nothing to you.

- Frank Barron

The surprising thing about dignity, as Frank Barron so aptly points out, is that taking a person's dignity away from him doesn't do you any good at all. It's worth nothing to the person who snatches it. But a customer losing his respect at the hands of your organizational representative, whether knowingly through rude words or rude behaviour, or unknowingly through careless attitude and behaviour on part of your staff, can lose your organization a lot of business in the bargain.

A relationship where one side does not respect the other, has no chance to develop and blossom into something mutually beneficial.

Your customer's self respect and dignity are the most fragile goods your organisation will ever deal with. Handle them with utmost care.

- Cyrus M Gonda, Kalim Khan

Treat your customer's self respect and dignity as you would treat a precious seed, give it the care and attention it deserves. Magic will then flower the relationship in unexpected ways.

And as the purpose of respect in a business relationship is to generate repeat business and positive word of mouth, we would do well to remember the ancient ***Persian Proverb :***

"He who wants a rose must respect the thorn."

All organizations and brands want the ***rose,*** that is, ***business and revenue*** from the customer. That is very desirable.

But the proverb reminds us that it is not possible to get the benefit of the rose, without respecting the thorn. The ***thorn*** in this case would be that which makes life a little difficult and possibly uncomfortable for the organization - the customer's unique requirements and customisation of needs, the importance the customer attaches to minute details, or for respecting the customer's valuable time.

Don't treat your customer's unique requirements as a thorn. Treat the thorns as an essential and inseparable part of the complete rose, which is so desirable to your organization, as ***without respect for the rose of revenue, your organization would cease to exist.***

The saying, ***No pain, No gain,*** holds very true for developing strong and healthy customer relationships.

3. FEAR

Fear is the third parameter of a lasting relationship. Surprised? Don't be.

We don't use the term ***fear*** in a negative context. Rather, we mean the fear one has of losing the opportunity to deal with the opposite person or organization.

Do your customers have a fear at the back of their mind that they may lose the opportunity to deal with your organization? That you may one day close down or shut shop?

A friend of ours was having his shop renovated. Carpentry work was in progress. A regular customer walked in and asked him, "What's going on?" Our friend said he was just having the place renovated. She replied, ***"Oh, I'm so relieved. I thought you were shutting shop."***

Have you created for yourself that position of being an indispensable or irreplaceable supplier to your customers?

Isn't it strange that the milkman, paper delivery boy, tailor, barber, make themselves indispensable to their customers, but large organisations with all the resources at their command find it difficult to do so?

Thus the word - ***fear,*** understood from this perspective is an important essential in any healthy relationship as it displays the ***level*** at which the bond between the two parties exists. The higher the level of fear of losing out on the benefits of the relationship,(if the relationship is terminated), the higher is the dependence on the other party, and ultimately the more is the strength of the relationship.

The presence of fear in the business relationship demonstrates that very few options are available to the opposite party to avail of the quality of products, services and personalized attention that your organization currently provides.

- Cyrus M Gonda, Kalim Khan

The higher the comfort level that exists between your organisation and the customer, the better you are able to cater to his needs, the higher will be the level of fear the customer will have of losing all these benefits.

Thus when we indicate that fear is an important component of a healthy relationship, it is from the perspective of acting as a barometer of the strength of the relationship.

When all three factors – Love, Respect and Fear, are present in a relationship in healthy measure, ***FAITH*** is the automatic result.

We strongly advocate that an organization have as its objective the goal of Customer Faith, rather than Customer Delight. Delight can be a one time activity. But Faith can only be built over a period of time.
And time is the true test of a relationship.

- Cyrus M Gonda, Kalim Khan

Too often, organizations attempt to leapfrog towards the concept of Customer Delight without first getting the basics right.

While individual heroics resulting in one time customer delight are great, they can never compare with consistently good performances on a regular basis which arise primarily from systemic strength.

As a wise man said – ***Today, customers don't want INSTANT, as much as they want CONSTANT.***

A feeling of faith can be generated by an organization amongst its customers through the following actions, if the following actions are repeated by the organizational representatives in their dealings with the customers time after time after time.

1. Informing and advising the customer about products and services which match his needs in an honest manner.
2. Acting first and foremost in the customer's interest. ***IN HIS INTEREST, LIES YOUR INTEREST.***
3. Listening attentively with mind, body and soul to what the customer has to say, and acting upon the same.
4. Genuine care, commitment and concern being demonstrated for the customer.
5. Keeping in touch with the customer even after the sale is complete and the money has come in.

When is a sale not Considered as a Deal?

In common parlance, a sale is equated with having struck a deal. But we feel this terminology needs a serious rethink.

A sale by itself does not imply that a deal has been made.

A sale classifies as a deal only if it creates room for further interaction with that customer or recommendation to other customers through that customer.

A sale, even if it generates revenue, may be classified as non-productive if it does not result in a good deal as far as the customer is concerned.

If the customer feels cheated, conned, and generally is left with a bad taste in the mouth once he has parted with his money, such a sale cannot be beneficial for the organization, as the relationship from the customer's end has obviously terminated.

An interaction can be termed as a deal even if it does not result into a sale, provided it has translated into goodwill which could result into further business opportunities.

- Cyrus M Gonda, Kalim Khan

In other words, a sale can be considered a deal only if the interaction has been a Win-Win. (We have covered more on Win-Win in ***Tenet Six, Moments of Truth.***)

***We may not always see eye to eye,
but we can try to see heart to heart.***

- Sam Levenson

We were in an electronics retail outlet the other day, and a customer came in asking for a particular model of air conditioner. The store didn't currently have the model in stock. The customer asked the salesperson he was dealing with if he knew where it would be immediately available. In most cases, a salesman would say, "I don't know." But here, this salesperson guided him to a nearby competitor, and patiently gave him directions to the competitor's store. This is a classic long term, relationship building exercise. It demonstrates a genuine desire to help a ***customer*** who has walked into your store. (He is the customer, as he has experienced your brand.) In this case, this excellent salesman may not have made a sale. ***The business happened for the competitor. But we say the deal happened for the shop this salesman represented.***

Therefore, a deal can be termed a ***bond of faith,*** wherein the customer realizes that your organization is worth ***DEALING*** with, and if he does not have a need ***NOW,*** when in future he ***DOES*** have a need, your organization will be the first one he will think of.

This will ensure that the stepping stone of the relationship has been successfully crossed.

The following real life example would do justice to this point.

A student of ours, who is a General Manager - Sales, with a leading construction firm, was once conversing about how he maintained a rapport with administration people in various companies, calling them up regularly just as a matter of courtesy, whether they gave him business or had requirements for commercial space or housing for their staff or not. He didn't sit to ***TARGET*** and ***SEGMENT*** and ***SEGREGATE*** and ***DISCARD*** those who weren't giving him business because they never seemed to have a requirement. He just kept in touch and maintained relationships. As a part of this continuous courtesy, he also kept in touch with an administration lady in a particular company, although that company never appeared to have any commercial space or housing requirement. One day, she got in touch with him saying, "Vithal, I'm now with another company, I've changed jobs, and we have a requirement here. The first person I thought of is you." And she gave him business of the value of 3,00,000 square feet. And that wasn't all. The next year, she again contacted him saying, "I'm now with yet another company," and she gave him even more business. Plus he now had an entry on an ongoing basis in both these large companies which had regular requirements. And all this because he kept in touch even with people who apparently had no potential for business.

Thus from the above example, we learn that while ***Targeting*** may appear to be a scientific and intellectual exercise, it ***can never beat good old fashioned courtesy and human relations and rapport.***

(In fact, when one sits to target and segment mindlessly and short sightedly, one is ignoring a huge chunk of the entire potential consumer base. As an example, the chocolate industry in India for many years segmented its customer base and targeted only children, before it realized that adults enjoy and consume chocolates too.)

Even looking at the issue of business relationships from a historical perspective, before the concept of money as a means of exchange was introduced, the barter system was in force. Money was introduced at a later stage in the business cycle to merely ***facilitate*** or ***smoothen*** the exchange transaction.

Thus in any business transaction, the first aim should be to facilitate and serve. Money will automatically be a by product of such a transaction, and so will a healthy relationship.

Higher your Employee Turnover, Lesser will be the Strength of your Customer Relationships

We have said this before, and we will say this again. It is your employees who make or break your brand. Once your brand has managed to secure the services of employees who gel and bond with your customers, it is imperative that management does all it can within its powers and beyond to retain these staff members. Customers develop relationships with individual employees first, and later feel a sense of belonging to the brand. Many customers at retail outlets, restaurants and hotels tell us they no longer go back once they find that a employee who understood their requirements is no longer with the organization.

When employee turnover in an organisation is rapid, even a regular customer starts to feel like an alien. A stranger in a strange land.

- Cyrus M Gonda, Kalim Khan

The European Model and the American Model of Customer Relationship Management

Relationship building is where the European concept of Customer Relationship Management scores over the American concept. Which is why excellent, personalized service is still referred to as ***old world hospitality.*** (Europe epitomizing the old world.)

While the American concept of CRM is more concerned with impersonal data collection and capturing, primarily in an electronic format, the

European concept focuses more on the process of interaction between the service provider and the customer, and ways and means to make it warmly glow with a personal touch.

Even though customer data is captured in the European model, the primary purpose of such data would be to enhance the customer experience by treating him as much of an individual as possible, so that he never feels the need to go to a competitor.

The concept of a ***Guest History Manager*** in a five star hotel chain brilliantly demonstrates this. Assume that a reserved room has been kept ready with a bouquet of flowers for a guest. The guest arrives, enters his room, and informs the reception that ***while he's grateful for the flowers, he's allergic to them, and so could they kindly be removed from his room. And could he have an extra pillow as well, please?***

Nothing unusual about these requests. They can be fulfilled by the hotel staff within minutes. ***But what happens after that is a matter which should be of interest to organizations in every industry.***

The Guest History Manager is informed by the operations staff that the guest is allergic to flowers and has requested for an extra pillow in his room. These bits of information are noted down in the guest database as points to be kept in mind whenever this particular guest checks-in the hotel in the future, not only in this particular hotel location, but at any location in this hotel chain.

Imagine the ***wow*** factor at work. The guest never has to repeat a request more than once with a particular hotel. He feels at home. He feels comfortable. He feels people here know him so well. And that they care for him. ***The relationship in such a scenario can only grow from strength to strength.***

This system can be implemented in every organization in any industry and it can be the best tool for relationship building, if used wisely and well.

The system ensures that every repeat customer gets royal treatment and is treated like a VIP.

We strongly recommend that every industry follow the example of the hotel industry and create a position similar to that of a Guest History Manager.

It saves the time, effort and energy required in repeating and understanding the same set of instructions time after time.

It makes the cost of moving away to a competitor much higher for a customer, as here he has already established a personalized relationship with the organization he is dealing with.

Thus, the ***Customer Retention rate is automatically strengthened.***

When the relationship is strong, in your customer's eyes you can do little wrong.

- Cyrus M Gonda, Kalim Khan.

Such a happy situation is also highly profitable for the organization as it ensures repeat business.

And it is very possible for every organisation to achieve these high customer retention rates through the process of relationship building.

It is not empty rhetoric.

What is required to reap profits through relationship building are first grade organisational systems, and a highly trained, customer focused staff across departments, who work in close co-ordination with one another, like a well designed, well oiled, well maintained and well serviced machine, with the heart and soul of a human being added for good measure.

- Cyrus M Gonda, Kalim Khan.

Thus what an organization which wishes to be known as the benchmark for customer retention in its industry needs to focus on is developing individual customer relationships, one at a time, rather than focus on mass market relationship building tools such as loyalty cards. Obviously, the individual relationships require more focus, time and effort from the side of the organization, but the added investment is well worth it.

As ***Joan Baez,*** the famous song writer and folk singer so aptly put it –

"The easiest kind of relationship for me is with ten thousand people. The hardest is with one."

Relationship Building

In any building, the elements of a strong foundation, well laid bricks, strong cement, and smooth exterior finish need to be present. In the same way, when it comes to strong and healthy customer relationships, the genuine liking for the customer is the foundation, understanding his unique needs comprise the bricks, customer centric systems form the cement, and polite and efficient service delivery complete the smooth exterior finish.

The Dream Resort at Devka

In Devka, a seaside resort town in the Union Territory of Daman, (about 200 kms. away from Mumbai), we have our very own Indian Cesar Ritz of the Hotel Industry in the form of Dosabhai Oliaji. He runs a family owned resort which can hardly compare in elegance and infrastructure with the five star resorts which surround it. Yet once a guest stays at Oliaji's Holiday Home, he would never stay elsewhere at Devka in future. Oliaji is almost ninety, and has been a fixture at the place as long as his oldest guests can remember. They come back year after year after year, and Oliaji delights in knowing, remembering and understanding each one of them personally. When one of us authors was about a year old, (forty years ago), his parents had taken him to visit this resort. The floor standing fan at Oliaji's resort in the room we had stayed made a jarring noise as the bearing in the fan was spoilt. (Obviously the author doesn't remember that as he was just a year old when this incident occurred.) The author's father had requested Oliaji if he could provide another fan as a replacement, as the noise wouldn't permit us to sleep. Oliaji didn't have a spare fan in the resort and all other rooms were occupied, but he immediately purchased a new fan from the market and placed it in the room.

Recently, ***forty years after this incident,*** the author and his parents visited Oliaji's resort again. Oliaji's first remark after the customary hug and greeting was addressed to the author's father, ***"The fan I got for you is still there and working well."*** That was enough to blow us away. What a memory. And how it made our family emotionally connect and bond with Oliaji.

Every family that has visited Oliaji's resort has a similar tale to tell. If it's a family with a small child, Oliaji ensures that two full glasses of milk are sent to that family in the morning and in the evening. They don't even need to ask. He knows the age, taste and preference of each individual staying in every resort room at all moments of time. And there is no charge for the milk. Oliaji wouldn't dream of taking it. In fact, he would be insulted if it was offered, During all meals, Oliaji personally takes a round of the meal tables, and if a guest has not had a particular dish, asks him what's wrong, and if the person isn't fond of that particular dish, he immediately sends some other dish to the table. ***It's a guarantee that in the more than sixty years Oliaji has run his resort, not a single guest would have gone away with an unresolved complaint,*** (that is, if they had a complaint in the first place.) ***Imagine the retention rate for this resort. World famous brands would give their eye teeth to secure half the retention rate that Oliaji manages.***

Inspite of several new resorts coming up in the vicinity, which offer everything from swimming pools, billiards and air conditioned bars on the premisies, Oliaji's regular and retained clients would never think of going anywhere else.

The wise man puts himself last and finds himself first.

- Lao Zi

To conclude this tenet, a thought provoking quote from the pen of ***Mark Twain,***

"One learns people through the heart; not the eyes or the intellect."

Tenet 6

ENSURE MEMORABLE MOMENTS OF TRUTH

Your organization creates Thousands of Moments of Truth a day

Why not make them all go the Win-Win Way

Brains Trust definition of 'Moment of Truth'

"Any interaction in any form, at any distance, that any individual has with any aspect of a brand or organization, which enables that individual an opportunity to formulate a certain opinion, either positive or negative, about that brand or organization."

A Moment of Truth is ***the*** defining moment in the life of a brand. In fact, collectively, Moments of Truth are what break or make a brand. As the saying goes, ***The Proof of the Pudding is in the Eating***.

The concept of Moments of Truth originated in the aviation industry, the formal christening of the term fittingly undertaken by a certain Jan Carlzon, the President of Scandinavian Airlines. A little background to the term would be in order.

The genesis of the concept of "Moments of Truth"

Jan took over Scandinavian Airlines when the organisation's image was at rock bottom. Service in the organization was a poor joke. Jan came in. The Customer Delight graph of the organization sky rocketed. As simple as that.

Aha !

But what was it that Jan ***DID*** to get the results he got? ***THAT'S*** the key. Jan was aware he was running an organization where his staff was individually interacting millions of times a day with passengers.

Jan termed each of these individual interactions between his staff and the passengers as a Moment of Truth, which he felt were the defining moments for the reputation of any brand.

His logic was spot on. If the outcomes of a large majority of these interactions were positive and satisfying, customer satisfaction, delight, and ultimately customer retention and positive word of mouth publicity would be the result.

Therefore, each passenger interaction would be a potential opportunity for Jan and his team to showcase their service philosophy and customer orientation.

Jan mentioned that in a customer driven company, the responsibility and authority needed to be delegated to those who until now may have comprised the order-obeying bottom level of the pyramid. Extensive changes would be required to shift from centering systems on the basis of organizational convenience, to now centering them around customer convenience.

And these changes would have no option but to originate at the top layer of management. ***The top executive would have to lead from the front, be constantly visible to staff, as well as to passengers.*** (Jan spent a majority of his time in the operational areas, interacting with passengers and front end staff.)

Sam Walton – Leading from the front

Another true leader of a similar caliber as Jan and possessing a similar philosophy was Sam Walton. It is a sad fact that CEOs across industries today argue that considering all the affairs of running a huge conglomerate, they have very little time to invest at the front end.

Sam Walton could easily have said the same.

As the head of the world's leading Fortune 500 Organisation, (Wal-Mart), Sam could reasonably argue that he was busier than most other CEOs. ***But Sam was very clear where his presence would be most inspiring, most needed, and most effective.***

At the front end.

Out of six working days in a week, Sam spent on an average three of them moving around from store to store at random. Investing his valuable time where he felt it would be most fruitful and productive. In the shopping area, assisting a shopper, or guiding a trainee as to the best and most efficient method to gift wrap a package.

Wal-Mart also has its own farms, where they grow their own fruits and vegetables. Sam would regularly drop in unannounced by helicopter at any of these farms with a big bag of doughnuts and flasks of steaming coffee. He would help the staff pluck the fruit from the trees, then sit down and share the doughnuts and coffee with them and have a good chat with his staff about the way things were going. This would give him valuable first hand insights as to the way in which the supply chain, the operational elements and the logistical aspects of his organization functioned. These data would prove invaluable in top management decision making at a later date.

This done, he would sit with the driver of the truck which would carry the picked fruit to the Wal-Mart store houses. All through the journey, he would use the opportunity to talk shop with the driver and get to know many inner details of work life in his organization at the operational level.

Sam Walton considered this time spent his greatest investment, not a waste.

Consistently great Moments of Truth lead to *'Six Sigma'*

In India, we have our very own ***Dabbawalas,*** (the world renowned tiffin (lunch box) carriers of Mumbai city), which comprise the ***ONLY organization in India acknowledged to operate at an efficiency level of Six Sigma.***

Six Sigma may appear a complex term, but in simple words it means ***operating at an efficiency level of around three errors per million transactions that the organization undertakes with its customers.***

Each of these one million transactions is nothing but an opportunity to provide a positive Moment of Truth, and that's the secret of the dabbawala's success.

THE SIGNIFICANCE OF SIX SIGMA IN ANY BUSINESS IS NOTHING BUT HOW MANY POSITIVE MOMENTS OF TRUTH PER MILLION THE ORGANISATIONAL SYSTEMS AND PEOPLE ARE CAPABLE OF DELIVERING TO CUSTOMERS.

In fact the dabbawalas operate at a level much above Six Sigma, as they are said to commit on an average only one error in every sixteen million transactions. And before you say that their scale of operations is negligible and that's the reason they can achieve this, the fact is that they deliver 1,60,000 tiffins a day. When you consider the fact that they also accurately and punctually return the empty tiffins they carry, back to the respective residences after the customer has finished his meal, the number of transactions they carry out daily comes up to 3,20,000.

And they consistently and successfully perform this magical feat although they depend on an external entity, (the local railways), and operate in sizzling heat or monsoon downpour. This merely goes to show the inherent strength and dependability and customer orientation of their systems.

If you were asked a question, ***"What ought to be the level of technology that India's ONLY Six Sigma organization should be possessing",*** your answer might well be, ***"State of the art technology, latest gadgetry, and similar things."***

If you were further asked, ***"What ought to be the level of qualifications***

of the senior functionaries at India's only Six Sigma organization", the answer again could possibly be, "MBAs from premier institutes in supply chain management and logistics, experienced Chartered Accountants, and the like."

The truth is, the average dabbawala is not technology savvy.

The average dabbawala's qualification has not reached beyond primary schooling.

The ***AVERAGE DABBAWALA IS NOT A BLACK BELT OR A GREEN BELT SIX SIGMA CERTIFIED EXPERT.***

In fact he doesn't have a belt. ***HE WEARS A WHITE DHOTI (LOIN CLOTH.)***

The dabbawalas literally put organizations which possess state of the art technology and highly qualified individuals at the helm of affairs in the shade as far as Moments of Truth involving customer interaction go.

So what makes ***THE DABBAWALAS*** India's only Six Sigma organization?

And what is the lesson from them that all other organizations could do well to learn?

IT'S PURE AND ABSOLUTE UNADULTERATED CUSTOMER FOCUS AND ORIENTATION, CENTERING OF ALL THEIR ORGANISATIONAL PROCESSES AROUND CUSTOMER CONVENIENCE, AND LEADERSHIP WHICH FOCUSES ON CUSTOMERS FIRST AND PROVIDING CUSTOMERS ERROR FREE MOMENTS OF TRUTH AS A PRIORITY.

Imagine a situation where you have a problem with the services of a leading private sector bank or a cellular service provider, ***and in spite of repeated complaints and interactions with staff at lower and mid levels; your problem is not resolved.*** And you as a dissatisfied customer of that bank or cellular service provider state a desire to meet with the CEO of that organisation to brief him about the same.

What would be the answer you would be likely to get?

"Sorry. Not possible to meet him."

Why?

"He's busy."

Busy doing what?

"Attending meetings, inaugurating new branches, addressing customer service seminars, giving interviews to media, deciding mergers and acquisitions, planning for expansion, (all this expansion, when the organisation is not even capable of catering to current existing customer's satisfaction), and so on."

Hold on. Hold on. Hold on.

Isn't the ***CUSTOMER*** supposed to be the King and the most important person around? And what could be more important for a CEO than a customer with a complaint which hasn't been resolved by his operational staff?

Shouldn't the CEO be eager to meet such a customer?

The answer to this valid query normally is, ***"If he did that he wouldn't have time for anything else. You're not the only customer with a complaint, you know. There are thousands of customers like you who have a pending problem."***

WOW. That fact alone should make this a priority issue for the CEO.

So what's the reason for the Dabbawala's success

Back to the Dabbawalas. A few years ago, Prince Charles of England was scheduled to visit Mumbai, and having heard so much about the efficiency of the dabbawalas, he expressed a desire to visit and meet them during his trip to Mumbai.

The head of the dabbawalas sent a polite reply to Prince Charles.

"We would be most happy to welcome you, provided you can come after two in the afternoon."

Why after two in the afternoon?

"Because until two in the afternoon, OUR CUSTOMERS ARE OUR PRINCES AND KINGS. They get total priority. It would be an honour to meet Prince Charles, but our customers come first, every time."

Compare this customer centric response with the statements in Chapter Five of this book, "Scenario Today," and you get the answer as to why the ***Dabbawalas are the only substantially large organisation in India***

able to operate at the level of Six Sigma.

The Customer Feels Cosy, When *Moments of Truth* are Rosy

Many senior executives in reputed organizations, for one reason or the other, allocate very little time to personal involvement at operational and grass root levels.

This important and vital activity is almost totally left to supervisors down the line. It sends a message throughout the hierarchy of the organization that customer interaction is not an important activity, nor a priority which requires top management time allocation.

Imagine a Corporate CEO who has no time for meeting his own customers who have complaints, getting a request from Prince Charles asking the CEO to meet him.

The expected reply?

"Yes Sir, Yes Sir, when would you like to meet up and where? Two in the afternoon? Two at night? Anything is fine with me, Sir, as long as it's convenient to YOU."

And ***THAT*** is the sole reason the Dabbawalas are the ***ONLY*** sizeable organization in India to operate at a level of Six Sigma.

To my customers, I may not have the answer, but I'll find it.

I may not have the time, but I'll make it.

- Unknown

A while ago, one of the dabbawalas, in the course of his duty, met with a fatal accident. His customers ***were not even aware that any calamity had befallen him.*** That's because their lunch boxes were delivered ***on time.*** Another dabbawala had immediately taken over, (this displays the planning, co-ordination, and super efficiency of their systems), delivered the lunch boxes on time, and ensured that even under such tragic circumstances, the customers would not go without their home cooked meals.

THIS is the true marketing philosophy at work. ***Centering all your organisational processes and systems to meet the customer's convenience and not your own. These are the lessons we can learn from this six sigma organisation.***

A simple two word strategy – CUSTOMER FIRST.

All that the Dabbawalas are doing as far as the customers are concerned, is providing excellent, error free Moments of Truth, time after time after time.

Unfortunately the concept of ***Six Sigma*** has been made unnecessarily complex and complicated and has been turned into a mathematician's domain and a non-mathematician's nightmare.

Logically, Six Sigma need not be a number driven philosophy.

The only thing which should be mathematical about the concept of Six Sigma is that Six Sigma indicates Positive Moments of Truth for the customers 99.9997 percent of the time. The rest of the concept of Six Sigma is all about gearing up organisational systems and people to meet this defect free level and possibly surpass it.

After all, the dabbawalas didn't sit to calculate whether they were at a level of Six Sigma. They just went ahead and geared their systems in place, focused on the customer and his requirements, and attained and surpassed Six Sigma levels.

Excellent organizations will strive to ensure that they never permit their customer to find a flaw in their functioning.

- Cyrus M Gonda, Kalim Khan

The behaviour of a brand, individually considered as separate components delivered by individual brand representatives, and then taken collectively as a whole, will be a reflection of organizational policy and culture.

Ultimately, the sum total of these behaviours will constitute the aggregate of the organisational Moments of Truth for the customers of that brand.

Win-Lose, Lose-Lose, Lose-Win, Win-Win

As we observed earlier, a Moment of Truth occurs each time there is an interaction between two parties.

Coming to the numerical aspects of the concept of Moments of Truth, since there are ***two parties*** involved in any Moment of Truth – On one hand the service provider or the representative of the organisation, and on the other hand the customer, there are ***four possible outcomes*** to any Moment of Truth.

Even while purchasing a bus ticket, a Moment of Truth occurs. If the bus conductor gives the right change without a fuss, gives the passenger a smile, is polite, answers any queries knowledgeably, then the passenger feels happy. Conversely, if the conductor is rude, sullen, refuses to give change, then the passenger feels disappointed.

In short, a Moment of Truth or a touch-point, is each, and every opportunity provided to the organisation because of its nature of business to directly interact with its client base to create a long lasting impact. The impact could be a positive or a negative one, depending on the behaviour of the service provider.

A Moment of Truth by its nature is a neutral entity.

It is the point at the customer crossroads.

Two paths originate here.

One path is the path to SERVICE DISASTER.

The second path is the path to SERVICE DELIGHT.

The choice lies with the organization which path it wishes to tread.

What the organisation and its representatives MAKE of the opportunity provided by a Moment of Truth, converts it into a positive memento or a negative backlash.

- Cyrus M Gonda, Kalim Khan

The four possible outcomes of any Moment of Truth are:

SERVICE PROVIDER	CUSTOMER	OCCURENCE	OUTCOME	ATTITUDE
Win	Lose	Regular	Short Term Profit	Aggressive
Lose	Win	Regular	Loss	Non - Assertive
Lose	Lose	Regular	Disaster	Aggressive
Win	Win	Rare	Recipe for Success	Assertive

There is no fifth outcome possible.

When we say ***Win*** and ***Lose,*** we do not mean a physical fight. Rather, when we say WIN, it indicates that the party which ***wins*** in the transaction is ***happy and satisfied, feels benefited by having participated in it, at an advantage, and would like to do business with the other party again.***

By contrast, the party that feels it has ***LOST,*** feels ***cheated, dissatisfied, would never like to deal with the other party ever again, and more importantly will spread a negative impression about the opposite party or brand*** which would spread to wherever that individual has a ***Circle of Influence.***

There is no rule that says that both parties involved in the Moment of Truth cannot win.

Think of it as a happily married couple, where both parties have mutually benefited, and would want the relationship to continue.

Winning and Losing in Moments of Truth are the result and outcome of ***three possible behaviours,*** any one of which could be at the forefront during the transaction. These three behaviours are:

1. **AGGRESSIVE**
2. **ASSERTIVE**
3. **NON-ASSERTIVE**

Let's see what these three terms mean:

- ## AGGRESSIVE

As discussed earlier in the chapter on Marketing Renaissance, being ***AGGRESSIVE*** means that an individual or an organization only looks for ***self*** convenience, ***personal*** benefit and is ***not*** bothered about whether the other party also benefits through the transaction or not.

The entire approach is a ***ME versus YOU*** point of view. Like opponents in a boxing ring.

One party will push, dominate, harrow and do everything possible to ensure that it ***wins*** at all costs, (and the cost is borne by the other party.)

In aggressive behaviour, the party which is being aggressive feels it has all the rights and feelings, and that the other party's rights and feelings don't matter. We are sure you could immediately think of multiple examples of this behaviour where you were at the receiving end.

One such classic example comes from the telemarketing industry, where the telemarketing end in most cases wants to make the call at all costs, ***irrespective whether the person at the other end is busy or not.***

The warped logic followed quite often is - "I win if I meet my daily quota of calls irrespective of how many people I have antagonised in the process." An ***AGGRESSIVE*** approach may result in a ***WIN-LOSE*** situation, (which by its very nature gets only short term benefits.) ***You may win the battle (by winning this particular transaction), but you definitely lose the war.*** This is primarily because a majority of such transactions where one party displays aggressive behaviour result into ***LOSE-LOSE*** if the other party responds equally aggressively.

The following example will better explain the aggressive, short term perspective.

Organizations mistake promotional and advertising activity as the marketing philosophy, whereas in effect the two are unrelated. ***Genuine marketing and customer oriented organizations ensure that customers are never exploited just because they have a need.*** Certain organizations believe that since the customer appears to be in a tight spot, they can milk him for all he is worth. This can never lead to retention or positive word of mouth. An example which a friend of ours quoted recently will prove the point. Our friend's brother had joined a gymnasium, paying Rs.16,000 as the fees for a year's membership. It's a reputed gymnasium, also very flashy, with quite an elite clientele. Unfortunately, six months into his membership period, our friend's brother developed a severe back problem, and was unable to continue his visits to the gymnasium. He requested them to transfer the balance six months of membership to his brother, who is our friend. The gymnasium authorities charged him Rs.1,600 as a transfer fee, which he paid, and he was told to come to the gym from the next day. The next day when he reached the gym, he was made to wait an hour at reception. The receptionist said she still had to clarify with her management whether he could start attending the gym in his brother's place (inspite of him already having paid the transfer fees.) Ultimately she said that he would have to pay a further Rs.5,500. When he asked the reason why, he was told bluntly that when his brother had taken the membership six months ago, the annual membership fees had been Rs.16,000, but now they had increased the fees to Rs. 21,500, so he would have to pay the difference. Crazy. Our friend walked off in disgust. He is a regular gym goer, and in fact had just finished his membership at his regular gym and wanted to try this one out. He had already paid the Rs.1,600 transfer fees and the next day, the gym management tried to extract still more juice out of him. It just didn't make any sense, logically or commercially. He has already spread a lot of negative publicity about this gym among his gym-going friend circle.

And this gymnasium spends a lot of money in advertising in newspapers and on expensive hoardings, but then loses such opportunities to generate goodwill by giving negative experiences. Definitely an attempt at ***WIN - LOSE*** from the gym's perspective, but as with all attempts at ***WIN - LOSE,*** ultimately results into a ***LOSE - LOSE,*** as the customer goes away never to return, spreading as much negative publicity as he can. What would it have cost the gym to let him continue the balance six months without an extra unnecessary charge, considering that he had already paid Rs.1,600 as a transfer fee? Nothing. It just tried to ***aggressively*** extract the maximum that it thought it could under the circumstances, and in the bargain didn't gain anything.

Another point our friend mentioned about this gym was that in the one day he was there, clarifying the issue about the additional fees, he could make out that the toilets there were stinking. Whereas, at the gym he regularly frequented, Talwalkars, he says the hygiene factor is given such extreme importance that there is an attendant waiting outside the washroom area, and each time a person enters and leaves the washroom, the attendant goes in with a mop. Never has he had a complaint with regards the hygiene and cleanliness at Talwalkars. Two gymnasiums, similar in terms of facilities offered and rates charged, differ so much on the issue of hygiene. Another Moment of Truth which impacts customer experience.

It matters not whether you win or lose,
what matters is whether I win or lose.

- Darrin Weinberg

The above quote, though said in sarcastic vein, explains the ***philosophy of the Win-Lose mentality.***

It has been ingrained in most of us as individuals as well as organisations, incorrectly, that for ***us*** to succeed, the other ***must*** fail. But in business and in customer interactions, your success ***cannot*** come as a result of the customer's dissatisfaction. If you aim for, or are satisfied with ***Win-Lose,*** that's the end of your relationship with that customer. So your ***'win'***, if you can call it that, is at best a hollow one, with more loss in it than gain, as you lose all future business that could have potentially accrued through that customer and through his Circle of Influence.

• NON-ASSERTIVE

Remember, it is Win-Win, not Give-In

In contrast to aggressive behaviour, being ***NON-ASSERTIVE*** indicates that one is ***meek, submissive, gives in or succumbs to the other party each time, and says a YES to everything,*** thereby losing on the transaction, but with the intention of keeping the other party happy. This situation is even more dangerous than ***AGGRESSIVE*** behaviour, because by saying ***YES*** to everything in a false attempt to please the customer, one ends up by ***over promising*** and ***under delivering,*** which is one of the ***gravest errors any marketer could make.*** In short, by displaying non-assertive behaviour, one feels that the other party has all the rights and feelings and one's own feelings don't matter, and one is willing to let the other person push and dominate at all costs, as long as the other person leaves the transaction feeling he has got the upper hand. ***The person behaving non-assertively feels he has secured business, irrespective of whether he can deliver what he has promised and committed.*** This also results in a short term relationship, as on non-performance or non-delivery as committed and promised, one immediately loses the trust of the other party. Thus, this behaviour ultimately results into ***LOSE-WIN,*** which ultimately converts into ***Lose-Lose,*** on non-delivery or non-performance.

• ASSERTIVE

Any business arrangement that is not profitable to the other fellow will in the end prove unprofitable for you. The bargain that yields mutual satisfaction is the only one that is apt to be repeated.

- B. C. Forbes

The third type of behaviour is termed as ***Assertive*** behaviour. The term assertive indicates ***self-confident, self-assured, forward looking and mature behaviour.*** It indicates that the party displaying assertiveness feels that it has rights and feelings, and acknowledges the same for the other party as well. Hence neither does the party displaying ***assertive*** behaviour push and dominate the other, nor does it let itself be pushed and dominated.

Rather, the objective of the interaction is to arrive at mutually beneficial outcomes, which shall primarily result in ***repeat business*** and secure all the other related benefits of ***customer retention.***

There is a misconception prevailing around the term ***repeat business,*** which needs to be cleared up. Repeat business does not only mean the same customer buying the same product over and over again, or even increasing the frequency of his purchase. For example, if a person purchases an expensive car or a watch, the assumption of the seller is – "How often would this person repeat this purchase? Therefore why should my focus be on after sales service and Win -Win in general?"

But the concept of Repeat Business is not as narrow as this. Repeat business has more to do with the philosophy – ***Once a customer, Always a customer.*** This implies that for whatever be the other future nature of businesses that the organisation as a conglomerate gets into, an existing customer of a particular business would love to patronise and recommend to others ***all the product and service categories falling under the umbrella brand,*** provided that the Moments of Truth with the Mother Brand have so far been positive ones. This magnifies the concept of repeat business from merely repurchase of the same category, to ***brand loyalty across categories.*** And for a Mother Brand such as the Tata Group, which has over a hundred brands and product categories under its umbrella, ***one positive*** Moment of Truth experienced by one customer can be a potential goldmine for all the other related brands as was demonstrated earlier in this book through the example of Tata Westside and Croma. The quality of Tata Steel will ensure that Tata Salt will also sell.

Successful collaborative negotiation lies in finding out what the other side really wants and showing them a way to get it, while you get what you want.

- Herb Cohen

The above statement distils the essence of Win-Win.

A point to note. Since training programmes in corporate houses are devised for positive and healthy reasons, we should bear in mind that there are ***rarely courses conducted on AGGRESSIVENESS training,*** but ***multiple training programmes conducted in the area of ASSERTIVENESS training,*** in which if a participant is overly aggressive, he is trained to tone down, or given more confidence if he falls within the non-assertive category.

Thus, training a person to become ASSERTIVE is considered desirable, whereas training a person to become AGGRESSIVE is not.

It is also important to bear in mind that although one cannot control the opposite party's behaviour, one ***can*** control one's own, and by doing so, one can often regulate the other party's behaviour as well.

You cannot be friends upon any other terms than upon the terms of equality.

\- Woodrow Wilson

Win-Win is not a strategy – It is a Way of Life

Many books mention that Win-Win is a strategy.

Nonsense.

Win-Win is not a strategy.

Win-Win can never be a strategy.

The reason for this is that the word strategy implies the presence of options.

We firmly believe that there can be no option to Win-Win.

Therefore, for the best brands, Win-Win can never be a strategy.

For the best brands, Win-Win will always be a philosophy.

Win-Win will be a ***way of life.***

EVERY SINGLE Moment of Truth Matters

Let us look at another important aspect with regards to Moments of Truth.

A question for you as a reader.

Do you feel that every Moment of Truth that every customer undergoes with a brand is a separate entity, having no connection with ones that go before or with ones which are to follow; ***or*** is each Moment of Truth that a customer has with a particular brand, irrespective of time period differential, connected with each other? ***In other words, is each subsequent Moment of Truth co-related with the preceding one, as far as the customer is concerned?***

Let's see.

As an example, if a customer has experienced ***fifty positive*** Moments of Truth with a particular brand, and ***THEN*** experiences ***one disgusting*** Moment of Truth, which one is he more likely to remember? The fifty positive ones or the one negative one? With most customers, it is the ***one negative moment that will stand out.***

Thus, a brand should never be complacent in feeling that since it has built up a bank balance of goodwill by providing many excellent experiences in the past, it can afford to be lethargic and slip up once in a while.

A case in point which will amply demonstrate the importance of each single Moment of Truth is that one particular one-day cricket match played at Sharjah between India and Pakistan – Cricket lovers will immediately be able to identify the match we refer to. In India, the game of cricket is equated with religion and the outcome of this match proves the point we wish to make, about ***ONE negative Moment of Truth wiping out all the good that the individual has previously done.*** This particular match was a see-saw tussle, with team fortunes fluctuating after every ball. The game reached a stage where Pakistan had to score five runs of the last delivery of the match to win the game and the tournament. The batsman at strike was Javed Miandad, and the unfortunate bowler to bowl the last delivery was Chetan Sharma, who till that delivery, had performed decently in that match. The only way Pakistan could have won was if Miandad could hit a sixer off the final delivery. And that he did. Pakistan won the match and the tournament, but the glory of this win did not shine for them as much as the agony of having conceded a six off the last ball haunted Chetan Sharma. His career and life thereafter got engraved in the memories of all concerned as the man who let us down. Worth mentioning here is the fact that Chetan Sharma was a protégé of the legendary Kapil Dev, and was a real good find as a pace bowler for the Indian team, which previously had a dearth of fast bowlers. Chetan had a good record in both forms of international cricket, (test matches as well as one-dayers), including the fact that he was the first Indian bowler to secure a hat-trick in one day cricket. ***But all the good he had previously done got wiped out of public memory due to his one last delivery at Sharjah, which Indian cricket fans still recall with agony two decades later.***

As ***Paul Foley*** put it:

"It is impossible to build up a backlog of goodwill: ill will, yes – but goodwill starts from scratch at nine o'clock every morning."

Whether we like it or not, we have to face the fact that the society we live in is getting increasingly intolerant of errors, defects, and mistakes in general. And customers are getting particularly more so. When they are paying for something, they have come to demand perfection.

This may not appear to be reasonable, but that is human nature.

And your customers belong to the human race. So after taking efforts and investing time, money and energy into creating fifty positive Moments of Truth, it is foolish to throw away that entire bank balance of fifty positives you have in that customer's account, by one irresponsible, careless act. Your brand loses that bank balance built with such difficulty over a period of time, and all the goodwill attached with it.

The reputation of a thousand years may be determined by the conduct of one hour.

- Japanese proverb

This point could be complemented with a wonderful example a participant in one of our seminars gave when he endorsed our stance, mentioning that ***a goalkeeper in a game of soccer is rarely remembered for the fifty wonderful saves he made, but rather he is always negatively associated with the one crucial shot he let past into the goal.***

Every snowflake in an avalanche pleads not guilty.

- Gordon Livingston

As Gordon Livingston puts it so beautifully and poetically, a life threatening avalanche is nothing but an accumulation of tiny, soft snowflakes. Individually each snowflake could say that it is the prettiest thing in the world, but what is an avalanche, if not a collection of tiny snowflakes? But each gentle soft snowflake plays its part in creating the destructive avalanche of snow.

Imagine ***each staff*** member making just ***one*** error each, with each customer they interact with. For the employee, its just one error per customer. Imagine the repercussions for the brand.

Every Moment of Truth matters.

Samuel Butler commented, ***"Friendship is like money, easier made than kept."***

One negative incident is sufficient to spoil a long standing relationship forever. The older the relationship, the more the effort and time you have invested in it. The more the reason to ensure that nothing occurs from your end which could sour the relationship.

Therefore, your organisation and its representatives need to be much more careful in dealing with existing customers, than they need to be with new prospects, in whom you have hardly invested anything as far as a relationship goes. Unfortunately it's the other way that most organizations tend to function.

As a leading psychologist mentioned, ***"We are not a very forgiving society. Very few mistakes, if any, are tolerated or permitted. Forgiveness has become, in a word, unfashionable."***

Why would ***your*** organization want to take the chance that the customer you're dealing with, does not fall into this category of being an unforgiving one?

And ***this*** is the reason why standardization of an organisation's staff and their scale of knowledge and level of people handling skills across branches, departments and outlets, ***including*** your franchisee's outlets is vital.

Franchising

There is a major problem with the way that most franchising operations are done today.

Take a look at most advertisements of big brands inviting franchisee partners.

The only two things required from the franchisee's end highlighted in the advertisement would be:

1. A premium commercial space in a premium locality, (preferably road facing.)
2. The potential franchisee's capacity to invest a certain amount of money.

That's it.

Rarely would expertise in the related field, relevant background of the potential franchisee, passion to operate in that particular field and similar issues be considered.

Which is why most franchisee run outlets very often slip up on issues of quality and service.

This is a vital area where brands that operate through the franchisee model need to be extremely alert, as it is their hard earned brand equity at stake.

The following illustrative example is derived from the book ***Brandscendence*** by Kevin A. Clark.

Kevin mentions how when vacationing in Colorado, he read the following newspaper story.

The Ritz-Carlton hotel in the town where he had been vacationing, a franchisee outlet, had apparently not been keeping up the maintenance standards set by the parent company. The management of Ritz-Carlton was worried that this might affect the brand image of the parent company. Unannounced, on a Saturday night, during peak business period, the Ritz-Carlton management conducted a surprise raid on the franchisee property. The hotel was found deficient in quality standards, and at midnight itself, the hotel staff was asked to hand over all Ritz-Carlton logo and signature elements.

All Ritz-Carlton letterheads were immediately removed from executive offices.

The floor mats and rugs with the Ritz-Carlton logo at the entrance and in the elevators were removed.

All articles with the Ritz-Carlton logo including cutlery, glassware, flower vases, towels, linen, etc., were taken away before dawn while the guests slept.

In the morning, each guest received a letter in his room stating that they were no longer staying at a Ritz-Carlton hotel, a polite reason and explanation for the change, and a thank you for the patronage.

Ritz-Carlton was serious to the point of being fanatical and paranoid about protecting it's brand image and equity across it's entire franchisee system.

The question is – ARE YOU?

Only with this attitude towards perfection and quality as a priority can your customers and guests expect to get positive Moments of Truth time and time again.

One negative experience received by a customer from any individual associated with your brand could be sufficient to lose you that customer and his entire Circle of Influence for all time.

This is why, for any organization, Win-Win has to be an attitude, a way of life, a philosophy, a religion.

Great movements lead to memorable moments

Let's take a peek into Jan Carlzon's mind and see why he gave this degree of importance to the concept of Moment of Truth. He headed SAS, which being in the aviation industry, has it's own unique points of interaction and customer contact. Let's understand this concept of Moment of Truth from a practical, operational viewpoint.

A few of the points of contact for a passenger when he deals with an airline could be:

1. The prospective passenger calls the airline for flight details.
2. If it is an international flight, the passenger could ask for help with

his roaming SIM card.

3. Similarly, he could ask for help with obtaining foreign exchange.
4. He could make multiple special requests such as carrying a pet dog to another country.
5. Passenger requests for pick up from his residence.
6. If the flight is delayed, the passenger needs to be provided immediate proactive information so that he doesn't leave home on time and waste time at the airport.
7. Once at the airport, assistance needs to be provided in terms of trolley services.
8. Baggage check in.
9. Choice of seat availability.
10. Interaction at the time of collecting his boarding pass.
11. Security check done smoothly and efficiently.
12. Announcements made clearly, accurately, and regularly.
13. Boarding the bus to the tarmac.
14. Welcomed on board and seated.
15. All the multiple requests and services the passenger may have on flight.
16. After landing, taking the bus to arrival bay.
17. Baggage received without delay.

These are just a few of the touch points that a passenger could undergo during a single flight.

It has been estimated by certain airlines that on an average there are ***more than a hundred and fifty touch points per passenger on every flight he takes.***

There are around two hundred seats or passengers per flight, and a well established airline conducts over a hundred flights a day.

This results into literally millions of Moments of Truth for an airline (and large organizations in other industries as well), each day; which are nothing in simple terms but ***opportunities for the organisation or service provider to delight and retain, or disgust and lose a passenger or customer forever.***

Especially in the presence of a competitive environment, ***regular positive Moments of Truth are the one ingredient most essential for ensuring repeat business.*** (Not that this element should be ignored in the absence of competition.)

Moments of Truth as far as the customer is concerned, could originate from the most unusual of sources, not necessarily from things which directly affect customers.

For example, we have always maintained that the quality of service that an external customer receives and the satisfaction he derives from interacting with representatives of a brand will be in direct proportion to the level that the staff themselves are satisfied and motivated. ***Happy, motivated and satisfied staff will result in happy, motivated and delighted customers. That's a basic formula for service excellence.***

'*The Class*' displays its class

To illustrate, there is this fantastic restaurant opposite the Marriott Hotel in Mumbai which serves the most fabulous ***thalis*** (complete Indian vegetarian meals.) It's appropriately called - ***The Class.*** We had recently been there for dinner, and were warmly greeted by the ever smiling manager, ***Tarakeshwar Rao.*** After the customary exchange of pleasantries, we casually asked him which day of the week he took his day off. Imagine our surprise when he responded by saying, ***"Sir, I enjoy my work so much that I don't take a day off. Once in a month when I feel tired, I just take a day's break and relax. But for me, the best tonic is coming to work each day. The owner of this restaurant, Mr. Saurabh Surana, takes such excellent care of each of us, that we feel like we're part of one happy family."*** And it shows. The service staff at The Class is so polite and persuasive, that even though a guest is stuffed, he can't refuse an extra helping.

And the fact and revelation that a staff member, after working in a grueling, demanding, restaurant environment, coming in at noon, and leaving well after midnight, forgoes his day off because he feels so happy about coming to work is a fantastic Moment of Truth which

ensures that the customers will be pampered like royalty.

Another Moment of Truth about ***The Class*** is created for a guest when the staff provide the guest comment book for him to pen his comments about the meal and the overall service experience. Flipping through the pages, one will notice that each guest who has added his comments, has been more delighted than the other, and almost every guest comment ends with the words, ***Waiting to come back again for another excellent experience.***

All these are samples of Moments of Truth. ***Any input or information that reinforces the customer's confidence in the ability of the service provider to deliver a memorable experience transforms into a Moment of Truth***.

The true job of a Brand Manager

Every brand should constantly be striving to identify areas in it's functioning and operations which customers and guests could identify as Moments of Truth, and then create systems to ensure that as many of them as possible are positive ones.

This is what we at ***Brains Trust*** feel should be the foremost job responsibility of any brand manager.

Consistent and Holistic Organisational Approach

It is also important that the customer gets a smooth, homogenous experience as far as information and inputs from different representatives of the organization go.

If one brand representative says right and another says left, this leaves the customer in a state of confusion.

More importantly, it gives a feeling to the customer that he cannot depend on ANY information or ANY communication provided by ANY representative of the organization. Even thinking about customer retention in such a scenario is impossible.

Just to illustrate the above, as we write this, we are seated in the lobby of a five star deluxe hotel in Mumbai, waiting for an acquaintance. As we entered the hotel, a lad carrying a motorbike helmet entered along with us. He asked the security guard right outside the hotel entrance if he could leave his helmet at the security desk while he attended a function in the hotel. We heard the guard clearly tell the lad that he could leave his helmet at the bell captain's desk which was situated just inside the hotel entrance, about five steps away from the security desk. The lad entered, and in our presence, repeated his request to the bell captain. The reply the lad got was, ***"Sorry, sir, we've strictly been instructed not to keep any helmets at the bell captain's desk. You can carry it with you while you attend the function."*** This as a matter of policy for a hotel is perfectly fine.

But to an unbiased observer, it would appear that ***the right hand of the hotel isn't aware of, and doesn't know, what the left hand is up to.***

And then the very systems and co-ordination of the entire hotel come into question.

Looking at a dish in the buffet in such a hotel, the guest might feel that even though it is marked as a vegetarian dish, it could well turn out to be non-vegetarian.

Or even though the reservation person tells him that his reservation is a confirmed one, the guest might very well doubt the same.

And when doubt sets in, faith is lost. And when faith is lost, customer retention can only be a distant dream.

Similar situations regularly arise where two different organizational representatives provide differing information to the same customer query in mobile companies, banks, insurance firms and the rest. ***These are all examples of negative Moments of Truth which can have such a devastating impact on the reputation and the revenue of the brand.***

Customers WILL form broad based, generic opinions about the brand based on single observations. That can't be prevented. It is similar to a situation of an applicant at a job interview being rejected simply because there is a spelling or grammatical error in his resume. The interviewer would make the assumption that the candidate is careless and irresponsible, and has no eye for detail. All these assumptions would be made based just on a single spelling or grammatical error.

Similar assumptions and perceptions are developed by customers when they witness one negative attribute about a brand. They transpose it to indicate that the brand may in many other ways too, not be able to deliver what it promises.

- Cyrus M Gonda, Kalim Khan

One weak link anywhere in the chain makes the entire chain lose its strength.

This is the most crucial lesson that any brand could carry as a takeaway from this tenet.

Every interaction that each customer has with an organization increases or decreases the image and reputation of the brand in the eyes of that customer.

Brands CANNOT prevent customers from making negative conclusions about every aspect of the brand's functioning based on one negative Moment of Truth they experience.

What brands CAN do is create excellent systems which ensure that customers do not receive a single negative Moment of Truth in the first place.

We have identified the five main reasons why the majority of Negative Moments of Truth occur:

1. Inadequate staff strength.
2. Existing staff not adequately trained.
3. Lack of simple, customer-centric systems in the organisation.

4. Lack of empowerment provided to operational staff.
5. Lack of adequate top management attention to activities on the shop-floor.

These negative Moments of Truth need to be reduced, minimized and ideally eliminated as regular positive Moments of Truth generate faith and confidence of the customer in your organisation and brand like nothing else can. Also, consistently positive Moments of Truth contribute to reducing the negative time and energy wasted by the organization in complaint resolution and also help the organisation's products and services to command a higher price.

Revenue is not generated in the organisation's board rooms.

Revenue is ONLY generated at the point of customer contact, which is where Moments of Truth occur.

This is why top management should have one foot and heel firmly dug into the shop floor at all times.

- Cyrus M Gonda, Kalim Khan

As O Bernard Small puts it so beautifully –

"Most customers today experience ***Many Moments of MISERY.***

It is the norm to experience ***Moments of MEDIOCRITY.***

Very few customers truly experience ***Moments of MAGIC."***

All will be well with your brand if you make Moments of Magic the expected norm for your customers.

The tenet of Moments of Truth will be followed by the tenet of the Circle of Influence, simply because Moments of Truth influence the entire Circle of Influence.

This is because ***Moments of Truth*** are nothing but experiences faced by your customers who generate either positive or negative word-of-mouth publicity, (***Public Relations***), which then reach and affect the ***Circle of Influence,*** which ultimately break or build your ***Brand***.

ENLARGE THE CIRCLE OF INFLUENCE

How large this circle is, none can tell
It just seems to grow and swell

If you don't know me, don't judge me.

- Tupac Shakoor

Another very, very important tenet we have identified which needs to be understood as a foundation to business success, one which is often ignored today due to the insane rush towards targeting and segmenting, relates to the concept of the ***Circle of Influence.***

The basic premise of this tenet and its impact on Customer Retention is that one never knows who's who. Also, one never knows who these unknown and ignored "who" can ultimately influence, due to the involved, complex connections that human beings share. A person you conveniently ignore may well turn out to be an individual who could influence your Key Account or your most important customer or client to shift over to your competitor.

This tenet will identify through multiple examples how human relationships entwine in the most unexpected ways. Like a pebble falling into water, the ripple effect is terrific.

We need the whole world as a friend.

- Herbert Hoover

As the saying goes, and as this tenet will demonstrate - ***It really IS a Small World.***

So let's examine what exactly does the fascinating concept of ***Circle of Influence*** indicate.

In simple terms, Circle of Influence is nothing but the people which an individual has in his acquaintance circle and those he can influence one way or another, through any form of word of mouth message, either positive or negative.

The relevant question on which this tenet is based is - ***HOW CAN YOU KNOW THE CIRCLE OR SPHERE OF INFLUENCE OF THE PERSON YOU ARE DEALING WITH OR INTERACTING WITH?***

The answer, as we will see through multiple examples, is - ***You just can't know.***

And it doesn't pay to have prejudged notions, prejudices, biases and perceptions about the individual you are dealing with. As Tupac Shakoor said, ***"If you don't know me, don't judge me."*** Such a powerful statement in the context of marketing.

The Six Person Theory

Let's begin this tenet with a theory which has a strong mathematical basis. It's called the ***Six Person Theory.*** This theory claims that any individual in this world can get in touch with anyone else in the world through a chain or link of a maximum of six persons separating them. Even if one wishes to connect with the Pope or Bruce Willis or the Queen of England, an average person anywhere in the world is separated from them by a narrow link of just ***six*** people.

How does this work in real life? Let us take a hypothetical example. You have a friend, who knows a doctor, or a lawyer, or a chartered accountant, who knows the brother of a local politician, who is connected with a Member of Parliament, who is in touch with the Prime Minister of your country, who can connect with the President of the United States. ***This***

is the type of intricate, complex web or network that exists among people on this planet. And all your customers are part of this intricate, well connected, network.

Think of it. Six billion people in the world. And all it takes for one of them to connect with any other is a maximum link of six individuals in between.

The six person theory is very clear on the fact that it is possible for any individual on planet Earth to get in touch with any other individual, using a link of a maximum of six intermediaries, the first of whom is personally known to him. The final link will fall in place within a chain consisting of five more links.

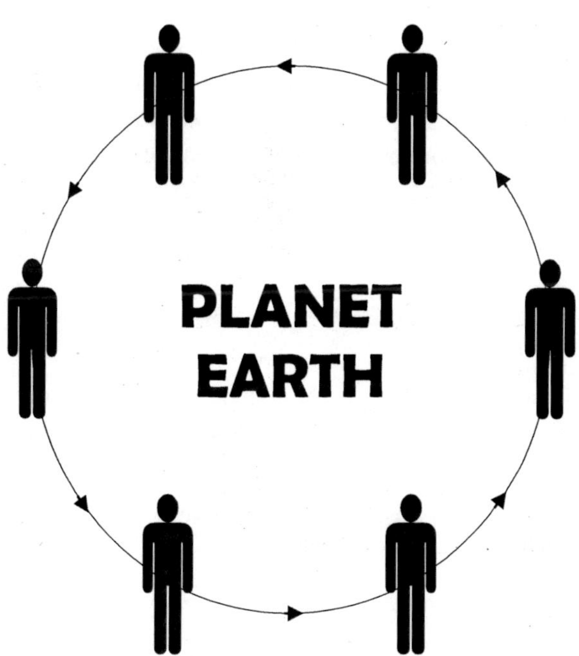

The Kevin Bacon Game

A verrrrry verrrrrry interesting game.

Brett Tjaden, a computer scientist with the University of Virginia, developed this game a few years ago.

Kevin Bacon is a Hollywood actor who has appeared in Hollywood movies along with stars such as Robert DeNiro and Jack Nicholson, and the game attempts to network the entire American acting fraternity by putting Kevin Bacon at the centre of its Universe.

This is how the game works:

1. Think of any American movie actor or actress from ***ANY*** era.
2. If they have appeared in a movie along with Kevin Bacon, they have a ***Bacon Number*** of ***ONE***.
3. If they have never appeared in a movie along with Kevin Bacon, but have appeared in a movie with another actor who has acted with Kevin Bacon, then they have a ***Bacon Number*** of ***TWO,*** and so on and on.

The verified claim is that there is ***no*** American actor who has ever appeared in a American movie and has a ***Bacon Number greater than FOUR.*** Tjaden has verified his claim by conducting a comprehensive survey of the Internet Movie Database, which contains data of almost any movie ever made. Tjaden has created a website that provides the Bacon Number for any American actor, however obscure.

The relevance of this game as far as the concept of the Circle of Influence is concerned is huge.

It tells us that any American actor across the last century is separated from acting alongside Kevin Bacon in a movie by a maximum link of four separations.

Kevin Bacon has been taken as a representative sample for the sake of this game.

With most other actors, the results would be similar.

And the results would be similar if we attempt to conduct this exercise for other industries and for social and business circles as well.

But organisations today are often so narrow minded when they conduct their segmentation and targeting exercises, that they don't look beyond the obvious and refuse to see beyond the fact that a particular individual they are interacting with may not need their product or not have the capacity to pay. That's all that most organizations are bothered about. Then they begin to ignore that individual.

Would this particular person we are speaking of be interested in purchasing our product or service, and does he have the capacity to pay? If not, we don't bother about him and we don't bother about how we treat him, and we don't bother what he may think of us, or what he may speak of us, and to whom – This in practicality is the purpose of targeting and segmentation.

This is such a narrow minded approach that it is surprising that organizations run by intelligent individuals could function on such a warped thought process. But this is what the mad rush of the quarterly target culture has brought organizations to, where there is very little time to even think about connecting with individuals if they don't appear to be immediate potential purchasers and sources of revenue.

Visualise the Power of the Circle of Influence

Our question to organizations is – "Even if an individual may not require your product or service, or buy it in large enough volumes for you to be interested in him, ***CAN YOU IDENTIFY WHO ELSE IS HE AN INFLUENCER TO?"*** This fact is rarely considered. Again, the root of the problem is ***short term thinking.*** Organizations and marketing departments feel it's a waste of time and effort to get into the depth of this apparently rhetorical question, which in reality has such far reaching ramifications and consequences for any organisation. Focusing on this ***one vital question*** and acting accordingly can be the best investment an organization can make.

We were impressed to read the following paragraph from the book, ***Prove It Before You Promote It*** by ***Steve Cuno,*** and would love to recommend this book to readers interested in the finer aspects of marketing.

"Crowd enough people into a room, and you may be surprised how many of them share a birthday. You may be less surprised however, when you think it through. Allowing for leap years, all it takes to guarantee a match is 367 days.... but there's no need for so many. A 1996 study by statisticians Persi Diaconis and Frederick Mosteller (cited in Robert Todd Carroll's, The Skeptic's dictionary, John Wiley and sons, 2003), shows that in a random selection of 23 people, there's a fifty percent chance of at least two matched birthdays. This brings us to the Law of Truly Large Numbers, a term statisticians use when the rest of us would have said COINCIDENCE.

In the Skeptics Dictionary, Robert Carroll explains the Law of Truly Large Numbers this way: "With a large enough sample, many seeming unlikely coincidences are LIKELY to happen."

--- from "Prove it Before you Promote it" - Steve Cuno

As ***Aldous Huxley*** aptly put it, so many years ago - ***If you let a monkey click away at the keys of a typewriter for a million years, it is highly possible that the monkey may in the midst of it all, type out a work to equal or even surpass the plays of Shakespeare. That would not make the monkey an erudite scholar.***

What Huxley aims to say is, that when a large mass or volume of any entity is considered, what may otherwise appear to be coincidence, will now become commonplace occurrences.

The point relevant for marketers is, when dealing with a sufficiently large customer base, (a customer has already been clearly defined by us as someone who need not buy your product or service, but merely experience or come in contact with some element of your organisation or brand), there is ***EVERY*** chance that ***quite a few of them will be directly connected, either personally or professionally, to someone in an organisation who would be a key decision maker as to whether to purchase goods or services from your organisation or not.***

And as you've witnessed in the tenets of ***Public Relations*** and ***Moments of Truth,*** all it takes is ***one*** bad experience for ***any*** of these influencers to pass on a negative word to the decision makers associated with your Key Accounts or Potential Key Accounts, and the damage is done.

Conversely, if each individual with whom your organisation's representatives interact is treated with tender loving care, (and there's no reason why this cannot be done. After all it's promised in most advertisements), then your organisational customer base and customer retention rate would sky rocket.

Organizations are dimly aware of the importance of all this, but somehow in the hustle of day to day proceedings, these gestures of goodwill towards all customers or persons interacted with, take a backseat.

By providing the following multiple examples and mathematically proven laws, we aim to reinforce the importance of simple, old fashioned courtesy to all concerned, and get courtesy and genuine concern for people back in the driver's seat of the business wagon, where they truly belong.

The Ghost-to-Ghost Hook-up

Let's start with the popular Alfred Hitchcock's ***Three Investigator Series*** of books, where three teenage detectives take up and successfully solve intriguing cases. The head of the Three Investigators, Jupiter Jones, introduces a brilliant technique to assist the three investigators in their work. He appropriately names it the 'Ghost to Ghost Hookup", (as opposed to the conventional Coast to Coast Hookup.) The three boys reside in a crowded suburb of Los Angeles, and normally accept assignments considered rather weird for conventional enforcement agencies. In their quest for solutions, they often have to locate for their clients a missing parrot, for example, or a vehicle in the city, of which they know the license number but not the location. The correct assumption that young Jones makes is that kids normally notice such new additions or intricacies in their neighbourhood. The technique they adopt is fiendishly simple but startlingly effective. Each of the three boys contacts five personal friends living in different parts of the city and asks them if they are aware of what the boys are looking for. If not, they tell each of their five friends to contact five of ***THEIR*** friends asking for this information, and the chain goes on. It is mathematically proven that within a period of a day, literally every boy in Los Angeles is part of the search. The boys have the entire teenage population of the huge city involved in their activity within a span of twenty four hours.

The mathematics remain the same, whether we talk of the three investigators, or of a corporate entity.

Imagine the power of the multiplier effect when it comes to word of mouth and the influence that it can wield to make or break your organization. (The Ghost here refers to the boys or assistants who silently do their work behind the scenes. The same as your customers do when they receive good or bad experiences from your organization.)

Five Star Hotels are not Defined by their Marble Flooring Alone

Another example. A real life one this time. One of us authors was once employed with a leading five star deluxe hotel in Mumbai. As a trainee at the Front Office reception desk, some evening shifts got really busy with guests crowding the counter. On one such evening, an elderly gentleman from Iran approached the reception counter. Although he was decently dressed, it was obvious from his attire that he would not be able to afford a five star hotel room, and he had no baggage with him either. He hesitantly approached the counter, and was greeted with a smile by the author. He was really a lovely old gentleman, and he looked very nervous and disturbed. He started to request, in broken English, if he could please be given the address of the Iranian Embassy in the city. He had been staying at a small hotel nearby, had lost his wallet and passport, and needed assistance. The hotel where he had been staying, being a mediocre one, hadn't been able to help him out, and he approached this hotel for assistance as it was supposed to be the best in the city, and he heard it had a fine reputation for hospitality, as indeed it had. He was almost in tears as he said this, being lost in a foreign land, with no money and passport, and hardly able to speak English, or any local Indian language. The author comforted him and made him wait at the reception counter, while a senior receptionist on duty was consulted as to how to get the Embassy address. The author was personally new at the job, and though the gentleman was comforted and calmed down, the author wasn't aware how to get the information the gentleman wanted. (This incident occurred before the easy access of the internet age.) The senior female receptionist on duty accompanying the author was a very nice lady. She comforted the gentleman as well, while she consulted a book on city information she had which contained the necessary address. While the elderly gent was being helped out, the Front Office Manager came up and asked what us receptionists were busy doing. When we explained, he curtly told us to stop wasting time on vagabonds and told us to go ahead with the job we were paid to do, which is attend to guests with the ability to pay who wanted to reserve a room in the hotel. He also rudely told the old man to get out of the lobby.

A great man shows his greatness
by the way he treats little men.

- Thomas Carlyle
(And we may add, so do great institutions.)

The old gentleman moved away, giving us a desperate, pleading look. We were helpless. And all this happened in a premier service industry institution. A hotel known for its legendary approach to service. A hotel which was an icon of hospitality. But when the Front Office Manger moved on, we caught the old man's eye, hurriedly called him back to the counter and handed him a paper on which we had scribbled the address of the embassy where he could hopefully get the assistance he required. He thanked us profusely, kissed our hands, tears of gratitude running down his cheeks and left. We felt that was the last we would see of him. The next day, the author and the female receptionist were once again on evening duty. The old man, now dressed handsomely in a smart suit, walked up with a young lady in tow. He handed both of us a huge gift wrapped box, (which we later found was filled with dry fruits), and once again thanked us, shaking our hands vigorously. Then the young lady accompanying him introduced herself. She was a senior functionary at the embassy we had directed him to, and also happened to be the old man's niece. After thanking us, she said that she appreciated the help extended to her uncle and would definitely be hosting her embassy's future functions with this hotel, seeing that it employed such friendly and helpful staff. (No thanks to the Front Office Manager, we may add.)

We thanked her in turn for her kind words, and thanked the old man for his thoughtful gift. After all, what had we done? Hardly a thing. ***But even this little thing had been grudged by the short-sighted front*** *office manager, who only viewed as a customer someone who had the capacity to pay and enter into a financial relationship with the hotel. I as an author didn't know this then, but now that I reflect on it, it fits in so beautifully with our current Customer Retention Model. The old man was a customer from the moment he first entered the lobby, whether he paid for, or used, the hotel services or not. As we have explained, it is not necessary for a person to buy before we term him a customer. It is sufficient that he experiences the ambience of the brand.*

In a casino or stock market, do we expect to hit the jackpot every single time? No. If we win seven times out of ten we are thrilled. Then why do we not feel the same way in business. Why do we expect to profit from every single interaction, that too immediately? Why can't we let the relationship flower for it's own sake? Why can't we let the opposite person experiencing our brand have a wonderful experience with us, irrespective of whether he buys from us today, tomorrow, or never.

When we spend millions on advertising expenditure, do we stop to think of the thousands of people who will flip the page or channel without even seeing or reading our advertisement? We don't mind the wastage then. Why then do we grudge it when it comes to providing excellent experiences? WHY DO WE RATION OUT GOOD EXPERIENCES AS THOUGH THEY WERE IN SHORT SUPPLY? Why do we tend to ignore and brush off individuals WE perceive as not having immediate financial potential?

Who ARE we to evaluate others in a split second? All our scriptures say that we take several lifetimes to know our own selves. How then, can we so quickly evaluate others whom we have never met before?

And where does all the targeting go then? TARGETING is just a polite way of saying, "Only be nice to those you think can benefit you financially and to hell with the rest." Is this the genuine Marketing Philosophy by any stretch of imagination?

And speaking of basing our opinion of individuals and their potential worth based on their external appearance alone, the following gives food for thought.

A Practical Piece of Journalism

A recent study conducted by a popular tabloid attempted to explore this general human perception of basing opinions on external appearances alone. The study was conducted in a unique, practical manner. Two of the reporters of that tabloid boarded the first class compartment of a local train. One of them, well dressed, was not carrying a first class ticket, and the other, very modestly clad, with a slightly tattered shirt and soiled and ill fitting trousers, carried a first class ticket on him. The results were as expected, proving the importance people attach to external appearance and all the related but incorrect assumptions thus conceived about individuals based on their attire. The well dressed individual who did not carry a ticket was not even given a second glance by his fellow commuters, who accepted him as one of their own, a man entitled to travel first class because of the crispness of his attire. But the second individual, comparatively ill clad for a first class passenger, was the object of dirty glances, and a couple of the fellow passengers even challenged his right to travel in the compartment. In fact he had to display his ticket to them as they were on the verge of ejecting him from the compartment.

This brings to mind a lovely Sufi story, full of deep meaning.

A person once came knocking at the door of the Sufi sage, Bayazid, and said – "I am seeking Bayazid." Bayazid himself opened the door, but he told the seeker, "I don't know who Bayazid really is. I too, have been seeking him for the past thirty years."

God Himself, sir, does not propose to judge a man until his life is over. Why should you and I?

- Samuel Johnson

A point to be clarified. It is important that your organizational representatives always project themselves at their neatest best, as one can't stop customers from making perceptions based on attire, however inaccurate and incorrect these assumptions may be. And this can lose your organisation a lot of business unnecessarily. But when your organization interacts with customers, it is imperative that your brand representatives don't get into the trap of evaluating customers based on their appearance alone.

Roll out the Royce

Another anecdote to cement the point we wish to make. Many years ago, so the story goes, the head of a princely state in India entered a Rolls Royce showroom in a foreign land to view the cars on display. The attendants in the showroom paid him no heed, perceiving for reasons best known to them from his appearance that he would be incapable of making a purchase there. The treatment he received so infuriated him that he bought several of the vehicles, converted them into garbage disposal vans and used them for that purpose in his state, thus bringing ridicule to the brand on a large scale.

This dairy learned its lesson the hard way

The following true story we recall reading some years ago makes for great reading. The location where this took place is not important. The message definitely is. It's a story about an old lady who used to be a regular customer at a local dairy. This dairy had a major client which was a nearby hotel. The hotel was a key account for the dairy and used to generate approximately seventy percent of the revenue of the dairy. Utmost care was taken by the dairy management while dealing with the hotel's account. The hotel in turn never had a problem with the dairy products provided, and even if they had, the complaints were immediately and politely resolved.

One day, an elderly lady, who used to shop at the dairy about twice a week, making small purchases such as half a liter of milk or a quarter kilo of cottage cheese, came to the dairy with a complaint. This was the first time that she had done so. The problem she stated was that the milk she had bought the day before had spoilt, despite proper storage at her end. It had turned sour. She had brought the spoilt milk with her and requested the dairy staff to replace it. The staff was indifferent to her request and refused to replace the milk. When she insisted, she was categorically told that in future she could make her dairy purchases elsewhere. It was also made clear to her that the dairy did not depend upon her business for its survival. She went away, upset that even as a regular customer with a genuine complaint, she was treated so rudely.

As far as the dairy was concerned that was the end of the matter, and the staff forgot all about it. Coincidentally (or apparently so), from next day on, the hotel which was the key account for the dairy, stopped purchasing any milk products from the dairy, without assigning any reason. The owner of the dairy was in a terrible state. If this situation continued, he would have to close shop. He sought an appointment with the purchase manager of the hotel and was granted one. He reached there well before time for the appointment, wearing his best suit, and nervously chewing his finger nails. The purchase manager kept him waiting for a long time. When at last he did meet the dairy owner, the purchase manager's manner was very cold and aloof. The dairy owner, after the customary greeting, anxiously asked the purchase manager the reason for their stopping purchase from the dairy. He asked if there had been any short coming from their end and said that he would do anything within his power to rectify it. The hotel manager said that as far as the hotel as a customer was concerned, there had been no problem. The dairy had treated it like a VIP customer, which indeed it was. The slightest complaint from the hotel's end had been promptly responded to. "But", continued the Purchase Manager, ***"WHEN MY MOTHER CAME TO YOUR DAIRY LAST WEEK WITH A GENUINE COMPLAINT......"***

THAT'S the Circle of Influence at work.

Silent. Behind the scene. But very effective.

One never knows which connection leads where. ***Therefore, we repeat that this entire theory of targeting and segmenting needs to be bundled out of the window or else at least seriously reexamined, because by ignoring customer segments which you feel are of no value, you are throwing the baby out with the bathwater.***

Focus on the Lifetime Value of Customer

We had once conducted a Customer Service workshop for the owners of petrol pumps of a leading oil firm. While we stressed the importance of treating every customer interaction as vital, some of the participants were unimpressed. One of the owners made the following comment. ***"So what if a customer is disappointed with the service he receives. I can afford to lose one sale."*** We told him that it would be far more than just one sale he would be losing. We then asked him how much worth of petrol an individual filled up on an average when he visited the petrol pump. He said the average bill would be in the range of five hundred rupees, and he also added that five hundred rupees was a small sum as far as he was concerned. He could afford to lose it. We then asked him how many times a month an average customer filled up five hundred rupees worth of petrol. "Around five times," he answered. We did the following calculation on the white board of the training room.

One bill	-	500 * 1	Rs. Five Hundred
Five times a month	-	500 * 5	Rs. Two thousand five hundred
Twelve months in a year	-	2500 * 12	Rs. Thirty thousand
Over a span of ten years	-	30000 * 10	Rs. Three lakhs
If the customer has two cars	-	300000 * 2	Rs Six lakhs

We then proceeded to explain the concept of ***Circle of Influence*** to the audience.

If, for example, the customer who receives poor service is one of the decision makers in a reasonably large organisation, he could prevent all fifty or maybe more vehicles of that organisation from using the services of that filling station. We have seen this happen in the past. This could result in a loss of millions of rupees of revenue for the petrol pump in a few years

Or if a ***single*** important decision maker of an organisation received poor service in an airline, he could stop his organisation from dealing with that airline as far as all official staff travel of his organisation was concerned. The travel bill of large organisations exceeds Rupees Ten Million a year, and ***more than three thousand staff have their travel and other decisions identified by one or two key persons***.

The Eighty : Twenty rule is applicable across time and place – It is Universal and Eternal

There is a concept termed as the 80 : 20 concept, which is a universally applicable philosophy.

It can be practically explained as follows.

Twenty percent of your customers get you eighty percent of your revenue.

Twenty percent of products in a company's offering generating eighty percent of total profits.

Twenty percent of repeat causes leading to eighty percent of defects.

Twenty percent of total footfalls in malls accounting for eighty percent of purchases.

Twenty percent of traffic signals causing eighty percent of the traffic jams.

Twenty percent of teeth doing eighty percent of the chewing.

Twenty percent of reasons that account for eighty percent of the delay.

Twenty percent of the intestine that does eighty percent of the digestion.

Twenty percent of people in your life with whom you share eighty percent of your time.

Twenty percent of the book which when read gives you eighty percent of the information.

Twenty percent of the authors who have eighty percent of the popularity.

Twenty percent of the numbers in your personal directory accounting for eighty percent of talk time.

Twenty percent of people giving you eighty percent of the trouble.

Twenty percent of teachers contributing to eighty percent of the knowledge gained.

Twenty percent of the alphabets on the keyboard used eighty percent of the time.

Twenty percent of the reasons due to which eighty percent of deaths occur.

Twenty percent of items in a restaurant menu ordered eighty percent of the time.

And twenty percent of organizations and brands giving us eighty percent of the examples of outstanding customer focus.

Whew. You get the idea.

It's now 80,000 : 20

But we strongly feel that it is no longer the 80 : 20 concept at work. Today, especially in business, the ratio is more in the range of 80,000 : 20.

This is because more organizational power and decision making is concentrated in fewer hands than ever before.

Twenty bad experiences that your customers face can well lose your organization the revenue of eighty thousand customers. It's happened too often for comfort.

For example, if a leading individual from another organisation received poor service in a hotel or a bank or a cellular company or an airline or an insurance company or any other sector, he could be influential enough to ensure that the organisation which has provided the poor service loses a key account.

A similar scenario could unfold with a bank and the bank could end up losing thousands of salary accounts of a particular corporate entity whose key decision maker has encountered poor service. A real life example pertains to a friend of ours who is the Head – Human Resources and Administration with a firm employing more than three thousand individuals. He recently shifted all the three thousand salary accounts from one bank to another after personally having an unpleasant encounter with an extremely rude bank staff where the three thousand salary accounts were initially held. His reasoning was very clear –

'I don't wish any of ***my*** employees to be served in such a rude manner ever.'

Similarly, if it is an insurance firm, it could lose thousands of policies in the form of group insurance.

Or thousands of organization bought cellular connections.

Or if is a hotel, hundreds or maybe thousands of room nights a year from a single large customer.

Or if an airline, the loss could be to the tune of thousands of seats a year, again from a Key Account.

Imagine losing a huge chunk of current and potential business, simply because one negative moment of truth was provided by someone in your airline, or your hotel, or your bank, or your cellular organisation or your insurance company; to someone who is a key influencer with one of your key accounts. As we said, it's a ***laaaaarge*** price to pay.

The question we posed at the beginning of this tenet still stands. ***"DO WE REALLY KNOW WHO WE ARE DEALING WITH EVERY TIME WE INTERACT WITH AN APPARENTLY AVERAGE CUSTOMER?"*** As we can see, the only answer is, ***"WE DON'T."*** And no organisation can afford to take the risk of antagonising a single customer or potential customer, however insignificant that customer may appear to be, at first or even at second glance.

It is rightly said, ***"They have sown the wind, and they shall reap the whirlwind."***

Concepts such as, ***ONLY KEEP AND SERVICE CUSTOMERS WHO ARE PROFITABLE,*** don't even ***begin*** to consider the impact of the Circle of Influence.

The following is a beautiful story. And every word of it is true. One stormy night, a middle aged couple entered a hotel lobby without a reservation and requested for a room. The reception clerk apologized that as there were many business conventions in town, the hotel didn't have a single empty room to let. After a short silence, the reception clerk felt sorry for the old couple, and asked them if they would mind sharing his own staff room, which was within the hotel premises. He said he wouldn't be using his staff room that night, as he was doing a night shift. The couple was worried about inconveniencing the reception clerk in this manner and imposing on his good nature, but the pouring rain outside made them gratefully accept his kind offer. The couple checked out the next afternoon. While leaving, the man sought out the receptionist and told him, ***"You are the kind of person every hotel owner dreams about having as an employee. Maybe someday I'll build a hotel for you to run."*** The receptionist smiled politely at what he thought was a well meant compliment. A few years later, the reception clerk, who was still employed at the same hotel, received a registered letter from the elderly gentleman. In the letter, the gentleman recalled the events of the stormy night and wanted the receptionist to visit him in New York. A return trip ticket had been enclosed. The receptionist had never been to New York. So with the ticket in hand, he decided to visit his elderly benefactor. The gentleman met him in New York at the corner of Fifth Avenue and Thirty Fourth Street, a posh location, where a grand, new hotel had been erected. ***"That," said the elderly gent, "is the hotel I have built for you to run. I told you a few years ago it might happen and today you must know I am serious."*** The clerk was flabbergasted. ***"You must be joking. What is the catch? Why me? Who are you anyway?"*** The reply was, ***"I am William Waldorf Astor. There is no catch. And you are the person I want to manage this entire hotel."***

The young clerk gratefully accepted. The clerk's name was George C Boldt.

The hotel was the original Waldorf Astoria, one of the most luxurious and reputed hotels in the world.

There are three vital lessons which any organisation can learn from the above:

1. Do good in all situations and on all occasions. Be nice. Don't bother to evaluate payback. And in most cases, how much extra does it cost to be nice anyway? And isn't any business all about genuinely creating and maintaining a healthy positive image for all stakeholders?

2. Employers must look for qualities of empathy and warmth in their prospective employees above all else. Forget about aggressive natures. Aggressive natures and behaviours belong in the dustbin as far as the genuine marketing philosophy is concerned.

3. Customers do remember and reciprocate the good you've done. Sometimes in unimaginable ways.

How much out of the way would YOUR Organization Go?

In this context, Akio Morita, the former head of the Sony Corporation, recollected a beautiful instance of not underestimating the power of a single walk-in customer which he was once privileged to witness. He recalls that he was once in a cosmetic store, and a customer walked in and asked for a particular shade of lipstick. The storekeeper did not have that shade at present, and he could easily have told the customer that and gone ahead with his other tasks. But what the storekeeper did was something amazing and worth emulating. He called over his salesman from behind the counter, wrote down the shade of lipstick the customer wanted, gave him some money, told him to catch a cab, reach another cosmetic store nearby, buy the shade of lipstick required at retail price, and rush back by cab. In the meantime, the store keeper made the customer comfortable and offered her a cup of tea and some biscuits. She waited, browsed around, made some other purchases in the meantime which she never had originally intended to make, and went off delighted when the salesman returned with the shade she wanted.

The point is, ***according to modern accounting theory,*** this action of the storekeeper would be termed a ***loss making activity.*** Spending more to make a particular sale than the revenue generated out of it would be considered foolish. ***But that's only when we don't add up the intangible benefits of customer delight converting into repeat patronage , loyalty, word of mouth and goodwill that most accountants wouldn't even begin to comprehend.*** When looked at objectively, ***this is the only USP a cosmetic store could create. A differentiator in terms of the added service element.***

All other things such as stock on shelf can rarely be considered differentiators. And this is what we have stressed in our next tenet on the ***Unique Selling Point.*** That the key differentiators of today, as far as customers are concerned, will be the service differentiators. The cosmetic store owner thoroughly understood this and was a brilliant proponent of the tenet of ***Circle of Influence.***

The goodwill the cosmetic store owner generated for himself through this simple act, the volume of future assured business generated through this particular customer and all others she could and would influence, would be far, far beyond the comprehension of traditional accounting methodologies.

In fact, we were once addressing the Small and Medium Scale Businessmen's Association – Cosmetic Division. The topic of the seminar was on how they could improve and enhance their cosmetic businesses. We did not know much about the technical aspects of the cosmetic industry, so we began our talk with the above example. And all these experienced cosmetic businessmen agreed that this sort of service orientation could be the ***only differentiator*** as far as a cosmetic store was concerned.

The Circle of Influence shows the importance that needs to be given to every single individual coming in contact with your brand.

None can measure the radius of its reference,
Critical is the Circle of Inference

- Cyrus M Gonda, Kalim Khan

ALL retained customers are Cash Cows. Even if they themselves don't generate too much profit, they can generate great word of mouth publicity to others on your behalf. Unfortunately, this aspect is rarely considered by marketers who decide to drop certain customers who don't on the surface appear to generate the level of profitability desired. But word of mouth publicity goes on under the surface, behind the scene.

In his bestseller, ***"Customers for Life,"*** ace automobile dealer Carl Sewell makes an estimate, that on an average, each customer that walks into the showroom of his car dealership for the first time is worth a potential lifetime value of three hundred thousand dollars. He arrives at this figure by simply putting the number of vehicles this customer would be expected to purchase over his lifetime, added with the service that his dealership could provide and charge for. ***But even Sewell, while arriving at this humongous figure, fails to consider and take into account the***

hugely enhanced figure that would accrue if recommendations and positive word-of-mouth publicity would have been considered.

All these examples and situations justify why we subtitled this tenet as, ***"How large is this circle, none can tell. It just seems to grow and swell."***

It is generally felt that it takes too long for the Circle of Influence to be covered to any appreciable extent to the level which it can affect the organization negatively. But it is definitely not a slow process. Rather, it is a rapid one. As we promised in the ***tenet of Public Relations,*** we will now demonstrate the speed at which this Circle of Influence can be covered.

Senna and the Grain of Rice

To clarify the misconceptions about word-of-mouth being a slow process, and the incorrect perception that covering the Circle of Influence would take too long a time, the following delightful folk tale from India gives a fitting reply. ***The tale may or may not have basis in reality, but the mathematics involved in the tale is definitely true and accurate.***

It brilliantly demonstrates the power of Geometric Progression, (the speed at which one person telling two, becomes two telling two others each, and so on.)

The tale goes as follows.

Senna was a citizen of a country who had performed a service for his King. The King wanted to return the favour, and asked Senna what he would like as a gift. In answer, Senna got along with him a chessboard, (a chessboard has sixty four squares), and told the King that the gift he would like would be a grain of rice to represent the first square, two grains of rice for the second, four for the third, eight for the fourth, sixteen for the fifth, and so on, till the same was true for the sixty fourth square. The King heard this and felt insulted.

He told Senna that he should have asked for a gift worthy of a King.

Gold, precious gems, some such thing, which the King would have been proud to bestow.

The King walked away after telling his courtiers to give Senna a sack of rice and send him away.

Senna respectfully spoke up and told the King that the gift he asked for would amount to more than a sack of rice. ***How much more?***, asked the King. ***Two sacks? Three sacks?***

Senna then replied that it would be much, much more than that. He himself didn't know the final total, as it was beyond him to comprehend such a vast figure.

Senna told the King that as far as he was aware, the number exceeded the grains of sand on all the beaches of the earth put together. Senna mentioned that so much rice had never been grown on Planet Earth, ever since organised cultivation began, five thousand years ago.

For your information as a reader, when we calculated this figure with the help of a computer, the value turned out to be a humongous twenty digit number. It is $18 * 10^{18}$ grains of rice to be precise. (We request you to perform the calculations.)

The Mathematics of the Grain of Rice

When we first read the tale, even we found the claim to be fanciful. To verify it, we physically counted the grains in a hundred grams of rice. We found that the figure came to approximately a thousand grains.

(A thousand grains is a figure on the higher side, that too with small grain rice used for the experiment.)

Then we found out the world production of rice in 2007. It was around 650 million tons. In 650 million tons, the approximate number of grains of rice would be a seventeen digit figure. Keeping in mind that the world population has increased five times in the last century alone, rice production every year through the ages has increased in proportion to the population. Thus basic mathematics will tell us that Senna was right. The amount of rice Senna asked for has truly not been produced on the face of this earth in the last five thousand years.

AND IT LOOKED SUCH AN INSIGNIFICANT FIGURE TO BEGIN WITH.

This is the power of Geometric Progression.

One person telling two, two telling four, four telling eight, and so on.

And organizations which fail to realize and take advantage of this force for their own good, are losing out on the most potent and virtually free power available in marketing.

To the contrary, organizations which realise the potential of the circle and harness the Circle of Influence to their advantage can reap untold goodwill and revenue.

Another brain teaser that sets you thinking

From the moment two frogs are put in a pond, their number starts to double every minute. One hour from the time the first two frogs were put in the well, the pond is full of frogs. The question is, when was the pond half full?

The immediate response most people give is, "At the half hour mark." But if you're one of those who got it right, you'll realize that ***the pond was half full just a minute before it became full.*** (That is, at the *fifty ninth minute.*) Remember, the number of frogs doubles every minute. ***Once a certain critical mass is reached, Word of Mouth takes on a speed and a life of its own.***

The Vital Importance and Points to Ponder about the '*Circle of Influence*'

1. How do you know in totality as to who the person you are dealing with actually is and what is the sphere or circle of influence he holds within him, at his command?

2. ***Why*** do you, as an organization, need to know the Circle of Influence of the person you are dealing with in the first place. Isn't marketing about basic courtesy, above all else? Do good to all who come in contact with your brand. The good comes back, manifold, often in unexpected ways and from unexpected sources. This is a basic law of the universe.

3. And if basic courtesy is provided to all who come into contact with and experience your brand at any touch point, then you need not ever worry about negative word-of-mouth publicity.

4. It is only when you sit to segregate and target whom you need to be courteous to, and whom not, do the organisation's problems begin in the first place.
5. Do you expect to make a profit on every share you purchase? Do you expect to win every lottery ticket you purchase? Then why when it comes to business does an organization expect that every bit of extra service provided needs to translate into immediate big bucks?
6. By doing good towards all customers, you automatically unleash the entire Circle of Influence at every customer's command in your favour.

The argument some organisations provide against focusing on the concept of Circle of Influence is that many feel that since it cannot be calculated, it is not worth focusing on, and ***consequently it should be ignored, as that which cannot be counted or calculated, does not matter.*** Nothing could be further from the truth.

As the following extract from a beautiful speech will prove beyond doubt, ***the power of the intangible, or that which cannot be counted and calculated, is far, far more than the power of the tangible.***

Thus, to conclude this tenet, the following powerful, thought provoking speech by ***Robert F Kennedy,*** proves that what is most important and vital need not necessarily be capable of being counted. But that in no way diminishes its importance.

In this speech, Robert Kennedy was addressing the students at the University of Kansas, and he brought out the futility of attempting to measure a country's progress by depending only on numerical and tangible data such as ***GDP.*** Concepts such as GDP are sadly lacking and woefully fall short of projecting the true overall scenario. As one example, the raw material and labour required to reconstruct the damage caused by a Tsunami or an earthquake is also added to the GDP and accounted for as progress or development. In reality, there is no development. Only what was lost is being rebuilt.

This is exactly what we wish to bring about through the tenet of the

Circle of Influence, that ***relying on numerical formulae alone can in no way bring about the true worth of an individual as a potential source of revenue for the organization.***

So do things which cannot be counted, matter?

As you will see, they matter most of all.

On with Robert Kennedy's speech.

'Too much and too long, we seem to have surrendered community excellence and community values in the mere accumulation of material things. Our Gross National Product... if we should judge America by that, counts and is enhanced by air pollution and the measures to control it, and by cigarette advertising, and ambulances to clear our highways of carnage. It counts special locks for our doors and the jails for those who break them. It counts the destruction of our redwood trees and the loss of our natural wonder in chaotic sprawl. It counts napalm and the cost of a nuclear warhead, and armoured cars for police who fight riots in our streets. It counts Whitman's rifle and Speck's knife, and the television programmes which glorify violence in order to sell toys to our children.

Yet the GNP does not allow for the health of our children, the quality of their education, or the joy of their play. It does not include the beauty of our poetry or the strength of our marriages, the intelligence of our public debate, or the integrity of our public officials. It measures neither our wit nor our courage, neither our wisdom nor our learning, neither our compassion nor our devotion to our country. It measures everything, in short, except that which makes life worthwhile.

And it tells us everything about America, except why we are proud that we are Americans.'

- Robert F Kennedy, Address : University of Kansas, March 18, 1968

Tenet 8

CONSTANTLY ENHANCE UNIQUE SELLING PROPOSITIONS

When there is something positively different about you, Your customers will stick like glue

The great thing a tiny lamp can do which the mighty Sun cannot, is to provide light at nighttime. USPs don't originate by accident, but by purpose and design.

- Unknown

Even the tiny mouse in Aesop's fable was of great use to the mighty lion

Leading from the tenet of the Circle of Influence, the next logical tenet in the sequence is the ubiquitous, ever present, but rarely understood in totality, tenet of the ***Unique Selling Point,*** (or ***Unique Selling Proposition,*** if you prefer.) ***USP*** is a phrase which rolls off very easily of the tongue of most advertising and marketing professionals. But it is also one of the most overused and unfortunately misused and abused terms floating around in the world of business.

Ask most people who glibly bandy around the phrase what it actually means, and they'll look at you with a condescending gaze as if you were illiterate. "Why, a USP is something that's different about your product. Surely that's obvious?", they respond sarcastically.

Well, that's the problem.
It's ***not*** that obvious, nor is it that simple.
The ***true definition*** of Unique Selling Point as originally conceived is:

"That parameter or characteristic, or set of parameters or characteristics which exist in your brand of product or service, that differ from your competitor's product or service in a positive way, creating a genuine benefit for your customers and end users, and which are not capable of being duplicated by your competitors in the short span of time, short span here meaning at least two to three years."

That's what the concept of USP is all about.

Now we can see a number of issues cropping up in this correct, complete and comprehensive definition that don't figure at all in the currently accepted, simplistic, mistaken and highly shortened explanation of a USP , which is - ***"Just something different."***

With the current prevailing misunderstanding of the definition, it's so easy to give a slight twist to a parameter of a product or service, which doesn't provide the least additional benefit to the customer, and which can also be easily replicated by a competitor in half a day, and then label this as a USP.

The Key Words in the Term - USP

The key word in the correct definition of USP is not the word unique.

Rather, the key words are the words and phrases:

- **positive**
- **genuine benefit**
- **not capable of duplication within two to three years**

Every individual, every organisation, every product, every service, every brand is by itself and by its very nature, unique.

No two individuals or organizations, no two fingerprints, no two snowflakes, can ever be the same. Each is unique.

The quality of being unique by itself does not make one better or worse or more beneficial or less beneficial than the other. The word ***Unique*** just means ***Different.*** And everyone and everything is already unique and different from the other in some way. ***That*** by itself cannot constitute a USP.

One individual weighs seventy kilograms, his friend weighs seventy two. Are both unique? Undoubtedly. Which one is better? There is no way to tell.

Thus, paradoxically, being ***UNIQUE,*** is a quality ***COMMON TO ALL.***

And this is where one of the main misconceptions about the term USP lies.

The question is, is your ***uniqueness*** sufficiently beneficial and attractive for a consumer to prefer and choose ***your*** brand over a competitors brand (which is also ***unique***), for his specific needs.

A crucial part of the correct definition therefore is - ***genuine benefit to the customer or end user.***

Thus all your slogans, punchlines, advertising campaigns and brand endorsers go out of the window. As far as the concept of genuine USP goes, these things just ***can't*** be considered as USPs, ***simply because they do not by themselves provide genuine benefits to the customer.***

And, even if the unique benefit your brand offers ***is*** providing a genuine benefit to the customer, and it ***does*** differ from competing brands in a ***positive*** way, that's not sufficient for it to be termed a USP. We still have the parameter of the ***differentiator sustaining for a minimum of two years to be considered.***

Why the Two Year Period

According to the original definition of the term USP, even if a genuine positive differential benefit exists, it has to be capable of being sustained as a differentiator over at least a two or three year period. This is essential in order to justify the effort and expense of creating it. Also, it's when the positive differentiator exists for a certain period of time that it gets talked about as a differentiator, and the brand can derive the benefits therefrom.

Thus, we may be the first to make a vibrating toothbrush or a one minute noodle and they ***are*** different and ***do*** provide a genuine positive benefit, ***but*** if they are capable of being replicated by a competitor within the span of a week or even a month, ***they cannot be termed as USPs.*** The definition is very clear on this. ***And this is where most brands claiming to have a USP fail.***

I may not be better than other people, but at least I'm different.

- Jean Jaques Rousseau

Rousseau, a Swiss philosopher and educationist, may have been sarcastic when he made this statement. Unfortunately, today most brands use this as their definition of USP.

Product USPs are rarely to be found today

When Sony came out with the first ever Walkman, it was almost immediately replicated by Philips of Holland.

Sony made it smaller, Philips made it smaller.

Sony added a recording facility, Philips added a recording facility.

Sony added stereo sound, Philips added stereo sound.

Sony added a radio, Philips added a radio.

Every feature that Sony added in a desperate bid to stay ahead was almost immediately replicated by Philips of Holland. In the end, Sony gave up trying to stay ahead.

The point here is that it is very, very difficult to have a product USP today.

The reason being that, today with levels of technology and communication having made rapid strides, and reverse engineering capability available, almost ***any*** product can be duplicated in a relatively short span of time.

Unless you're considering something on the scale of the ***Palm Islands of Dubai.***

Or an exceptional and outstanding series of products like the ***BBC***

nature documentaries, which accrue through ***years and decades*** of archival, intellectual and proprietary resources. As the Daily Telegraph newspaper put it so aptly, ***"The BBC can still make programmes no other television company could dream off." That's*** Product USP. And that's ***rare.***

Toil to make yourself remarkable by some talent or other.

- Seneca

For over five centuries, the source of economic dominance had been leadership in the fields of science and technology. ***Daniel H Pink,*** author of ***A Whole New Mind : Why Right Brainers Will Rule The Future,*** and ***Virginia Postrel,*** author of ***The Substance Of Style,*** suggest that this ***era based on technological dominance may well be over.*** Their reasoning being that technological advances in this modern era will be stripped bare and reverse engineered the moment they are developed and commoditised by countries such as China and India and put out to the masses. ***Products,*** which obviously are based on some technology or the other, ***will no longer be capable of differentiating from each other and will not find it possible to possess tangible USPs.***

These two authors argue that the future source of economic value will arise from Right Brain powers and characteristics such as ***empathy, sense of aesthetics, creativity, passion and imagination.***

These are all intangible attributes. And these are the attributes that form the roots of world class service and provide an organization with USPs which can be sustained.

A few rare examples of possible Product USPs, or USPs based on the tangible element

If you own a resort overlooking a lovely valley view, and your resort covers ***all*** the land overlooking that view, ***that*** could be a USP.

Or, if the zoo in a particular city has the ***only*** animal of that species in the country available on display, ***that*** could be a USP.

In the Iran Iraq war in the 1980s, USA was a country that sided with Iraq.

In the nightly bombings exchanged between the two countries, Iraq ensured that it avoided targeting areas surrounding embassies in Iran of countries which were close in ties to USA. Iranian citizens who were multi millionaires, who had palatial bungalows, would pay huge sums every night for the privilege of sleeping on the foothpaths adjacent to these embassies as these were considered the only few safe zones. ***These*** were USPs throughout the duration of the war.

As we said, true USPs are almost impossible to find as far as products or tangibles are concerned.

Then what use is the term 'USP', today?

Good question.

If you want to be truly successful, invest in yourself to get the knowledge you need to find your unique factor. When you find it and focus on it and persevere, your success will blossom.

- Sidney Madwed

The true USPs in today's times are the Service USPs

Since USPs are rarely attainable through product alone, the brand perforce has to focus on ***differentiating*** itself through the element of ***service,*** or through the ***intangible element.*** And this cannot be replicated or copied as easily or as rapidly as a product or a tangible difference can. Therefore, the only ***sustainable*** USPs today are the ***service*** USPs.

Product USPs are based on tangible elements such as technological capability and physical resources. Service USPs are derived from attitude, philosophy and mindset.

- Cyrus M Gonda, Kalim Khan

The ***culture and orientation*** of service that has seeped into every pore and entered every crevice of the organization flowing from top to bottom, until every atom of the organization lives and breathes service orientation and customer focus may be ***impossible for competitors to replicate till the crack of doom.***

Excellence in the areas of tenets propagated in this book are the source of genuine and sustainable USPs.

- Following ethical practices towards customers.
- Generating genuine positive public relations (word of mouth publicity), through customer delight.
- Generating continuous, consistent, positive moments of truth.
- Devising flexibility in approach to suit customer interest.
- Trusting the customer.
- Empowering front end staff.

All the above, which comprise some of our tenets which have each been elaborated at length, can and will be the ***only true source of differentiators*** in world class organizations today.

Disney has got this element right. It has become the benchmark for a world class entertainment experience.

So has Nordstrom, the department store chain known for its fantastic service culture.

The Ritz-Carlton chain of hotels has it's own unique culture of customer dedication.

These are by far the leaders in their field and industry, and ***not because their physical assets differentiate them from their competitors.*** That's not the differentiator, nor their USP.

As far as physical layout goes, one five star deluxe hotel would be as grand and opulent as another. So would a premium department store. But whereas in many other hotel chains, the answer to a certain out of the way guest request could be a polite but firm ***"No",*** as we have seen at the Ritz-Carlton the response will always be, ***"The answer is Yes, now what is the question."*** And at the Ritz-Carlton, this is not just a catchy phrase. It's treated on par with the tenets of a religion. A supreme commandment that cannot be ignored, come hell or highwater. ***That*** is a USP that may not be duplicated for decades or possibly generations by competing hotel chains, however grand and opulent their façade may be.

It is not the outer shell or exterior that determines true USPs. It is the inner core, the soul, the culture, the top management philosophy, which determine USPs.

- Cyrus M Gonda, Kalim Khan

The soul and the culture of an organisation cannot be bought off a shelf. They have to be imbibed and soaked into the DNA of the organisation. And the process has to initiate at the very top. No external brand endorser can give an organisation that vital leading edge.

And if you recall the ***tenet on Ethics,*** these elements of culture and customer orientation were ***Arthur Andersen's original USP.***

It is not that other Chartered Analysts did not know the tangible elements of accounting principles and procedures. These are common knowledge to even amateur accountants. But putting into practice the ***true customer orientation over short term profitability*** is something which positively differentiated the original Arthur Andersen from the rest of the pack.

Thus, it's evident that the intangibles, the culture which permeates from the top, the true customer first focus, is rare and not easy to replicate and ***these are the*** USPs an organization needs to strive to achieve.

People will pay a higher price at Nordstrom to purchase the ***same*** goods they could have bought elsewhere but many still prefer to go to Nordstrom – for the excellent service they are guaranteed to receive.

True USPs help you tower giantlike over the rest of the field.

If a man writes a better book, preaches a better sermon, or builds a better mousetrap than his neighbour, the world will make a beaten path to his door.

- Ralph Waldo Emerson

It is your genuine USPs which make you irreplaceable in the eyes of your retained customers.

The Giant of Jazz

Years ago, one of the most popular musicians in the world was a clarinet player by the name of Benny Goodman. An icon who is still revered today by followers of jazz. We remember reading an article about him somewhere.

It said that Benny Goodman was a simple looking man.

He could blend in a crowd of office goers and be literally invisible.

Neatly trimmed, well combed hair.

Basic, simple framed spectacles.

Well polished, simple lace shoes.

A sober suit and an even more sober tie.

Today, some people would call him plain, dull, uninteresting based on his external appearance.

But when Benny Goodman went on stage and put that clarinet to his lips, the world stopped and listened. He played that damn clarinet better than anybody else in the world. He literally made it speak. And it wasn't a special clarinet either. Physically, it was the same clarinet as any other.

In other hands, and on other lips, it would not have sounded half as sweet. That's what intangible USPs are all about.

They are not about the physical assets and the resources at one's command, but are about what one DOES with those assets and resources. That decides the strength of an organisation's USPs.

In the Indian context, the example of Benny Goodman could be replaced by Hemant Kumar, Manna De and Mohamed Rafi.

Did Benny Goodman have customers? Sure he did. Every individual who ***experienced*** the melody of his music was, and even today is, his customer, long after Benny Goodman has left this world behind.

An averagely talented musician out to promote himself, streaking his hair green, pink and yellow, tattooing every available inch of his body, putting on the most outlandish clothes, ***is under a misconception if he feels he has achieved a USP.***

These external appearances can be easily duplicated by a five year old child. The playing ability and skill cannot. They take years.

BE A BENNY GOODMAN.

CLASS WILL TELL.

TALENT WILL SPEAK FOR ITSELF.

Develop that talent and skill of service till everyone talks with pride about being YOUR customer, the same way that people talked with pride about having a front row seat at a Benny Goodman performance.

Laurel and Hardy – The geniuses of comedy

Take the all time favourite comedy duo of Laurel and Hardy. At the end of the movie, ***'The Laughing Twenties',*** which is a compilation of the best work of the two comedians, the narrator mentions – ***"Into the distance and into memory. NEVER WILL WE SEE THEIR LIKE AGAIN."***

That's USP. Imagine a customer confidently saying about the service levels and personal touch that your brand provides, 'Never will we see a similar level elsewhere.'

It's the greatest compliment that could ever be paid to your brand.

If a Barber Shop can have a USP, then ANYONE can

It doesn't require you to possess a Research and Development laboratory and huge research budgets to develop a USP. The smallest and simplest form of organisation can achieve it, ***provided they have the will.***

Let's look at a simple barber shop.

What could an average barber saloon, charging the minimum Rupees Thirty for a haircut do, to differentiate in a positive way? Not much, you would say. But let's explore the subject a little in depth.

There is this small barber shop we know of, a five seater place, that we know of and frequent, very simple in its exterior and decor. What could they possibly do to create customer delight that other barber saloons don't? They do something very simple but yet highly effective.

They have understood the customer's genuine latent needs to the highest degree. Granted, a customer does visit a saloon for a haircut and a shave. But while that's what he needs, ***what else could delight him?***

That's what these ***geniuses,*** (yes, geniuses), at this saloon have identified.

In this day and age of contagious disease, ideally, a customer would prefer a separate pair of scissors, comb and razor to be reserved and used only on him and no one else. Not possible, you say? Think again. That's precisely the USP that this saloon is offering its regular, retained customers.

The customers are told to provide their own scissors, razor and comb, as well as a small box, (the size of a child's tiffin box), labeled with the customer's own name to store these items in. The saloon has kept aside a cupboard where it stores about three hundred such boxes alphabetically, for its regular clients, and keeps them safe for use only when these clients arrive.

Look at the multiple benefits this activity provides:

1. The saloon saves on equipment wear and tear as its regular clients provide their own equipment at their own expense.
2. It brings a feeling of delight to the regular clientele. An area which is of concern to them, (hygiene), is taken care of in brilliant fashion.
3. It's such a ***lovely recipe for customer retention.*** In other circumstances, a customer would be tempted to visit another saloon once in a while. But in this case, he is held captive since his equipment is already stored with the saloon itself.
4. And what does it cost the saloon? Just the space it takes to place one cupboard. Benefits? Three hundred retained customers at any given time.

Is it that it would take a competitor two years to emulate this simple USP?

In theory – Not at all.

It wouldn't even take a day.

Physically, all that needs to be ordered is a cupboard. But it's a bet from our end that we'll see very few, if any, saloons emulating this USP.

Because the stumbling block lies not in the lack of availability of the required physical resource, (a single cupboard), but in the lack of a proper attitude, lack of customer orientation and lack of a culture which is rarely directed towards genuine customer delight.

Thus, it is a customer focused culture that is the key to genuine, lasting USPs.

Attitude is a little thing that makes a big difference.

- Winston Churchill

USP in a Grocery Store

Another example of a genuine USP we witnessed is brilliant in its simplicity and concept. The credit goes to a small grocery store, one among many similar stores in its neighbourhood, all stocking almost the same inventory at almost the same price. But ***this*** particular store does a lot more business than the rest, as it has identified a need in its customer base and tapped it.

The need per se has nothing to do with the produce that it stocks. It has to do with the fact that in the city of Mumbai, it is very difficult to get somebody to accept soiled, worn out currency notes. Even bus conductors refuse to accept them, and it becomes difficult for someone possessing such notes to use them to purchase anything. And these notes abound in large numbers.

This store has capitalized on this need of people to spend these soiled notes as fast as possible and rid themselves of them.

There is a bold ***signboard*** outside this store, mentioning, ***"All old and torn notes accepted here (as per Reserve Bank of India regulations) against purchase."***

Brilliant.

Guess where most customers in the neighbourhood, and even casual passers by with even slightly soiled notes go? And once they enter the store, (primarily with the objective to dispose their soiled notes), they buy all the groceries they need. Just taking advantage of the opportunity the store has given them to unload their soiled notes. Again, it doesn't cost the store a thing. As the soiled notes accepted by the store are within RBI regulations, any nationalized bank would accept the soiled notes from the store. So the store doesn't lose out in any way. All it takes the store is a little extra effort to send someone to the bank to deposit the notes in bulk.

From Tailor to Fashion Designer

For most tailors, the function of alteration appears to be below the dignity and more trouble than it is worth. Its almost impossible to find a tailor who does alteration work, this despite the fact that there are many customers willing to pay a decent amount for this type of work. A trouser waist to be tucked in, or the trouser length to be slightly increased. A tailor we used to know rightly identified this as an area with ***HUGE*** potential for business, and advertised himself as a tailor specializing in alteration work. He soon got more business than he could handle, so he hired a couple of assistants to help him. He soon started getting business for shirts and trousers and even jackets from the very same customers who used to come to him purely for alteration work. Their existing tailors had refused to provide them with this alteration service, and had axed their own feet. Soon this tailor moved upscale and is now quite a reputed fashion designer in his own right, simply because he identified a genuine need which his existing competitors had considered below their dignity to service.

The Auto Rickshaw with USPs

There is an auto rickshaw we have seen in Mumbai, one among thousands of other rickshaws in the city. But this particular rickshaw is a masterpiece in providing the customer with amenities that even most airlines wouldn't provide.

- A pen and chits of paper in case a passenger wants to take notes.
- Paper tissues for the passenger to use stored in a plastic cup screwed to the back of the driver's seat.
- An ashtray.
- A small black and white television.
- A fire extinguisher.
- A small clock.
- A calendar.
- A magazine and a newspaper for him to read.
- A headache tablet and band-aids.
- Flavoured mints.
- A twenty five percent discount offered for senior citizen passengers.
- A mirror and a small comb.
- The driver keeps sufficient change in case the customer doesn't have any.

The list is literally endless. In short, like the Little Drummer Boy in the Christmas story, ***this driver is giving all he has.*** And as a result of this, this rickshaw owner is flooded with requests from passengers to regularly ferry them to office and back. He literally has to refuse customers, although regretfully, as he simply doesn't have time to serve them all.

And today, other rickshaw drivers feel, "We are getting enough business anyway. We don't ***need*** to go the extra mile." But it is predicted that with the Mumbai suburban Metro railway line due to commence operations, the volume of passengers traveling by rickshaw are due to see a huge drop because of this competition from the new railway line.

The same holds true for big brands. For multiple reasons, they will see their individual market shares plummet in the near future, unless they treat current scenarios as a wake up call.

If Big Brands adopt a similar proactive attitude towards their customers which this rickshaw owner displays, with the volumes of resources the big brands have at their command, they'll never be short of loyal, retained customers.

Tenet 9

TAKE PERSONAL PRIDE IN YOUR BRAND

Serve grand
For a better brand

Business is a lot like a game of tennis –
those who SERVE well usually end up winning.

- Anonymous

Let us commence this tenet by clearly understanding that logos, jingles, taglines, package designs, advertisements etc., do NOT make or define a brand. These are merely a BRAND IDENTITY. A Brand Identity is the tangible element that is within the control of the brand.

THESE ELEMENTS CAN EVEN BE BRILLIANTLY MADE AS A HYPOTHETICAL CLASSROOM EXERCISE FOR A BRAND WHICH IN REALITY DOES NOT EVEN EXIST.

Therefore, in the ultimate analysis, it's NOT the brand identity that matters. What DO matter are the experiences that your brand provides to customers.
These experiences are what shape and make your brand.

- Cyrus M Gonda, Kalim Khan

What is a Brand?

Who owns it?

How does one strengthen it?

These questions lie at the heart of every marketer's career.

There are many explanations provided as to what a Brand is and how it could be made strong as steel. Billions of dollars have been poured down the proverbial drain in the pursuit of brand building, very often to no avail.

One route to brand building which is quite commonly adopted is through the route of expensive advertising campaigns.

It is obviously to the advantage of advertising agencies to suggest that the best way to build a brand is through a blitzkrieg of advertising. Naturally that's what they would suggest. But the truth of the matter is, the advertising industry has double standards, and thus can hardly be relied upon in case of claims pertaining to value addition in brand building.

We wish to demonstrate why we feel so with the following example:

When it comes to ***any other product category apart from cigarettes,*** the advertising industry is very categorical in stating that the more the visibility of the advertisement, more will non-users of that product category be converted into users. (After all, that's why advertising charges are so high.)

Say for example, the advertising industry claims that a housewife who is in the habit of providing hot, home cooked breakfast for her family, could be convinced through repetitive advertising to serve a breakfast of any nutritious, packaged cereal instead. Once she is convinced that cereals are a good option, now the task of making her choose a particular brand of cereal can be commenced through clever advertising. This is what the advertising agencies claim they are good at.

Next example. Another claim made by advertisers is, segments of the society which traditionally have never used shampoos for washing their hair, could be convinced through repetitive advertising that shampoos are good for keeping hair clean. Once a person is convinced that shampoos are the best option for hair care, now the task of convincing him to use a particular brand of shampoo which is being advertised could commence.

BUT WHEN IT COMES TO THE PRODUCT CATEGORY OF CIGARETTES, where there is strong public opinion against the product category itself, ***THE ADVERTISING INDUSTRY CHANGES ITS STANCE WITH THE FINESSE OF A HOUDINI***.

NOW the stand taken by the industry is that ***MERE ADVERTISING CANNOT CONVERT A NON-USER*** (of cigarettes), ***INTO BECOMING A USER. THE ADVERTISING AGENCIES CLAIM THAT THE ONLY PURPOSE CIGARETTE ADVERTISING SERVES*** is that it helps to ***CONVERT A PERSON WHO ALREADY SMOKES CIGARETTES, (YOUR COMPETITOR'S BRAND), INTO NOW SMOKING YOUR BRAND. IT SAYS THAT IT REALLY CANNOT MAKE A CURRENT NON-SMOKER TAKE UP CIGARETTE SMOKING SIMPLY THROUGH ADVERTISING CIGARETTES.***

WOW. These sudden turnarounds as per convenience make the head spin.

Advertising agencies say this in the case of this particular product category, (cigarettes), because they know that if they claim in ***THIS*** instance that non-users can be converted to users through the "power" of advertising, then the anti smoking lobby and parents of teenagers would be down on them like a ton of bricks.

Advertising agencies want to absolve themselves of all responsibility of converting non- smokers to smokers. Therefore, when it comes to the category of cigarettes, they say advertising has very little power to convert a non-user to a user.

But when it comes to other product categories which are not injurious to health, they want to claim credit for converting non-users to users.

So they go the way the wind blows. Which stand of theirs are we to believe?

The point we raise is - ***NO ONE IS ULTIMATELY RESPONSIBLE FOR THE SUCCESS OF THE BRAND APART FROM THE BRAND ITSELF.***

External agencies can at best be support systems in the crucial task of brand building. The responsibility for building a brand cannot be abdicated and surrendered to some outside agency which is merely a generic communication specialist.

We are all aware that the way in which a child is raised and reared by its biological mother in an environment of genuine bonding and affection can never be duplicated by an army of impersonal, paid caretakers. And that's how a child is raised in the best possible manner. The adult that the child will blossom into, will be the result of the sum total of care, affection, nutrition, discipline, support, and nurture that has been provided primarily by its parents, or immediate family through its formative years.

And a Brand is nothing but a child

A Brand is nothing but the sum total of the values, affection and support it has received, primarily from its founders and immediate family members, which if done in the right way, will result into terrific experiences for the customers of the brand, regularly and repeatedly. On the hour, every hour, as the news broadcasters say. This is what will make the brand a rock solid one.

We would like you to think of a few ***world famous brands.*** Take a couple of minutes and ponder.

Now read further.

Which are some of the brands you thought of and what images did they conjure up?

Maybe you thought of Nike, Coca Cola, IBM, McDonalds, Wrangler and the like. And what did your mind's eye visualize as you thought of these or maybe other brands? Probably the colours, logos, jingles, punch-lines, associated with these brands.

Rarely would the first thoughts these brands evoke be related to the positive experiences that have accrued to the individual while consuming these products or services.

We would term such a brand as relatively weak, having to depend on external appearances, and not actual experiences, for its survival and recall factor.

How does one Determine the Strength of a Brand?

In fact we at ***Brains Trust*** have devised our own practical, qualitative, formula for evaluating the strength of a brand in the minds of it's customers.

'Brains Trust' Brand Strength Evaluation Formula

The LESSER the brand needs to rely on self-created external parameters (including endorsers, symbols, slogans, logos, jingles, punch-lines), to make it's customers think of it positively and in glowing terms, the STRONGER is the value and image of that particular brand in the eyes of it's customer base.

In fact, the above is an area in which we at Brains Trust regularly provide qualitative and quantitative consultancy services to our corporate clientele, helping them understand and then enhance the strength of their brand.

The following examples would well demonstrate our formula of strong brand building.

First - a question for the reader.

Have you heard of a ***brand*** called ***Japan?*** Yes, ***Japan.***

Let us say you wish to purchase a television or a music system and walk into a showroom. You select the model of your choice and then you may ask the sales attendant, ***"Is it Japanese assembled? I'd prefer a piece that is assembled in Japan rather than Korea, Indonesia or Taiwan. I'M WILLING TO PAY TWENTY PERCENT MORE FOR SUCH A PIECE. I'M EVEN WILLING TO WAIT FOR A WEEK IF IT'S NOT IN STOCK RIGHT NOW."***

Brilliant.

The customer has faith in a product because it has been assembled in a country he has never visited and assembled by a man he has never met in a factory he has never seen.

What could be a better example of a solid brand building exercise?

The customer is willing to pay twenty percent more, wait a week for delivery, just because it's been assembled in Japan.

And, we rarely see advertisements saying Japanese products are the best in quality.

The Japanese do not need to say it. Others say it on their behalf.

The customer demanding a Japanese product may never have visited Japan or interacted with a Japanese national in his life. He doesn't recall a logo or a tagline associated with Brand Japan.

But yet see the goodwill generated and the confidence the customer has in ***THE BRAND CALLED JAPAN.***

It's the little things that make the big things possible. Only close attention to the fine details of any operation makes the operation first class.

- J Willard Marriott

It wasn't always this way for Japan though. Building a good, solid, reputed brand takes time, persistence, devotion to customer needs, and sustained honest effort. In short, brand building is not a haphazard activity achieving results through advertising spend, but through a systematic approach involving personal and constant attention of the top management, requiring the decision making layer to be constantly in touch with the customers and with ground level realities. Initially when Japanese companies started off in the field of ***Consumer*** Electronics (not customer), the name of the brand was embossed in large print on the product and ***Made in Japan*** didn't feature at all. Gradually, as the confidence of consumers grew, **Made in Japan** started featuring on the product, and today the words ***MADE IN JAPAN*** hit you boldly in the face even larger than the name of the brand itself in many instances. But it takes some time for this confidence to be generated. And its only because the Japanese were obsessed to the point of being fanatical about the quality their brands stood for that this confidence was passed on to every single customer of Brand Japan.

And ***Brand Japan*** wasn't built on the fragile "power" of advertising, but on the rock solid foundation of positive word-of-mouth.

Further Examples of how Customers Subconsciously Identify Strong Brands

As we explained in our ***formula of Brand Strength Evaluation,*** it is in the brand's long term interest to let customers identify with it by the quality of its product and service, and by the ***USPs*** the brand offers, and ***NOT*** by the logo or Brand endorser (which give no genuine benefit to the customer in themselves.)

For example, we don't even recall having seen the ***flag*** of Singapore, (the logo of Brand Singapore), nor hearing its ***National Anthem,*** (the jingle of Brand Singapore), nor having seen its currency. (***All these are part of Singapore's Brand Identity, which really don't convey much to the customer by themselves***). But we ***do know*** that ***Brand Singapore*** stands for cleanliness, discipline, regard for rules and superior quality of life for its customers, (citizens).

Anything Worthwhile Takes a Little Time

Yes, building a solid brand does take a little time.

Anything worthwhile and good in quality, takes time. If you invite an honoured guest over to your house for dinner, would you hurriedly prepare and serve him two minute noodles or would you take the effort to prepare a delicious, memorable, home cooked meal?

A good brand is built on the ***BEDROCK OF CREDIBILITY.*** And credibility itself is built on a foundation of ***quality consciousness, customer orientation, healthy innovation, attention to customer feedback, consistency in product, process and delivery, and positive word of mouth publicity.***

There are no short cuts to all this, and there never will be.

People who have heard music from a pair of Bose speakers are aware of the image of quality that this brand name evokes. They don't recall whether Bose speakers even ***have*** a logo or a tagline, but they ***do*** recall their crisp, clear sound and the many memorable pieces of music they would have heard through them.

And rarely, if ever, have we seen an advertisement for a Rolls Royce either.

Similarly, Swiss watches and chocolates are renowned, appreciated and sought after the world over.

So is porcelain from Dresden in Germany.

As is crystal from Swarovski.

The point is, as far as all these rock solid brands are concerned, what matters most to their customers is the quality and consistency that the brands stand for.

Truly strong brands have very little to do with logos, slogans and catch phrases.

Rather, such brands depend on their ability to continuously provide a quality product, service and experience. This is where the bulk of the resources of such brands are invested.

Personal Branding

To further elaborate, we'd like to bring up the issue of ***Personal Branding,*** which has gained such importance today. We rarely associate outstanding individuals with a personal logo or a catch phrase, but we ***can*** single them out and identify them for their positive qualities and the unique benefits they have developed and stand for.

As an example, we'd like to bring up the difference between the work done by a ***Recruitment Agency*** and that done by a ***Headhunter***.

The way a ***Recruitment Agency*** functions is that it receives a request from a client organisation stating that it has a vacancy and is looking for ***any*** suitable candidate who meets the pre-decided requirements of age, qualifications and experience to fill up the vacancy. If five candidates meet the requirements set by the organisation, any one of them could potentially be good enough. The organization here is in a stronger position than the candidate, as it has a wider choice, and it can dictate terms.

The ***Headhunter's*** job, on the other hand, is quite different. He receives a request from an organization, ***not*** to fill up a vacancy with ***any*** suitable candidate who meets the requirements, but to get for the organisation ***a specific, particular candidate*** who has already been identified, who may currently be employed with a competitor. So in this case the organization does not want any Tom, Dick or Harry, just because he is thirty years of age, has an MBA degree, and has ten years of experience. The organisation wants Mr. ABC and no one else, and it's willing to pay the price that Mr. ABC asks, provided he is willing to join the organisation.

In this case, it is the candidate and not the organization who is in the happy position of being sought after. The candidate is not the one doing the job search. He has five organisations running after him to avail of his services. He is no longer one among five applicants chasing one job in an organization.

But all this is possible ***not*** because Mr. ABC has merely ***advertised*** the fact that he is available, or devised a catchy logo or jingle or tagline which uniquely identifies him or separates him from the rest.

Rather, this situation transpires because Mr. ABC has spent his time, effort, energy and other resources ***BUILDING HIMSELF UP AS A STRONG, SOUGHT AFTER BRAND, CAPABLE OF DELIVERING WHAT OTHER CANDIDATES CANNOT.*** It is not his physical, tangible attributes such as age and height that put him in this position but the knowledge and expertise he has acquired through relentless practice, study, experience, thus making him capable of delivering that extra edge. ***HE IS NOW A SOUGHT AFTER, PERSONAL BRAND.***

As we said, great brands are built on the bedrock of intangibles

Consider certain individuals who have strived and succeeded in creating a ***Personal Brand Worth*** for themselves. This, despite the fact that externally they appear to possess similar physical attributes as the rest of the human race. Two arms, two legs, one brain, and so on.

Authors, inventors, military leaders, medical personnel, and sporting greats. In each profession there are individuals who have utilized to the highest level the physical and mental capabilities with which they were endowed. ***They could not physically enhance their natural assets by growing an extra head or two, or an extra pair of hands.***

So they excelled at their chosen profession by optimally using the limited physical assets they possessed.

As research has shown, an average individual utilizes barely five percent of the brain power he has at his disposal. The balance ninety five percent lies vacant, unless conscious efforts are made to develop the same. ***Similarly, we have observed that rarely do organisations exploit and fully utilize the talent and potential their employees possess to a suitable degree.***

While on the subject of personal branding, take a man called ***Harry Houdini,*** who died decades ago. His name is even today synonymous with perfection and beyond in the art of the skilled escape. Houdini has entered the English dictionary as a word which epitomizes the apex of skill as an escape artist. One man. Through his single minded determination and dedication, learning as much about his chosen profession as possible, and even beyond. Practicing till he became perfect. A man with just two arms and two legs like any other man. ***He became a brand and a legend in his own lifetime.*** There has never again been another Houdini.

Sir Winston Churchill, one of the greatest exponents of the English language ever, whose eloquent speeches are still a delight to read, ***spent three years getting through eighth grade at school as he had trouble learning English.*** But he persevered, developed a quality vocabulary, and progressed to become one of the finest orators and exponents of the English language of all time.

In the same way, organizations, rather than attempting to increase the existing customer base by focusing on attracting new customers, can generate much more business at lesser cost, by focusing on and becoming better at activities which will delight and retain existing customers, who will then also spread positive word of mouth. Thus, organizations can make optimal use of the latent potential waiting to be tapped among the currently existing customer base and its Circle of Influence.

It is mostly a myth to believe that ***some people just have it and other people do not.***

Success in building a strong, sought after brand, whether as an organization or as an individual, or as a nation, has always been the result of hard work and dedication.

This is what surges certain individuals and organizations ahead of the rest.

It is not talent, (which is inborn and cannot be duplicated), that makes the difference.

It is in most cases a sheer, sustained, dedicated effort which does the trick. A one track mind as far as perfection and quality are concerned.

A case in point will prove this beyond all reasonable doubt.

The Polgar Family

In the 1960s, Laszlo Polgar, a Hungarian educational psychologist, propounded the theory that ***great performers are made, not born.*** To prove the validity of his theory, he married a woman who would have children with him to forward his theory. At random, he selected the field of chess in which he would make his children champions. The couple had three daughters, Susan, Sophia and Judith. Laszlo and his wife, Klara, devoted their lives to making their three daughters chess experts. The three daughters were tutored at home, their education while covering basic school curriculum, focused sharply on imbibing the niceties of chess. Hours and hours of chess practice daily were part of the three daughter's routine.

The results followed as a matter of course.

At the age of seventeen, Susan became the first woman ever to qualify for what was then called the Men's World Chess Championship.

When Susan was nineteen, Sophia fourteen and Judith twelve, they competed as a team in the World Women's Chess Olympiad and scored Hungary's first ever victory against the Soviet Union team.

When Susan was twenty one, she became the first woman ever to be ranked as a grand master, the highest possible rank in world chess.

Judith became a grand master at age fifteen.

The point to note is, neither Lazslo nor his wife were chess players of any repute. They did not hereditarily pass on any chess ability to their children.

What made the three girls such a force to be reckoned with in their field was the hard work, effort, dedication and sustained practice they put in to achieve these heights.

As Susan Polgar says, "My father firmly believes that innate talent is nothing. That success is ninety percent hard work. I agree with him."

The Polgar family example can definitely be replicated in the field of genuine Brand Building as well.

Strong Brand, thy name is Consistency

As we saw in the case of Brand Japan, and Brand Singapore, (among others), a solid brand is built on the bedrock of consistency.

While an individual, one-off, lone ranger kind of instance, resulting in one time delight is great, such instances of delight can never compete with consistently good performances on a regular basis, which arise from systemic strength. There is a fantastic example about systemic strength coming from Jan Carlzon's airline, SAS, which is elaborated in the ***Tenet on Empowerment.***

Your Brand can be identified as a strong brand if the entire Brand Team is filled with good players, functioning efficiently within a customer oriented system, rather than your team revolving around a handful of great players fighting desperately against a self centred, and not a customer centered, system.

- Cyrus M Gonda, Kalim Khan

Where the need for heroes exists, it indicates that the system has failed.

Great brands do not go weak when good performers leave them. Rather, great brands ensure a constant inflowing stream of consistent performers geared up and backed by a system which permits and indeed encourages them to remain united and give their best.

Faith in the brand will be generated through the brand acting first and foremost in the customer's interest.

If there is a conflict between the brand's interests and a genuine customer's interests, it is the genuine customer's interests which should get priority.

Not surprisingly, by doing this, the brand itself will benefit over a period of time, ***for the brand's interests and success are linked with it's customer's interests and success.*** For example, if a particular product or service doesn't match a particular customer's requirements, no attempts should be made to sell such products and services to him, irrespective of the short term loss of revenue that could accrue from such a ***mis-sale.***

(We use the term mis-sale to indicate a mis-match between the customer's requirements, and a product or service being attempted to be sold to him.)

A strong brand also needs to display a genuine concern for the customer and his needs, making efforts to understand his genuine needs better, and developing improved and enhanced products and services to cater to the same. Needless to say, this activity, like all other true brand building activities, needs to be done on an ongoing basis. We find it ridiculous when certain organizations publicise a certain period as ***Customer Service Week.***

The only implication one can derive from this farcical statement is that in the rest of the weeks of the year, it is okay to ignore the customer, and that in other weeks, the customer service is ***WEAK.***

A strong brand also ensures that it's representatives take pain and effort to go out of the way for the customer. This is at times difficult and inconvenient for the brand, but an absolute imperative for long term brand success.

We recently attended a seminar on the subject of brand building. The crème de la crème of the advertising world was present. The troubled times for the economy were in full swing. And everyone on the dais and in the audience agreed on one thing. ***Now in these troubled times, we need to get back to the basics.***

In short, get feet back on ground, where they rightfully always belong.

Great. No doubting that statement.

The question is, ***"Why are basics resorted to only in bad times. And in times of plenty, we leave the ground realities behind, (including focusing on the customer), and fly up and away to construct castles in the sky."***

The Brand's Feet at all Times Need to be On The Ground

For that is where the customer's feet are.

And if the brand can remember to do this basic activity in good times and bad, the value and worth of the brand will grow manifold.

How does one calculate the value of a brand?

Very simple. Recall the example of Brand Japan? And how most customers are willing to pay a premium for and wait some time if they can be assured of purchasing a Japanese assembled product? ***That determines the value of the brand.***

Are your customers willing to pay a premium for the privilege of purchasing your product or availing of your service? As an example, since both of us used to be fans of the Dell brand of laptops, we waited for Dell to launch its version of the nine inch mini laptop before we went ahead with our purchase decision for a mini laptop, although other brands had launched their nine inch mini version much before Dell had done so. That we ultimately didn't purchase the Dell nine inch mini is another story, which has been related elsewhere in this book.

If your product is not currently available for some valid reason, are your customers willing to wait a while for it, or do they immediately purchase a competitor's product or avail of a competitor's service as a substitute?

The premium amount that your loyal customers are willing to pay, and the period which they are willing to wait for it to be available, determine the value of your brand in your ***customer's eyes.***

And believe us, ***those are the only eyes that matter.***

While on the subject of developing a strong, sustainable brand through consistency and quality, it is possible that all brands may not achieve or aspire to this high level.

It's a fact that every organization and brand is not interested in being the best, or anywhere near the best.

Such brands may not find focusing on issues of perfection and quality fitting in with their objective of competing on price alone. Fair enough.

But for the rest of the brands who wish to compete on quality, (as most brands worth their salt say they do), the message of our tenets is imperative.

A great brand is never built by accident, always by design.

Great brands constantly benchmark themselves as far as their systems and processes go, with the best in class, not only in their own industry, but also from apparently unrelated industries. Ideas and true learning can and do come from any direction.

For example, Lexus dealers had benchmarked the processes of Mercedes (auto industry), Nordstrom (retail industry) and Ritz Carlton (hotel industry), for identifying best practices in customer handling and satisfaction.

Lexus dealers then started providing free car washes, complimentary weekend stays, breakfast buffets at the dealer's premises and also constructed mini golf courses at the dealer's outlets. All this, to get customers keep coming back.

Giving the best to your customers pays off exponentially. By hiring staff at lower rates, an organization may feel its bringing down its operational costs. But ultimately what such things tend to do is dilute the value of the brand in the eyes of its customers.

Nordstrom, the quality retail chain, pays its staff a higher salary than their competitors do, but despite this, Nordstrom's profit margins are higher than most of its competing brands, simply because of the quality of service their staff are able to provide customers, who keep coming back, and get others with them.

'Brains Trust' Five C's of Branding

- ***Creativity*** (in ensuring improved products and service delivery systems.)
- ***Clarity*** (of the message of the brand as to what it stands for.)
- ***Convenience*** (of availability, usage, features of the product or service.)
- ***Consistency*** (of product and service delivery.)
- ***Credibility*** (which comes through excellent experiences over a period of time.)

The individual founder's philosophy is crucial to strong brand building

A point to consider. The truly strong brands, the ones which fulfill genuine customer needs in a quality manner - Disney, Wal-Mart, IBM, Microsoft, Bank of America, Mary Kay Ash, Tata, are brands initially built by individuals with the vision and foresight to provide a great product, quality service, customer focus, personal involvement and involving very little, if any, advertising spend.

PART TWO of this tenet - 'BRAND', will deal with a related sub-area which in today's times, needs a lot of clear thinking.

Part Two of this tenet will deal with the concept of the BRAND ENDORSER.

A TRUE EXPERT'S WORD IS ALWAYS HEARD

A very common myth prevailing today among organizations is that the presence of a CELEBRITY (however unrelated), is vital for successful branding. Nothing could be further from the truth.

This book is the second joint venture of ours as co-authors. Our first book was the best selling book on how to give and receive excellent customer service, entitled ***"Where is my Ketchup."***

At the reading of ***Where Is My Ketchup*** at Crossword bookstore, one of the members seated in the audience asked us a very pertinent question.

Her question was, "Your book has beautifully explained in a story form as to how any organization can create a great brand image for itself by providing superior customer service. But in your book there is no mention of the concept and role of a celebrity brand endorser in the process of brand building. ***Do you think that in today's age, a strong brand can be built and sustained without having a celebrity brand endorser to promote it?"***

We were very glad she asked this question, and we spontaneously replied as follows.

"We are hosting this event at a ***Crossword*** bookstore, which is India's largest and most wide reaching chain of bookstores.

The parent company which owns the Crossword brand is ***Shopper's Stop,*** the largest chain of shopping malls in the country.

To the best of our knowledge, neither Crossword, nor Shopper's Stop, have used the services of a celebrity brand endorser to propel them into the first position in their categories. And these are just two examples of brands which immediately come to mind as we are conducting this event under their auspices. There are multiple other strong brands today, which have made it to the big league, without the shoulder of an unrelated celebrity on which to ride piggy back."

The current usage of Brand Endorsers is at best a half baked tool for short term attraction

Unfortunately, in the current scenario ***brand endorsers have been taken on for VISIBILITY and NOT CREDIBILITY. If nude women would have been permitted under advertising standards, they would easily have replaced the current lot of endorsers.*** It is unfortunate that even several so-called leading brands have been unable to develop or identify genuine USPs to utilise as attractors.

It is a fact that brands which have genuine USPs prefer to put them at the forefront of their publicity campaigns. It is only when USPs fail to exist or have not been developed, that this easy, but short-term and expensive method of celebrity endorsement is adopted. We pity such brands which are apparently bereft and poverty stricken when it comes to the matter of possessing genuine marketable USPs to project to the public.

Brand Endorser? Or Rubber Stamp?

In the sorry sort of sick scenario which exists today (where individual celebrities are personally endorsing more than twenty five brands each), celebrities sell off their name to a celebrity agent to use as he sees fit. The agent, to recover the amount he has paid the celebrity, signs deals involving the celebrity to endorse everything from A for Aardvarks to Z for Zanzibar. ***A cricketer endorses every product category from hair oil to car oil.*** Little do the brands hiring such celebrities recall the statement – ***"When one stands for everything, one ends up standing for nothing."***

The celebrity is in effect reduced to a rubber stamp as far as his choice to select brands to endorse is concerned. Not that he or she is bothered, else he or she would have been judicious about selecting quality brands to endorse, used the same brands that they endorsed, and kept selection rights as to which brands to endorse with themselves and not given away these rights to an agent.

Brand Endorsement – The Professional Way

In USA, the home of Marketing as a formal discipline, professional guidelines have been specifically formulated for the different marketing activities and sub-disciplines. The same holds true for the Brand Endorsers as well. And the first guideline for professionally selecting a Brand Endorser to endorse a brand is very clear.

THE PERSON HAS TO BE AN EXPERT IN THE FIELD HE OR SHE IS ENDORSING. This guideline is crystal clear. If, for example, an individual is endorsing a bank or a financial institution, ***THAT PERSON HAS TO BE A PERSON OF EMINENCE, STANDING AND EXPERTISE IN THE FIELD OF FINANCE, CAPABLE OF UNDERSTANDING THE INTRICACIES OF THE INDUSTRY, AND CAPABLE OF OFFERING SOUND ADVICE TO POTENTIAL CUSTOMERS ON THE SAME.***

In India, we have self proclaimed financial failures and certified bankrupts endorsing the efficiency and expertise leading banks and financial institutions.

It is like The Blind Leading The Blind.

A private sector bank, which utilized the services of such a film star to promote itself, is in a major problem today, because it has focused more on glamour and hype rather than on core banking and customer service.

The logic of the endorser being an expert in the field he is endorsing is that ***HE IS SUPPOSED TO BE A GUIDE FOR THE LAYMAN, NOT JUST A PRETTY FACE.***

The assumption of spending millions on ***RENTING*** a endorser is that the consumer base makes it's purchase decision based on the endorser making claims on behalf of the brand.

A person can be in a solid position to make a claim only when he or she has in-depth knowledge of the product he or she is endorsing.

Let us at thus stage clarify that the majority of celebrity endorsers of brands today are in no way even close to being experts in the products and services they endorse.

In India, forget having in-depth knowledge of the product or service, in many cases the so called endorser obviously doesn't even ***USE*** the product he or she is endorsing. In fact, in products such as 100 cc motorbikes and scooters, which are endorsed by leading cricketers and Bollywood celebrities, never have these endorsers been seen on these bikes anywhere other than in the advertisement. Obviously, these small two wheelers are considered beneath their dignity to be used in public.

One of the stars endorsing such a motorbike has even given a ***personal guarantee*** for the motorbike, boldly stating in the advertisement, ***"I am there if something goes wrong with the bike."*** This is such a ridiculous statement and so blatantly insulting to the intelligence of the consumer base, that one would have laughed if the statement didn't make one cry.

What is he going to do if something ***does*** go wrong with a bike that a customer has purchased?

- Repair it?
- Take it to a service centre?
- Attend to the customer's complaint?
- Refund the customer's money?
- And most important, where does one get in touch with him in case something goes wrong with the bike?

Organizations must understand that ***a Guarantee is not a Gimmick***. A true guarantee is a fantastic marketing tool.

A Guarantee is a strong confidence building mechanism that should never be devalued and reduced to the level of a cheap stunt.

- Cyrus M Gonda, Kalim Khan

Satellite Television

A recent news report mentioned how a leading celebrity endorser, who endorses the satellite television services of a particular brand, actually uses the competing brand, the dish of which is clearly visible on the terrace of his bungalow. By no means would such a act be termed as 'professional'.

Thus, obviously apart from consistently being seen using the brand one is endorsing, the first rule for selecting a ***professional*** brand endorser is - He should be an expert in the field he is endorsing.

We need to understand what the term "PROFESSIONALISM" truly means

In USA, the Society for Public Relation Professionals, (a non-statutory body), has a test for membership, mentioning that one's personal values should not clash with the industry or product one chooses to work for and represent or endorse. For example, one of the parameters in the test for membership states that if one's personal values are against smoking and the highest paying job one is offered as a PR professional is with a tobacco company, doing PR for it, should the person take up the offer? If the answer provided by the applicant is "Yes", then the person is denied membership to the society ***as it is not considered professional to promote, endorse and defend a product or service which is against one's personal values.*** They cannot clash. The logic is clear. There would be a clear conflict of interest between the individual values or beliefs and the product that the person is endorsing and promoting.

In India, we have the example of a leading Hindi soap opera actress being asked in a magazine interview if she would permit her children to consume soft drinks. Her answer was, ***"Of course not, surveys have shown that soft drinks are not good for health."***

In the same interview, she is further asked if she would endorse soft drinks if paid to do so. Her immediate response was, ***"Of course I would. My professional life has nothing to do with my personal values."***

That by itself is such an unprofessional statement. The implication of the statement is, ***"I need to safeguard my children's health. But I don't mind trying to convince other people's children to consume the same, provided I am heftily paid for it."***

We would call that anything but professional.

P Gopichand, Anil Kapoor and Rajnikant show the light

In this regard, ***hats off*** to truly professional celebrities such as ***Puella Gopichand (former All England Badminton champion), Bollywood film star Anil Kapoor, and the South Indian film star Rajnikant,*** who refuse to endorse aerated soft drinks, as they personally believe, (and as sufficient research has proved), that consumption of aerated soft drinks is neither in any way nutritious nor conducive to good health.

It is not that the money they would have been paid to endorse aerated drinks would not be of use to these gentlemen. But they rightly feel that as role models and icons for youth, they would not wish to wrongly influence their fan following to consume such products. ***These gentlemen (yes, gentlemen), put their personal values and ethics and the welfare of their fans at a priority above short term monetary considerations, and thus strengthen their own personal credibility and brand value.***

In case Anil Kapoor, Rajnikant and P Gopichand ***ever*** decide to endorse any brand in future, the highest amount of credibility would be attached to their word.

Unlike some endorsers who endorse and stand for everything.

Because when a person stands for everything, he stands for nothing.

We even have a Bollywood star who endorses soft drinks, (which are proven to be bad for health), and the same star also endorses health products. Wow.

While on the subject of soft drink commercials and Bollywood endorsers, the following example is a highly ironical one.

A Bollywood actor, who himself regularly appears in cola advertisements, claiming and shouting that the cola he represents and endorses is the best, passed a comment against another actor, (his competitor in the movie industry.) This other actor, (the competitor), had gone around portraying to the media that he himself was the greatest actor in the industry. Our first friend, who endorses colas, commented about this competitor, ***"IF ONE IS THE GREATEST, ONE NEEDS NOT TO SHOUT IT FROM THE ROOFTOPS."***

So very true.

But when it comes to this very same actor getting paid to endorse colas, shouting from roof tops and train tops that ***This Cola is the Greatest,*** how soon he forgets his own words of wisdom. It proves that even the celebrity endorsers themselves are aware that if a thing is the best, it need not say so about itself.

Hometrade

A decade ago, in the late 1990's, there existed for a ***very*** brief period of time a company called Hometrade. What business it exactly was into, only the founder of Hometrade and God may know. ***(It's three brand endorsers were certainly in the dark.)***

It was vaguely into some sort of financial and investment shenanigans. The fact of the matter is, the company induced members of the public to invest their money in it, promising very high rates of return. In order to convince the public that the company was a sound investment bet, it hired three leading celebrities, two leading Bollywood stars and one leading Indian cricketer. These three faces flashed on every Hometrade hoarding in the city, and these hoardings were all over the place.

The message these three celebrities were hired to provide was very clear, ***"We have utmost faith in this brand. It's a good company in which to invest."***

At that time, the concept of celebrities unrelated to the product they were endorsing was comparatively a novelty in India, and this is why many members of the public got carried away. Some retired individuals even invested their entire life savings in Hometrade.

Hometrade, it was later discovered, was a fraud since day one.

It collapsed.

Like a pack of cheap cards.

Taking along with it the life savings of the trusting individuals who had invested in it, based primarily on the message of its three brand endorsers.

If these three endorsers had done their homework well about the background of the brand they were endorsing instead of focusing on their endorsement fees, they could have prevented public money from going down a fraudulent drain. They didn't. The only answer one of them had after the entire sordid episode was, "Even I didn't receive the complete payment I had been promised from Hometrade for my endorsement."

The Core Message of this Sub-Tenet on Brand Endorsers

This is the only one of our thirteen tenets which carries within it a sub-tenet.

This is because today, the faulty mechanism of brand building by the thoughtless usage of unrelated celebrity endorsers has reached epidemic proportions, and needs to be stopped at the earliest. Neither does it benefit the customer, nor does it benefit the brand.

If at all an organization feels the need to utilize the services of a Brand Endorser, there are ***two excellent options available,*** which are increasingly gaining popularity worldwide.

The two options are:

1. ***Animated characters as Brand Endorsers.***
2. ***Experts from that field or industry.***

Let's see examples of both of these and how leading brands have used them to good advantage.

Animated Characters

Let us begin with the ***animated characters,*** which connect immediately with the young as well as the old.

R. K. Laxman, the celebrated cartoonist of the Times of India group, has created a brand through his animated character, ***The Common Man.*** The common man has now been taken on as the brand endorser for the airline, ***Deccan Air,*** which has slotted itself as the ***Common Man's Airline.*** The common man endorses the common man's carrier. That's such a great fit.

Other memorable animated Brand Endorsers of Indian brands include the Amul Butter Girl, the Air India Maharajah, and Gattu, representing

Asian Paints, all of which have been around for decades, successfully representing their brands.

In fact the trend in Western countries is strongly moving towards using animated characters as brand endorsers. ***The advantages of animated characters as brand endorsers over celebrities are multiple:***

1. They are much, much more cost effective. There is only a one time development cost attached to them. That too is far lower than the fee paid to a celebrity, which runs to the tune of millions. Of course, needless to say, it is the customer who ultimately pays for all this. (As everyone knows, the cost of manufacturing aerated drinks is less than a rupee, yet they sell for ten times as much.)
2. Animated characters have a terrifically long shelf life. Generation after generation can identify a brand with the same animated character.
3. Negative actions of a celebrity impact the brand. (For example, cricketers not attending the Padma Bhushan award ceremony, leading to the brand equity of the brands they endorse being diluted. The same can never ever happen in the case of an animated character.)
4. Even a small firm can afford to avail of the services of an animated character as a brand endorser.
5. Different segments of customers may love and hate a particular celebrity. But no segment can have ill feeling towards an animated character.
6. An animated character is totally within the brand's control in terms of body language, expressions, actions and so on.
7. There can be no confusion in the mind of the customer as to the brand being endorsed. ***In India, confusion galore prevails when it comes to certain celebrities, who endorse more than thirty brands each year.*** In many cases, it is only the celebrity's presence on screen which is recalled by the viewer, not the brand he is endorsing. This can never occur with an animated character, which belongs to and is loyal to one brand alone. ***(In fact, many advertising people we have spoken to have mentioned that they***

would like to see a scenario where every celebrity is restricted to endorsing just one brand a year, to cut the clutter.)

8. An animated character, which is the brand's property, can never leave the brand and endorse a competitior's brand for a higher fee. A recent example of this is a film-star shifting his loyalties from Brand Pepsi to Brand Coke. There are multiple such examples we have seen where a celebrity has endorsed a particular brand, and a few years later has endorsed a competing brand, all for the sake of a higher fee.

9. Animated characters come with no star tantrums and attitudes as unwanted baggage.

10. The animated character can truly be moulded to suit the brand's personality. In case of celebrities, pseudo attempts are made to match the brand's personality traits with those of the celebrity. It is as bad as trying to hammer square pegs into round holes. ***It is amazing to see a celebrity endorsing over thirty brands, and each brand claiming that the celebrity matches their own, special brand personality.***

11. Animated characters don't have a fatigue value as far as the audience is concerned.

12. There is no fear of brand value getting lost through poor performance of the endorser in his own field. (For example, a cricketer who is an endorser performing poorly on the cricket field.)

Animated characters are clearly the road ahead when it comes to the issue of Brand Endorsement.

Actual Experts

Next, let's have a look and see how ***actual experts*** can be utilized by a brand to great advantage. Let's take an example of the famous brand, ***Volvo.*** Volvo is a fantastic brand, having its ***strategy*** or ***what it stands for,*** clearly in place.

Brand Volvo stands for safety.

Volvo is genuinely committed to its core brand value - ***Safety.*** It is currently developing radar controlled cars to prevent accidents, and the brand has a very ***specific vision statement -***

"By the year 2020, no driver or passenger should die or be injured in a Volvo car."

As an example, whom does ***Volvo*** choose as a ***Brand Endorser*** to endorse the safety of its trucks? Not some movie star or sportsperson. Volvo selects ***actual truck drivers*** who have been driving Volvo's trucks on the highways for decades, to appear in the Volvo commercials, endorsing the safety of the Volvo trucks, and speaking their heart out to the entranced audience, who listens attentively, knowing that ***this is a true expert on the brand speaking.***

Does your brand behave badly or well?
Only your customers have the right to decide and tell.

- Cyrus M Gonda, Kalim Khan

A Wonderful Piece of Research (When unrelated brand endorsers are used, the following is the reason why)

The following research from the field of psychology and behavioural science, deals with the issue as to why celebrity Brand Endorsers have become popular with organizations and brands today.

Petty, Cacioppo, and their colleagues have done sterling work on the aspects of ***understanding the nature of persuasion.*** According to their ***Elaboration Likelihood Model*** (ELM), ***two different approaches to persuasion exist.***

ONE - The ***Central route,*** which occurs when recipients find a message ***INTERESTING, IMPORTANT*** or ***PERSONALLY RELEVANT*** and they thus devote careful importance to the message. In this case, they examine the message in a thoughtful and rational manner, evaluating the strength or the rationality of the argument it contains. (The genuine USP depicted in an advertisement.)

(We call this route the ***straightforward*** and ***honest*** route.)

TWO - In contrast, ***if recipients are likely to find the core message as being uninteresting or uninvolving, they would not be motivated to process it carefully or give it their due attention.***

(This would most likely happen when there is ***no genuine USP*** to speak of.)

In this case, ***persuasion is sought to be done from the backdoor,*** or the ***Peripheral route***. This route could be undertaken by attempting to have the message passed on through an attractive model or a celebrity, ***to make up for lack of attention paid by the recipient due to lack of core content in the message in the first place.***

Under these conditions, the person who is communicating the message, (the advertiser), hopes to get a positive reaction from the recipient without the recipient making a critical and rational analysis of the message. ***If the recipient had made a critical and rational appraisal of the message, he would have most likely rejected it.*** As Petty and Cacioppo state, - ***"ADVERTISERS, SALESPERSONS AND OTHERS WISHING TO CHANGE OUR ATTITUDES ARE WELL AWARE OF THIS ALTERNATIVE ROUTE TO PERSUASION, AND OFTEN TRY TO USE IT WHEN THEY REALISE THAT THE ARGUMENTS THEY HAVE GATHERED IN SUPPORT OF THEIR PRODUCT OR BRAND ARE NOT STRONG OR CONVINCING."***

IN SUCH CASES AND SITUATIONS, THEY TRY TO WOW YOU WITH CELEBRITIES, BEAUTIFUL PEOPLE, CLEVER SLOGANS OR CATCHY TUNES. THIS IS NEVER A LONG TERM STRATEGY AND WOULD BE SCORNED BY AN ORGANISATION OR INDIVIDUAL ATTEMPTING TO BUILD A STRONG BRAND ON THE STRENGTH OF GENUINE USP.

Keeping the results of this research in mind, we would do well to reflect on a message in Tenet Two, which mentions the high popularity of Chinese products. The Chinese products, we saw, are highly functional and provide value for money. This is the reason why they do not need to depend upon a celebrity to promote them. The products speak for themselves, which is why, rarely, if ever, would you see a Chinese product being promoted by a celebrity endorser.

Maybe this is one reason why the Chinese products are priced so reasonably as well. The millions of dollars which other brands pay to their celebrities are not added or included in the pricing of Chinese products.

The Proof of the Pudding

An important point to consider before investing heavily in Brand Endorsers is to verify whether celebrities are effective in getting viewers to take the action that their message is inducing the viewer to take. After all, the purpose of using a celebrity to pass on a message is so that the viewer would take some action favourable to the brand which is paying for the message. Are Celebrity Endorsers effective in delivery when they make an appeal to the general public? This issue was finally laid to rest after the Mumbai electorate cast, (or didn't cast), their votes at the 2009 Indian Parliamentary Lok Sabha elections.

Prior to the elections, prolonged and highly vocal campaigning was undertaken by almost the entire Bollywood celebrity circuit, exhorting the electorate to come out and vote in large numbers on voting day. ***This was truly a noble gesture on their part.***

(A majority of the celebrities involved in this campaign are the same ones who also are currently endorsing most of the big brands.)

The celebrities were very visible throughout the campaign, pleading with, and urging the citizens of Mumbai to vote, making desperate personal appeals to the eligible voters. All very noble, as we mentioned before.

But, and this is the shocker, this particular election saw one of the ***lowest ever voter turnouts*** in the city of Mumbai. Much lesser than even fifty percent of eligible voters cast their vote on election day. Whatever be the other reasons for this debacle, this should settle once and for all the question of whether the Bollywood celebrity has the power to spur the general public into action by its very presence. The dice are sadly not loaded in their favour.

The sour icing on this messy cake is that a large number of Bollywood celebrities from Mumbai who were inducing other to vote, didn't turn out to vote themselves, although they were very much in Mumbai on voting day, as newspapers reported.

A similar situation exists where celebrities endorsing brands and encouraging the public to purchase and use them, themselves do not use the brands they endorse. It is sufficient proof for all concerned, that ultimately the general public, (which constitutes the entire consumer base for the brands that these celebrities endorse), will continue to act in the way that it chooses, irrespective of celebrities exhorting them to do otherwise.

If the focal point of a brand as far as the public image goes is an unrelated celebrity endorser, ***it displays a miserable and pathetic lack of faith by the brand in the strength of its own product or service.*** It then appears that the only alternative for the brand is to ride piggy back on an unrelated celebrity's back, cashing in on the celebrity's popularity in a totally unrelated field.

That ***definitely*** is not the sort of signal that a strong, confident brand which has a genuine USP to offer it's customers would project.

A recent survey conducted by one of India's leading research agencies on this same subject, results of which appeared in the national press, backs up our thought process and proves beyond all doubt, reasonable and unreasonable, that ***IN NO WAY DOES USAGE OF A BRAND ENDORSER INFLUENCE THE PURCHASE DECISION OF A CONSUMER AS TO WHICH BRAND TO PURCHASE.*** This survey was conducted scientifically, covering a huge number of respondents, who were regular purchasers of brands which spend huge amounts on celebrity endorsers. The responses of almost all the participants were unanimous. "We do not base our purchase decisions based on whether a paid celebrity tells us to do so. We prefer to use our own judgment and rely on word of mouth from friends, relatives and acquaintances. We have no faith in someone who is paid to tell us to make a purchase."

But then, when many brand managers admit in private that most brands in any industry score somewhere close to a four on ten when it comes to the overall level of quality of service delivery, what else can a brand manager do to enhance the bottomline?

The answer is simple.

Follow the messages in our tenets. It would take a little time to get things on track and for customers to have total faith in your brand, but once this is achieved, your brand will now have a strong base on which to stand. And it will stand on its own, strong legs, and will not need the crutch and weak support offered by an unrelated celebrity.

The same holds true even for internal customers, or employees.

Take the organization, General Motors. They had run a brilliant advertising campaign portraying a set of people as ***Team General Motors.*** The team here comprised some of the most senior employees of General Motors, with the maximum experience. The oldest existing employees of the organisation were portrayed in the advertisement, mentioning the departments they worked for, and the number of years of experience that they individually and collectively held at General Motors. This advertisement served a dual purpose.

One - it motivated the most senior employees, as they were projected to the outside world as the face of the organization, and also sent across a message to junior employees that the organization cared for and valued senior employees, so employee retention automatically improved.

And second – it sent across a strong message to customers that this was the wealth of experience behind every product that the organization produced. The organization used its own existing human assets to great effect.

Contrast this brilliant example with a frivolous one, adopted by a current white goods firm, manufacturing refrigerators, air conditioners, and similar goods. This firm also adopted a similar approach in its advertisements, portraying a team as representing the organization. Unfortunately, this team consisted of five members of the Indian cricket team as representatives of the organization. We have spoken with senior employees of this organization. They are thoroughly disgusted and disheartened with this approach. They felt that they don't matter at all as far as the management of their own organization is concerned. It showed that the management had more faith in five cricketers rather than the five most senior and experienced employees in order to represent the brand.

While on the subject of modern cricketers, it appears as if the primary purpose why people take up cricket as a career today is to endorse brands. Some time ago, the mother of a young cricketer representing the country was interviewed by a newspaper as to how she felt now that her son was representing the country.

Her response was shocking. ***"I am glad he is playing for the country, but I'm wondering why so far no brand has approached him for an endorsement."***

Look at the response.

It's not that she has a specific brand in mind which suits her son's personality, or a brand providing a product or service in which her son is an acknowledged expert. To parody that old nursery rhyme:

Cock - a - doodle - doo

ANY brand will do.

This tells us more than any other example as to what the root problem is with the way that celebrity endorsement is being done today.

We would like to conclude this tenet by mentioning the fact that the best and strongest brands are of the firm opinion that the best Brand Endorsers they could ever engage to ably represent them in the market place are their very own employees and satisfied customers.

Tenet 10

QUALITY IS KEY

All is lost in the race for cost
But customers will pay for a better way

We have no argument with competitors who charge less.
They realise what their product is worth.

- The Motto of the Quality Service Provider

We were conducting a training programme on marketing for a leading financial institution, and the topic of quality was being discussed and debated. One of the participants argued that he felt that quality was not of such a concern to customers. He felt that what customers were primarily bothered about was a lower cost. That's when the CEO of the organization, who was also a participant in the programme, mentioned that if such was the case, why would a majority of travelers pay a stiff toll and prefer to travel by the well made Mumbai-Pune expressway, rather than go by the bumpy freeway, by which they could travel to the same destination, ***free of cost?***

What a wonderful argument in favour of quality.

Come to think of it, when one travels by train, the first class fare is at least four times higher that of the second class fare. Just try getting a first class seat on a long distance train. The seats get filled up before the second class seats do. And it is not that passengers in the first class compartment arrive at their destination earlier than the second class passengers, or take a shorter route. To the best of our knowledge the first class compartment reaches the destination at the same time as the other compartments do. Yet there are many people willing to pay more than four times a higher price simply so that the ***quality*** of their journey is superior.

The same holds true for air travel.

And also holds true in most other walks of life.

Today, most customers realize the value of the time tested concept where the buyer weighs his options between a cheaper product and a more expensive one of the same category, and decides to go for the latter, fully aware that in most cases it is cheaper in the long run to pay a little more for the enhanced quality, as by purchasing a cheaper alternative ***merely because it is lower in price,*** in most cases it would fail to perform up to the desired level of expectation.

Cutting elements of cost that would have directly or indirectly contributed to customer delight, end up in destroying customer value, which leads to destruction of customer faith, which ultimately results in loss of customer's share of wallet for the organisation.

- Cyrus M Gonda, Kalim Khan

Customers are now more aware than ever that by making purchase decisions purely on the basis of cost they inevitably end up compromising on quality and the added benefits that enhanced quality can provide.

While writing this book, we were sitting in a restaurant. Coincidentally, while we were having a meal and structuring this tenet on quality, the neighbouring restaurant's exhaust chimney, (poorly and cheaply constructed, we later learned), caught fire. The restaurant owner of the place where we were seated, who is a friend of ours, told us that the neighbouring restaurant's chimney had been constructed by a contractor who was slightly cheaper than the contractor who had constructed the chimney of the restaurant where we were seated. This low price was the reason why the neighbouring restaurant's owner had opted for that contractor. Our friend had even then had advised his neighbour to use the contractor who was slightly more expensive, as he guaranteed a quality job and was very experienced in this particular line of business. But the neighbour had tried to save a buck. In the process he got a bad quality job and ended up spending much more in the long run. The work had to be done all over again and the restaurant lost three day's revenue while it had to be shut for repairs. He vowed in future to listen to our friend and get all work in his restaurant and also at his residence done through contractors of repute, who came highly recommended.

Deliver.

Don't deliver excuses.

Deliver quality products and service.

- Cyrus M Gonda, Kalim Khan

Customers will pay for a better way

At the Taj Mahal Hotel, Mumbai, when the restaurant, the Zodiac Grill initially opened, for a few months the patrons were not presented with a bill, but asked to pay what they thought the meal was worth. The revenue generated was far in excess of what the management had anticipated. People in general don't mind paying extra for quality.

The very expensive 'Blue Drink'

No organization or brand can continue to survive on past glory and goodwill. Overcharging customers by overpricing products and services simply because of past repute, and then compromising on quality, is a sure recipe to disaster. A leading Five Star Hotel in Mumbai literally survives on temporary labour and staffing when it comes to its banquet functions, which generate a major chunk of the hotel revenue. The hotel literally resorts to hiring temporary staff from the street, and the only things these temporary staff are provided with are a white shirt, black trouser and a black bow. There is very little, if any training provided. ***Obviously in such a scenario, it is impossible for this temporary, contract staff to imbibe the service culture, the service tradition, and the service philosophy of the hotel.***

And these are the untrained staff who are the contact points for and interact with and serve guests in the function who are being charged Rupees Three Thousand a plate for their meal. As a disgusted former executive of this hotel told us in confidence, "They built a good name through quality service. Now the policy of the current management is to spend Rupees Twenty Five and earn Rupees Thousand. Rather than spend Rupees Hundred and generate Rupees Two Hundred, which should be the done thing.

This was validated by a friend of ours, who is a General Manager in charge of Administration with a leading corporate house. He mentioned how he had organised a corporate dinner for around five hundred of his guests at that same hotel. During the function, he realized that the waiters attending to the guests did not know anything about the beverages and drinks that were being served. Our friend said that it appeared that the waiters lacked confidence to interact with guests, and rather than come forward and ask guests if they needed assistance, the reverse occurred. Even when a guest requiring assistance managed to catch a waiter's eye, the waiter in most cases shied away and managed to disappear into the crowd. When at last our friend managed to get to speak to a waiter, he asked him what the cocktail he was serving contained and was called. The waiter stared hard at it, and ultimately blurted out, ***"Sir, this is a BLUE DRINK."***

As far as our friend was concerned, this was the final straw. That was the ***Moment of Truth*** where he firmly decided never to host his office functions in this hotel ever again.

And if one calculates the bill for each such function, where five hundred people are having their meal at three thousand rupees a plate, ***the bill works out to Rupees Fifteen Lakhs*** (Dollars one and a half million), for a single function.

Our friend mentioned to us later that he could have got far better food and service at a four star hotel at half the rate. He said he felt that over here, he was only paying for the hotel's brand name which thrived on past glory.

Never let this feeling percolate to your customers –
That they're only paying for the brand name and
past glory of the brand.

- Cyrus M Gonda, Kalim Khan

Value for money is an entity that needs to be provided in every transaction. Don't try to save a buck when you have no right to do so.

The management of the hotel in the above anecdote has paid dearly for this practice of trying to save a buck where it had no business in doing so.

This is precisely why this tenet is sub-titled as, ***"All is lost in the race for cost."***

Don't worry about profits, worry about service.

- Thomas Watson, Sr. (Founder of IBM)

If your organisation wishes to charge a premium for its products and services, fair enough. There are many customers willing to shell out a premium. But in return for that premium, what they rightly expect is quality and value for money. Your front end staff need to have the competency and product knowledge to respond efficiently to customer queries, especially if you're charging a premium to your customers.

One of the ***critical parameters*** of ***evaluating*** the ***quality*** of a product or service goes as follows:

"Does your product or service, (including your service staff), live up in actual usage to what it's committed to deliver according to all your marketing communication, including your advertising message?" When advertising uses ***CREATIVE LICENCE,*** and ***EXAGGERATION*** becomes ***FICTION,*** then this crucial parameter of quality is violated.

The Indian Nightingale – Lata Mangeshkar

Quality is never achieved by accident. It is always the result of intelligent, honest and sustained effort.

Lata Mangeshkar - A Guinness book record holder for the maximum number of songs sung. Her career has spanned over half a century. Even in her seventies, she maintains the sweet angelic voice of a youthful twenty year old.

Definitely, part of this success has to be attributed to the God given voice she possesses.

But there are many others who are born with similar talent. It is not by coincidence that she cannot be matched by the singers of today. Quality is never an accident. It is always the result of sustained effort. Genius contains a minimum of ninety nine percent perspiration.

When Lata Mangeshkar was in the initial stages of her career, the songs she sang were composed in chaste Hindi and Urdu. Composers such as Naushad, a perfectionist, held sway.

Naushad made Lata Mangeshkar sing the songs over and over and over again till he felt they were of an acceptable standard.

So Lata Mangeshkar practiced and redid the songs she was to sing till she became perfect.

Goodness in singing during that golden era was largely based on the singer's pronunciation. So Lata appointed an Urdu teacher to teach her Urdu. She did regular ***riyaaz,*** (practice.) (She still practices her singing regularly, even though she is almost eighty.) Her pronunciations in Urdu became impeccable. By the way, she can read and write Urdu, which is not her mother tongue. A leading Urdu poet has gone on record as saying that she has a better understanding of the Urdu language than most people for whom Urdu is their mother tongue. Her work speaks for itself.

She has managed to achieve all this as she was proactive and took efforts to develop her skill till she reached the pinnacle of her profession, and no one has been able to dislodge her from that position for over fifty years.

I have offended God and mankind because my work didn't reach the QUALITY it should have.

- Leonardo Da Vinci

(Last words of this great man. Even on his deathbed, his focus was on the enhanced quality he felt he had been capable of achieving. Which is why his name is remembered in glowing terms even centuries after he lived.)

Similarly, there are other famous playback singers from the old school, who mention that even before their coaches focused on improving their singing ability and voice quality, they were made to run several laps around a race track. The purpose of doing this was to develop stamina and a powerful set of lungs, so that they wouldn't gasp for breath while singing lengthy verses as most singers of today, who lack this disciplined approach tend to do.

And it is a fact, that along with the parameter of ***true quality earned through sustained dedication and practice,*** comes the related parameter of ***humility.***

Lata Mangeshkar has acquired humility to the core.

When she goes to a temple to offer her prayers, she asks for no special privileges. She waits her turn in line with the other devotees, sometimes for up to three hours. This is so unlike the media created celebrities of today, who break the line even for a sacred affair such as offering prayers and enter a temple like VIPs. This quality of humility brings added respect and luster to Lata Mangeshkar's personality.

All these attributes which make Lata Mangeshkar tower over her competitors, apply equally to organizations.

Acquiring and sustaining a culture of hard work and sustained efforts leads to genuine humility, which is observed and noted by customers. Your work then speaks for itself. And your ***customers also notice and appreciate this added benefit of humility that your organization displays and will respond to it positively.***

Only a fool thinks price and value are the same.

- Antonio Machado

As we saw in the example of the ***Blue Drink,*** there are many customers who are ***willing to pay a premium, but naturally they expect value in return.***

They expect a customized product or service.

They expect flexibility in organizational processes pertaining to them.

They expect minimized levels of defects and errors in the product or service provided.

They expect prompt redressal of their grievances if things go wrong.

They expect their needs, likes, dislikes and priorities, their feedback and their relevant suggestions, their complaints, to be given priority by the top management.

If organizations can't do all the above for the customer, some other organization is always more than willing to do so.

And in a competitive environment, some other organisation will always be willing to go the extra mile.

If the word BRAND could be defined in one word,
that one word would be QUALITY.

- Cyrus M Gonda, Kalim Khan

A Marketing Lesson from Real Life

Organizations have to realize that the customer is any organisation's ***only source of revenue.***

The following is a vital message upon which all organizations need to reflect and ruminate.

Many organisations mistakenly believe that even if they provide a below average product or service, they are still apparently surviving and they still have customers. In short, revenue is coming in. So the general attitude is - ***why take the effort to improve?***

There is a very good answer for such myopic thinking.

It is very like the following analogy.

Imagine a person residing in a polluted city, and having to commute to and fro from work every day on a two wheeler. To lessen the impact of the polluted surroundings, our friend ties a white handkerchief over his face to cover his nostrils. At the end of his commute, the handkerchief around his face would have turned black in colour, or at least a dark shade of grey. This is due to the pollutants abounding in the environment. The handkerchief only partially absorbs the impact of the pollution on the lungs, which must similarly be feeling the ill effect of pollution. The only difference between the handkerchief and the lungs is that the ***daily damage caused to the lungs is not externally visible,*** and the ***individual is complacent under the incorrect assumption that the pollution has not affected him; yet.***

How much healthier would this same individual be, and how much better the state of his lungs, if he resided in a healthful environment of a pollution-free hill station.

The point of this analogy is, ***DESPITE THE DAILY ASSAULT ON, AND DAMAGE TO THE LUNGS, THE INDIVIDUAL IS STILL ALIVE.***

In the same way, organizations which don't nurture their relationships with their existing customers, and which are fast losing a large chunk of their current customer base, ***are still surviving.*** Thus, organisations which are aware that their service levels and attempts at Customer Retention leave much to be desired, become complacent with the fact that they still exist.

Their arrogance is evident in the attitude, ***"So what if my service is lousy or unacceptable. I'M STILL SURVIVING. I STILL HAVE CUSTOMERS."***

The question remains, ***"For how long will they continue to survive? How long will customers continue to come?"***

And the second question, ***"Even if they DO exist, how much healthier and stronger and financially better off would these organisations currently be, if they followed the strategy of customer sensitivity and customer retention, rather than focusing on cutting costs by providing bare minimum service levels?"***

Organisations, like individuals, should bear in mind that the impact of a polluted environment does not show up in the short term.

- Cyrus M Gonda, Kalim Khan

It is very much like an express train which is speeding at over a hundred miles an hour. When the driver applies the brakes, the train does not stop immediately.

BUT THE PROCESS OF STOPPING HAS BEGUN.

In the same way, a large organization which has started slipping up on quality would be losing a large slice of customers and generating negative word of mouth publicity on a regular basis. Till this volume of loss of customers reaches critical mass, it would not be noticeable, ***in the same way that tooth decay also is not noticeable until it reaches a critical stage.***

This is the message pertaining to quality on which organizations need to focus.

If you believe in unlimited quality and act in all your business dealings with total integrity, the rest will take care of itself.

- Frank Perdue

How Motorola reaped the benefits of honestly focusing on its own poor quality of product and service

The brand which formally introduced the concept of Six Sigma, (the epitome of quality), to the world, is Motorola.

Motorola, which today is a brand whose very name conjures up images of a quality product, didn't always have things so good.

As ***Art Sundry,*** a senior functionary of Motorola once mentioned, ***"The real problem at Motorola is that our quality stinks."***

And this ***honest introspection*** and ***self analysis*** was the start of the Quality Journey at Motorola. From this intense soul searching, the concept of Six Sigma grew. The management at Motorola realized that it was no use hiding one's head in a hole in the ground like the ostrich, hoping that the quality related problems the brand faced would vanish on their own.

Understanding quality from the customer's perspective, and accepting the fact that enhancement of quality at every stage of the customer process and cycle is imperative, puts an organization on the right path to quality.

And from this understanding and admission, the concept of Six Sigma at Motorola grew.

Acceptance of poor quality from the customer's perspective is the starting point of an organisation's Quality Journey.

- Cyrus M. Gonda, Kalim Khan

If Motorola could reap huge benefits from such simple, honest, ***proactive introspection,*** why is it that we don't find more organizations taking a similar route?

The answer is, that unfortunately, ***human DNA is wired towards being reactive rather than proactive.***

A simple example will suffice. Honestly ask yourself the question, ***"How often do I visit the dentist?*** Every six months in a systematic manner, whether I feel the need for a visit or not. ***Or when I feel I can no longer bear the pain."***

That tells us everything about the mode (whether proactive or reactive), in which most of us normally operate. It requires a conscious effort from our end to formulate a habit and culture of proactiveness.

A Single Straw can Break The Customer Relationship

In a parable in the Bible, there was a camel which was overburdened with a bundle on its back. The bundle consisted of hundreds of straws (sticks), which the camel was carrying. The camel was still standing. ***But one new straw which was added to the bundle finally caused the camel to collapse.***

As with the camel, an organization never knows which negative Moment of Truth would finally cause the customer to sever his relationship with the organization.

Don't wait to identify the straw which will break your customer's back before you start to act to rectify and improve quality in your organisation.
Straws don't have labels mentioning details, as to whether they are the last straw or not.
To your organization, all straws appear the same.
But to the customer? Aha! They are NOT all the same.
Only your customer will decide which straw is too heavy to now continue the burden with dealing with your organisation any longer.

- Cyrus M Gonda, Kalim Khan

The Myth of Customer Tolerance

A college canteen, which had a large captive audience of students, began compromising on food quality. The attitude was one of - ***where else will the students go, irrespective of the quality we provide?*** They will have to eat something, somewhere to fill their stomachs, and in the short breaks they get between lectures, ***this is the only eating place that fits their time constraint.*** Thus, under this mistaken assumption, ***quality and service kept plummeting, and yet the revenue was pouring in.***

Seeing the constant stream of customers, the management of the canteen made the mistake of believing that it's quality was actually good, considering the amount of eatables they sold everyday. ***They failed to realize that it was compulsion and not goodwill that contributed to the continuing sales.***

A hungry man will eat anything.
A thirsty man will drink anything.

- Mencius

Sensing an opportunity, an entrepreneur opened a fast food joint right outside the college gates and started providing hot, simple but tasty fare, which is just what the students wanted, but had never got in their college canteen. Almost overnight, the canteen started bearing the look of a deserted ghost town. The canteen management started to improve their food quality, but by then it was too late.

There is no fury like a once ignored customer.

- Cyrus M Gonda, Kalim Khan

The students were now more than happy with this new service provider, who had accurately placed his hands on their hurting nerve.

The above tale is a common one. It is likely to get more and more common in the coming years.

And the tale is definitely not going to be restricted to canteens and colleges, but will be the fate of all organizations large or small, old or new, in the manufacturing or service sector, which fail to provide quality and value for money by taking advantage of the customers helplessness due to current non-availability of a better option. Similar scenarios could well happen, and are happening, with banks, airlines, hotels, auto manufacturers, mobile service providers, insurance firms; in short ***any organization in any industry which continues to treat the customer with arrogance, contempt and impunity.***

Competition may currently exist and yet an organization may still be having it's customer base. ***That still does not indicate that the existing customers are satisfied.***

If the level of all existing service providers in that sector or industry is on the lower side, each service provider will have some market share by default. It is a sad but true reality that this is indeed the prevailing scenario in most sectors. Looking at abysmal levels of service provided by existing competitors, lethargy then sets in. ***Thus, the overall service bar for the industry is lowered rather than raised.***

Why do anything extra - is the philosophy adopted.

Where else can the customer go, the rest of the service providers are equally bad - becomes the motto.

Highest Unique Differentiator

The gravitation of all players in such a scenario tends toward the ***Lowest Common Denominator*** in service, rather than being the ***Highest Unique Differentiator.***

(***Highest Unique Differentiator*** is a term we at ***Brains Trust*** have coined to identify the organization in any industry which has currently created the maximum genuine USPs, and is thus currently at the highest level of trust and quality in the minds of customers.)

As observed, organisations ought to avoid at all costs falling under the Myth of Customer Tolerance. Customer tolerance can be perfectly equated to the parable of the straw that broke the camels back. We never know which one will do it.

Is bigger really better?

Smaller organizations by their very nature, tend to pay more attention to their customers, treating them as the individuals they are, and generally providing them with more personalized attention and service.

It is due to this factor that their existing customers are retained and a positive word of mouth gets more customers to the smaller firm.

This is when the firm starts to ***grow***.

And this, we strongly believe, is the danger point for most firms.

Not that there is anything wrong with growth per se, provided it is a controlled growth.

But there are such things as uncontrolled or very rapid growths.

One name for such uncontrolled and rapid growth is cancer.

It is at this stage of growth, where ironically an organization and its management feel most triumphant and victorious, that the organisation is actually at its most vulnerable.

There ***are*** cures to ward of this danger. But these cures need to be the priority and focus of the management at this crucial stage.

Most firms fail with rapid growth, as the very reason for which they grew, (providing quality products and services), disappears, as now the growing firm's priorities shift. Responsiveness to customer needs and personalized service, maintaining the quality that helped the firm sustain and grow; all these characteristics which symbolized the small firm, now unfortunately take a backseat.

In the driver's seat are now the priorities of even faster growth, more branches, more footfalls, more publicity, opening franchisee outlets, and the rest.

As we said, growth is good. But along with this growth, there need to be proportionate increases in infrastructure and capable staff to handle this enhanced customer base as efficiently as the organization did when it was relatively small.

Correction.

The infrastructure and staff should ***not*** increase in a ratio proportional to growth, but at a ***higher ratio*** than the rate of growth. The reason? Now the organisation has a reputation to uphold, and everything to lose if quality drops.

We have multiple such sad tales to narrate. The following one is representative of this epidemic and gives a good idea of what we speak.

The irony of shrinking while growing

There used to be this very popular coaching class not so very long ago, a favourite with students in that stream of education. Why it was popular among its customers was not a mystery. ***The focus of the management was on providing quality education.*** The faculty was brilliant. And every batch of students that passed out from this class used to pass on the word to the other students that this was the class to attend if they wanted great results. The fees this class charged were the highest among any class in this field of study. But students and their parents didn't mind. They were getting value for money with respect to quality of education. Seeing this popularity, the management of the class started to think in terms of expansion. From this one famous branch of this coaching class which attracted students from all over the place, the class within a short span of three months spread its tentacles by opening six other branches in the city, to take rapid and speedy advantage of the goodwill it had developed in it's client base.

Finding new locations was easy. Paying for them was also not so difficult. Neither were getting the interior décor and the furniture. The class had made sufficient profits over the years to pay for the expansion.

What could ***not*** be purchased in the short term with money was more faculty of the same caliber who had been instrumental in making the class what it was.

The initial euphoria among students and existing goodwill ensured that the first batches in all the new branches were filled to capacity. Then the grumbling started, increasing in pitch and volume, till unhappy students and their parents started demanding a refund, as the quality they had expected simply did not come their way. The management had no option but to refund a part of the fees. ***But that alone did not bring back lost goodwill.*** In a couple of years, all branches, including the initial one, closed down.

Does that mean that one should never expand? No way are we suggesting that. Growth is the engine of commerce. But for growth to remain and sustain, it is imperative that the growth result into win-win scenarios, both for the organization, and for its customers, who ought to be able to look forward to enhanced quality, superior service and more positive Moments of Truth.

Unfortunately, as we have observed in Chapter 5, ***The Scenario Today,*** the warped logic of unplanned growth is passed off with the following explanation by large brands when they provide poor service. - ***We Have So Many Customers. How Can We Be Expected To Pay Attention To All And Satisfy Each One.***

This attitude begins the downward slide for any brand. Then organizations in a panic mode will shell out millions on film stars and cricketers as Brand Ambassadors to attract back these lost customers. ***Little do they realize that the same amount they are spending on these brand ambassadors could be far more sensibly invested in better trained and better paid staff, and on technology and infrastructure that would give exponentially more returns in terms of profits.***

Come to think of it, what matters to a customer when he purchases a product or service that an organization has to offer? The quality of product and service and the value that he receives; or the paid Brand

Ambassador who endorses it. (And who would have endorsed a competing brand just as easily if he or she had got more money for doing so.)

It's all a matter of management priorities.

If organizational growth is planned, steady and gradual, your brand is a winner.

If not......***as Hsi Tang Chih-Tsang, the Zen Chinese master said:***

"ALTHOUGH GOLD DUST IS PRECIOUS, WHEN IT GETS IN YOUR EYES, IT OBSTRUCTS YOUR VISION."

It may be all right to be content with what you have; never with what you are.

- B C Forbes

We may not have given many positive examples of Indian brands, (especially large ones), when it comes to the aspect of quality. Not that Indian brands haven't been providing excellent products and services to their customers. They have. But it is not just a one-off example of a positive Moment of Truth that raises the brand image.

Quality has to be consistent across customer, time, place, and service representatives.

- Cyrus M Gonda, Kalim Khan

Even when it comes to a question of international brands, the same few names keep coming up again and again with regard to consistent quality and excellence.

Once again, we reiterate that if a brand truly wishes to become world class, it has to move ahead of focusing on cost cutting in areas which affect product and service quality.

It is far easier to become the cheapest service provider in any industry rather than the best. But the benefits of being the best far outweigh those of being the cheapest.

- Cyrus M Gonda, Kalim Khan

Competing on low cost alone is a dangerous policy and is seldom sustainable. Discounts and special low prices cannot be offered for a long period of time without bleeding the organization dry.

And a buyer who is attracted to purchase a product or service on the basis of low price alone, is seldom likely to be loyal to the brand. If the customer's sole reason for purchasing a product or service is to go for low price, the moment he finds a competing brand offering a slightly lower price, he moves away.

This would not be the case with a customer whose focus is on a quality product or service. And this is the chunk from which loyal and retained customers are created.

As Claes Fornell put it, ***because price discounts can only be temporary, the customers they attract are also temporary.***

All would be Lost in the Race for Cost

Ernan Roman and Scott Hornstein, in their wonderful book, ***Opt-In Marketing***, provide a lovely little real life case study of a quality conscious manufacturing firm which suddenly found itself amid a price war. Competitors had suddenly begun slashing their prices and were boldly advertising the same. The President of this company was very worried and started to consider his options. He realized that responding to competitors with a further price cut of his own would lead to a vicious cycle of ever reducing prices throughout the industry, and dilution in quality of product and service, and also loss of profitability for all firms in the industry would be the end result.

He couldn't very well just ignore his competitor's actions, as price sensitivity among customers exists in every industry. The President realized that his organization was definitely not the cheapest in its industry. In fact, it took pride in the fact that it invested heavily in research and development, and dedicated itself to providing a better product and achieving superior customer satisfaction.

The President immediately initiated a quick research among his customers, to find out the view and priorities of the firm's large and long term customers.

The research results gave the President relief. The findings were that the firm's current long term customers, or who matched the profile of the firm's long term customers – clearly stated that ***PRICE WAS IMPORTANT, BUT QUALITY WAS FAR MORE IMPORTANT. Customer quotes as response to the survey included the following:***

- ***a. "Of course I look at price, but if the quality and delivery aren't there, the price means nothing."***
- ***b. "We pay for quality."***
- ***c. "Quality is number one. I would not sacrifice quality for price."***
- ***d. "Service is at the top of my list. Responsiveness, get me answers quick."***

In fact, what emerged from the customer survey was a hierarchy of priorities from the customer's end. The hierarchy was as follows:

1. ***Quality***
2. ***Price***
3. ***Delivery***

The Key Customers of the firm stated as response to the survey that they would ***pay between 5 and 15 percent more*** to do business with this firm. A typical customer comment was - "***I would pay more for consistently high quality and on time delivery***."

As Ernan Roman and Scott Hornstein mention, "Given the research results, it would have been disastrous if the firm had changed its marketing strategy from quality to price competition, from a value added supplier to a commodity that competes on the basis of price alone."

Do not just do a job. Do a quality job.
You and your customer will both have a sound night's sleep.

- Cyrus M Gonda, Kalim Khan

Tenet 11

ONE 'C' IS GREATER THAN THE FOUR P's

Think in terms of the one 'C'
Think in terms of 'YOU', not 'ME'

We have covered the concept of the difference between the ***Selling*** philosophy and mindset, and the ***Marketing*** philosophy and mindset, in great detail in Tenet Two.

We have seen the important role that attitude and mindset play in deciding organizational strategy, policies and ultimately actions.

If the organizational attitude is focused on self, and is inward looking; by default all sets of policies and actions of that organization will be internally focused.

By contrast, if the focus is on the other party (the customer), and is outward looking in nature, policies will be framed and actions will be conducted keeping the other party in mind.

The concept of the ***Four P's,*** by it's very nature and terminology, causes an organization to focus internally on it's own products and their features, it's own pricing policies, it's own place or method of distribution, and it's own promotional activities. In short, the language an organization will use when it focuses on the Four P's will be - ***My*** Product, ***My*** Pricing, ***My*** Place and ***My*** Promotion.

Naturally, this will lead to the organization consciously and subconsciously adopting the ***Selling Philosophy,*** by focusing internally on itself.

We can never say MY customer. The moment we say MY customer, we begin to take him for granted.

- Cyrus M Gonda, Kalim Khan

Since long, marketers have been heard extolling the virtues of the Four P's, virtually to the exclusion of any other concept. It is as if the Four P's have attained the status of a Marketing God, and are to be propitiated at all costs. There is almost no room left for anything else when it comes to a discussion on a marketing related issue. As things stand today, the four P's appear to reign supreme.

We agree that the Four P's do play a role in marketing decision making, ***but their role should be subservient and subordinate to a certain 'C'.***

This 'C' which we speak of, stands for the humble but omnipresent and all important ***customer***.

We feel that pride of place when it comes to focus of decision making in a marketing context belongs to this 'C' before all else.

Why the 'C' should precede the Four P's

It has been rightly observed by psychologists that the words and terms we use have a deep impact on our minds. The words we use regularly and repeatedly tend to become the focus and center of our thought processes.

Keeping this in mind, is it not strange that we as marketing professionals speak so much of Promotion, Price, Place and Product, but comparatively so little of the Customer?

It is not in the dictionary alone where the **C** rightfully ought to precede the **P**, the same should hold true of the marketing mindset.

Until and unless we constantly think in terms of the CUSTOMER, we will be subconsciously relegating him, and correspondingly his interests, into the background.

- Cyrus M Gonda, Kalim Khan

This is a major reason why customers are so disconnected with organizations in general today. The decision making process in organizations tends to centre less around the customer's interests and more around the organization's immediate needs.

This is a natural outcome of the mindset which tends to think in terms of P's rather than the C.

Move away from the P's and chase the 'C'

It's doubtful that any organisation or marketer would deny the customer pride of place in the business context. Yet when it comes to marketing theory, the four P's are still the primary basis of all decision making. And it is always theory that leads to practice. Theory is the foundation stone of implementation.

And even when most marketers ***do focus on a 'C',*** unfortunately that C tends to be the ***Competitor,*** rather than the ***Customer.***

Even advertising agencies advise clients to spend humongous amounts on prime time advertising, and hiring celebrity brand endorsers, simply because, "Since competitors have done so, we can't be left behind." The ***Me-Too concept***.

The problem with this is, when the focus is on the competitor, the end result will be a duplication of the competitor's actions. This is ***a reactive philosophy, and not an independent, proactive one.***

Focusing on Competitor's Price

"Has our competitor reduced his price? Then we need to do so as well immediately." – This is the typical manner in which pricing decisions are taken in organizations.

We are of the firm opinion that pricing is a function which should be left more in the hands of finance people, specifically cost accountants, and statisticians, rather than pricing decisions being taken in isolation by Marketing department personnel.

We have the following rationale for this belief:

As we mentioned in a particular tenet, what should be charged to the customer is a fair or a reasonable price.

By a fair price, we don't mean a ***low*** price. Rather, what should be charged is a price which will give the customer ***value for money.*** The following will explain our rationale for believing so.

Some time ago, we met an Indian national who had settled in a Gulf country for a substantial period of time. In the course of conversing with him, we casually enquired whether he had any intention of coming back and spending the rest of his days in India. Didn't he miss being away from his motherland? He said he definitely missed being away from home, but he was still very sure that he would prefer to stay in the part of the world he was in now. The one reason he spontaneously provided for being so clear about his decision should give a lot of thought to businessmen in India.

He said, "If I wish to get my house painted in a Gulf country, a contractor may provide me with two options.

Option one. The contractor quotes Rupees Twenty per square foot of wall for painting, and this would be for a superior quality of paint.

Option two would be quoted as a rate of Rupees Fifteen per square foot, and this would be for a paint of a slightly lesser quality.

Fair enough. Similar options may be provided to me by a contractor back home in India.

But whereas in the Gulf, if I as a customer opt for the superior option and pay Rupees Twenty per square foot, ***I actually get a superior quality.*** There is an actual difference between the two options in terms of quality. But back home in India, I have experienced that though many contractors provide differentials in quotations and promise a superior level of quality for a higher price, in reality, the quality provided will be the same. Even if I select the option which quotes the higher rate, I will still in all probability get the same level of quality as I would have if I selected the option of Rupees Fifteen per square foot."

Whether right or wrong, this is the perception carried by a large section of the population, and this would have been based on some such negative experience in the past. As a wise man said – ***The customer's perception is your reality.***

Any organisation that wishes to succeed in breaking this perception and mindset from the customer's end, has to first and foremost create an environment of trust and faith in the minds of its customers. The organization has to clearly send across the message that irrespective of competitors resorting to manipulation of this type, ***OUR*** organization can be trusted blindfolded to deliver what has been promised or committed.

Over a period of time, overpricing and overcharging the customer, just because competition is limited or does not currently exist, will not be possible.

Nor is it sensible to resort to foolish discount schemes, giving away the store, just because your competitor does so.

By the way, when it comes to pricing, there are two types of price.

1. **Cost Price**
2. **Selling Price**

The ***Japanese*** played with ***cost price*** brilliantly. ***Whereas the world played with competing on selling price, the Japanese focused on cost price.*** The Japanese focused on improving and enhancing manufacturing and service delivery processes and systems to eliminate waste, and thus could control their cost price, which automatically had a positive impact on profitability. The amount of wastage that occurs in most organizations has to be seen to be believed. If half this wastage is curtailed, cost price of most products and services could be substantially reduced. And the organization as well as the customer both could benefit.

But when it comes to a Selling Price war, all the players involved in it lose. (Including the customer, because in a price war, the quality of product or service always drops.)

Focusing on Competitor's Product

Has our competitor come up with a new product? Let us immediately make a similar one.

Has our competitor improved his product by adding a new feature? Let us copy it and duplicate it and add that feature to our product as well.

If this be the scenario, your organization will never attain the benefit of having a first mover advantage.

Focusing on Competitor's Place

Has our competitor entered a new geographical region or place? Let's rush there immediately. We can't be left behind.

Has he opened an outlet at a new location? Let's open an outlet opposite his.

We forget, fools rush in where angels fear to tread.

Focusing on Competitor's Promotion

This is another area where the ***Me-Too*** concept holds sway.

Has our competitor resorted to a new promotional activity? Is he giving two for the price of one? Let us give three for the price of one.

Has he picked a celebrity to endorse his brand? We have to get one too.

As we saw in the ***Tenet of Brand,*** the celebrities by themselves have little power to swing the consumer's choice in favour of the brand they endorse. In most cases of brands undertaking celebrity endorsement, it is money down the drain. This whole business of selecting celebrities to endorse a brand happens in large measure due to the me-too effect. The ***me-too effect*** comes into play when a brand's focus is on the wrong C, (the competitor), incorrectly assuming that if a competitor has hired a celebrity to endorse his brand, our brand can't be left out.

Why doesn't the organizational logic instead work in the right direction and think, ***"My competitor must have selected a celebrity to endorse his brand, as his brand may not have any USP to speak of. To cover that, he needs a celebrity. My brand has a strong USP. I don't need a celebrity to be the focal point of my promotional campaign."***

The Me-Too concept can be likened to the behaviour of a small child who shows no interest in a particular plaything, until his kid brother begins to play with it. Only then does reaction set in, and the first child immediately wants to play with that same plaything as well. In children, this trait can be overlooked, but when intelligent brands begin to act in a similar fashion, it's time for serious rethinking.

- Cyrus M Gonda, Kalim Khan

As you see, ***when the mode of thinking is in '4P' Gear,*** then it's mostly the competitor's actions that decide our own. Such organisations will by default be reactive. Always in second place. ***Losing out on the first mover advantage.***

We will have to be satisfied with the silver or the bronze medal, never the Gold.

But if organsiations shift their thinking mode to the correct 'C' gear, (the ***Customer***), then the organisation will be on the right track.

Decision making will then gradually shift from being self and competitor centred, to being customer centred, and it is ***this mindset shift, as negligible as it sounds, which can spell the difference between success and failure for an organization, because it is this mindset shift that is so important to the vital C, the CUSTOMER.***

As *Pat Veal* says –

"Out of the heart, the mind speaks. The mouth is the vessel through which the words come. As we become more health conscious, we may fast to flush our system and rid our bodies of toxins, after which we change habits to stay clean. We can apply the same principle to our language and words."

It's as the time tested proverb tells us, ***What We Think, We Become.***

By focusing on the Four P's, the organisation's ***primary focus*** subconsciously, if not consciously, becomes ***competitor tracking.***

Simply because your competitors are capable of, and can and do perform some activity, it doesn't indicate that you can and should and need to do it yourself.

And after seeing your competitor do it, if your organisation feels you can and should do it, then why didn't you do it in the first place? (For example, once Tata Motors announced the Rupees One Lakh Nano car, we had a host of competing car manufacturers announcing similar plans of their own. But it is only the Tata project which the average individual recalls favourably.)

Why did the organization wait for the competitor to do it first?

Yes, keeping track of competitors does make sense, but it has to be kept within perspective.

It is not our intention to advise organizations to ignore competitor actions. But organizations should not base all decisions and actions as reactions to competitor's actions.

Proactive behaviour is all about saying, ***"Can I think for myself and take actions, irrespective whether others around me have not done the same, because I believe these actions will be beneficial for me?" You won't wait for a neighbour to exhibit similar medical symptoms you have before you visit a doctor, will you?***

Do ***not*** get overawed by your competitors and feel that you have to immediately react to whatever steps your competitors take.

If organizations keep as much focus, pay as much attention, and are as responsive to customer's needs as they are to their competitor's actions, then customer delight and customer retention rates would zoom.

As an example, we were recently outside an outlet of a leading fast food chain which had just launched a new chicken delicacy. Right opposite this outlet lies the outlet of a competing fast food chain. The first outlet was conducting a promotional activity in which four to five individuals dressed up as chickens were being instructed by their supervisor to stand outside the outlet of the competitor and lure over the competitor's customers. Very cheap trick in itself. Definitely not worthy of a fast food chain which is a world renowned brand. But what happened a few hours later was unbelievable. We were once again passing that outlet and saw a huge board outside mentioning that due to huge demand, the chicken delicacy was sold out. Out of curiosity we went in and enquired when it would be available again. Even the manager was unaware. The same situation continued for a week. The chicken delicacy was still out of stock.

Why did the organization need to lure away competitor's customers when it didn't have the ability to service them? Why couldn't it focus on it's own inventory, supply chain, logistics and delivery systems?

One who is so constantly obsessed about reacting to competitor's actions is apparently not confident of the quality of his own product and service, and has little faith in the strength and depth of his own organization's customer relationships.

True gold fears not the test of fire.

- Ancient Chinese saying

And who says that the competitor would be right in what he is always doing? Why should his actions be taken as Gospel?

Children so often make the mistake during examinations of peering into someone else's answer sheet, seeing that someone's answer was different from their own, canceling out the answer they had themselves written, write the other person's answer, only to find later that their original answer which they cancelled out had been the correct one.

A Lovely Lesson from a Little Lizard

We were taught a brilliant lesson related to this by a participant in one of our corporate training workshops on marketing. The programme was being conducted in a location where there was a lot of greenery around. In the course of the programme, a chameleon, (a type of lizard), entered the training room. The lady participants in the programme were shaken up. Fortunately, one of the male participants was an expert snake and lizard handling expert. He got up, expertly caught the chameleon without harming it, and left it outside in the lawn and came back. We asked him how he got to be such an expert at this. Wasn't he worried that the snakes and lizards would harm him? ***His answer contained a wealth of meaning.***

He said that he used to see programmes related to snakes and lizards on television and realized that ***these snakes and lizards also were a vital and integral part of the eco-system,*** and meant him no harm. This is when he began to view them with empathy and realized that ***they too had an equal right to exist and survive, and started to practice handling them with care.***

Coincidentally, the topic being discussed when the chameleon had interrupted the programme was the topic of dealing with competition in business. Participants had been mentioning that competition needed to be eliminated as soon as possible as it was bad for any business and prevented their own businesses from growing.

We explained to the participants that in the same way that the snakes and lizards were a natural and inherent part of the eco-system, similarly, ***the presence and existence of competitors was a natural and inherent part of the eco-system of the business world,*** and competitors did not primarily exist for the purpose of harming others, but to provide consumers with a choice and option and service them in the best way possible.

Brands which indulge in marketing warfare towards their competitors have so much in terms of areas of improvement possible when it comes to their own product and service delivery. The valuable, limited resources which they wrongly divert towards competitors, could much more profitably have been diverted to improving quality of product and service.

Most Marketing Today has Truly Ignored the Customer

The 4 P's tend to gain focus when marketing as a function incorrectly sees itself only in the ***customer acquisition*** area, rather than as part of the holistic customer life cycle. It is apparent that the 4 P's bring the attention of a business on acquisition rather than on retention. As a simple example, the concept of ***after sales service*** cannot be slotted into any of the P's as they currently exist.

Multiple text books on the subject of Marketing have approximately one chapter or section devoted to the Customer, in most cases located towards the end of the book.

Seminars and workshops on the topic of Marketing have a single session devoted to the topic of the Customer.

These are not-so-subtle messages which give a clear indication that the discipline and function of Marketing bestows comparatively little attention to the Customer as compared to the 4 P's.

This is the root cause of a majority of problems that most marketers face – that much more attention is paid to the Four 'P's' and not enough importance to the one 'C', the Customer.

Four against one does sound a little unfair, but in this case, the One C, the Customer, if given its rightful attention, is more than a match for the four P's.

- Cyrus M Gonda, Kalim Khan

The Four P's in any brand exist by default. Every brand ***will*** have a ***Product*** which is sold at a particular ***Price*** at a particular ***Place*** and which is ***Promoted*** in a particular way. These will happen by default. ***These 4 P's are by default attributes of every brand, every product, every service.***

But CUSTOMERS do not exist by default

As we have just seen, every brand contains within itself the 4 P's by default.

BUT NO BRAND CAN HAVE CUSTOMERS BY DEFAULT.

Customers have to be focused on, made the centre of attention, pampered, and ***retained*** through careful nurturing.

If brands shift their focus from the 'Ps' towards the 'C', the brands will then provide:

CONSTANT, COMMITTED, CUSTOMISED, CUSTOMER COLLABARATION.

Also, brands will then:

CREATE and CONSOLIDATE CUSTOMER CONFIDENCE.

We would like to conclude this tenet by thanking our esteemed corporate clients who have demonstrated faith in our thought processes and have suggested that our tenets, rather than the 4 P's, form the heart and core of their organisation's genuine marketing philosophy, because our tenets deal with aspects that are at the heart of customer retention. Happily, we have seen our client organizations, large and small, who have implemented our tenets with heart and soul, achieve great success.

If any organisation gives importance to, and genuinely practices all the tenets we have explained and enumerated, the organisation's focus and resource allocation by default will automatically be towards the customer.

THE DAYS OF THE FOUR P's ARE OVER,
IT'S NOW TIME FOR THE 'C' TO FLOWER

Tenet 12

LET 'FLEXIBILITY' BE YOUR ORGANISATIONAL BUZZWORD

Customers are frigid when organisations are rigid Customers spend when organisations bend

The bend in the road is not the end of the road unless you refuse to take the turn.

- Anon

This is one of the most crucial parameters when it comes to a customer's decision to stick with a particular brand or to shift to other options. Flexibility and customisation can be said to be at the core of the marketing philosophy. In fact it's the reason why certain Mom and Pop stores, single location outlets and small family run businesses which are attentive, responsive and flexible to individual customer needs still survive and even thrive in the face of stiff competition from organised retail.

A simple but true example will brilliantly illustrate what this tenet means.

Some time ago, we had been to a fairly decent restaurant for a snack. On the menu, among other dishes, was listed the item, "Omelette", and also the item "Bread and butter sandwich." We were looking for an omelette sandwich, but that item was not specifically listed on the menu. We requested for an omelette sandwich, but the order taker said that would not be possible as it was not listed on the menu. We agreed it wasn't. We suggested a simple way out which we felt he could have thought out for himself. We said we would pay for an omelette, as well as the bread and butter sandwich. He could just place the omelette inside the bread and butter and serve it as an omelette sandwich. His reply stunned us. ***"That's not possible. The kitchen staff won't agree to make it since it's not on the menu. We can serve you an omelette, and bread and butter separately on your table. YOU can make the sandwich yourself by putting the omelette between the bread and butter."*** We walked out immediately to look for another place for our snack.

While this may be an extreme example, every word of it is true, and in no way are such experiences uncommon. Big brands also behave in similar ways with their customers very often, refusing to bend their rigid rules, which very often are representative of nothing but bureaucracy and a stubbornness to abide by policies created in an ivory tower, where very little understanding of ground realities at the operational level may prevail.

You want to set rules, but with a lot of flexibility.

- Frederic Mishkin

The practice of rigidity and inflexibility is not restricted to small brands alone. It has spread like an unwanted epidemic, and literally every brand at some time or other exposes it's customers to the statement – ***"We can't do it the way you want it. We can't explain why. What you're asking for sounds rational and logical. It's just that our organisational rule says we can't do it."***

In short - ***"We don't know why. We don't mind breaking. But we won't bend."***

When statements such as these come our way, we are reminded of two classic poems from English literature.

One of them is - ***"The Charge of the Light Brigade,"*** which is a true story of an incident from the Crimean war, where six hundred soldiers rush to their death without understanding why they were doing so. Their management, (or Military Leadership in this case), had badly let them down by giving them half-baked orders and little or no information on the ***WHY*** aspect of their job. The immortal lines from the poem -

"Ours not to question why,

Ours but to do and die."

are synonymous with lack of clarity and understanding on the part of many frontline staff when it comes to the issues of knowledge or authority to take decisions on an issue where the customer requests for some flexibility in product, service,delivery or some other aspect of the transaction.

The other poem which comes to mind is ***Invictus*** by the British poet William Ernest Henley. Interestingly, ***Invictus*** in Latin stands for ***unconquered,*** a word that reminds one of a ***Win-Lose*** mindset. The line from the poem which is most relevant in the context of lack of flexibility goes as -

"My head is bloody but unbowed."

This is very indicative of the lack of flexibility with regards to customers that many organisations indulge in today. Some organisations prefer to lose customers through their stubbornly rigid attitude, but will hold their financially bleeding head high with false pride.

It is pertinent to note that the poem ***'Invictus'*** was the text selected by Timothy James McVeigh, the Oklahoma Bomber, (who blew up the Alfred P. Murrah Federal Building in Oklahoma in 1995, killing over a hundred and seventy innocent people in the process), to be his last testament to the world before he was executed.

Attitudes such as ***"My head is bloody but unbowed,"*** are associated with rabid and rigid radicals such as the Oklahoma Bomber, but they have little role to play when it comes to organisational flexibility and understanding customer needs. Such an attitude can never lead to Win-Win outcomes.

Your organisational processes should resemble grass, not trees, at least as far as customers are concerned. When storms come, (as they surely will), it is the rigid trees which are uprooted, and the flexible grass that survives.

- Cyrus M Gonda, Kalim Khan

The grass, which is flexible at the tip, but rock solid in its roots, is never destroyed, however intense the storm.

As the traditional Chinese proverb goes –

"Stoop if the roof is low."

If we see a room with a low ceiling, we won't deliberately bump our head against the low ceiling, will we? ***We adjust, temporarily bend, and accommodate.***

It is your customers who define your product and service parameters.

If your customers require a low roof, then as a service provider, you have to be flexible enough to reach under it, of course ***not at the cost of your organisation's dignity or self esteem. (Remember the grass, its tip is flexible but its foundations and principles are solidly rooted under the ground.)***

But in most cases we have observed where rigidity rules the roost, it is not dignity or self esteem at stake, but rather ego, obstinacy, short sightedness and self importance which result in rigidity.

Leaders honour their core values but they are flexible in how they execute them.

- Colin Powell

The following example will serve to justify:

One of us authors had an account with a leading foreign bank. As an add-on to this account, an ATM card had been provided. One day, the author noticed that the ATM card was slightly cracked, but still functional. The ATM machine still recognised and accepted it. The crack was as yet not sufficiently large for the machine to reject the card, but this would happen sooner or later. Being a proactive individual, the author immediately went to the main branch of that bank in Mumbai city and said that he would like to have it replaced before it cracked further and could not be used at all. This was done so there would be no inconvenience and interrupted service if the card cracked further and stopped functioning. The person at the bank said, ***"We will provide you a fresh card within five working days, but you will have to surrender your existing card immediately."*** The author was naturally upset at this, as the reason he had been proactive in asking for a replacement was so that he could continue using the ATM card without interrupted service, and now a functioning card was being taken away.

"Why can't I keep the card till the new one arrives," was the natural query. ***"Because there can't be two cards for the same account existing at the same time,"*** was the curt response. Now, if this was an accurate statement, it meant that the new card was already prepared, or else why block the existing card right now itself?

She had no answer to this.

Then she was asked why this entire process took so long. Her mumbled response was, ***"Today is Friday. The card is not prepared here in Mumbai. No processing will take place over the weekend. The request from our end will be sent to our back office in Chennai. They will take a few days to process it. We don't know how long. Then they send it to Hyderabad for further processing and they will courier it to your residence."***

"Well", I asked, ***"if no processing is going to take place over the next three days and obviously the new card won't be ready before that, then why is the existing card being blocked right now? Am I being penalised for being a proactive customer?"*** She glared nastily and then made a concession. ***"Okay. I'll make a provision that your card can remain active for the next three days. Is that fine?"***

Sure that was fine. But why couldn't she have done that in the first place? In fact that was the reason for the proactiveness from our end - To reduce the down time of the card by having a new one prepared while the old one was still functional.

The author added, ***"Also, I would like to pick up the new card from your bank. Please don't send it home as I leave for work early in the morning and reach home late at night and there's no one else at home***

to receive it when it comes. Tell me when I could pick it up from the bank and I'll be here."

Her reply probed the depths of rigidity and inflexibility.

"We can't do that. It's our policy that the new card is dispatched directly to the customer's residence from our back office in Hyderabad. We have no control over it. You can't pick it up from here."

Unbelievable.

And this comes from a bank which boldly advertised its customer centric and customer friendly policies. After arguing for literally a quarter of an hour, she agreed as a special favour that I could pick it up from the bank. ***"Great, when should I come?"*** The reply was - FIVE working days from this day, which exclude the weekend, a Public holiday next week, and therefore the next weekend as well. In short, the Monday after next was when I was told it would be ready. This meant a total of ten days taken to renew an ATM card.

Well, on Monday after next when the author reached the bank, the card hadn't arrived. Neither did it come on Tuesday. When the lady was queried, her response was, ***"How should I know. The back office says it has been couriered. I can't trace it now. What's your hurry anyway? You can always enter the branch and withdraw cash from the cash counter."*** (The ***friendly*** bank.)

To cut the story short, when I went to the bank a couple of days later, I received my card. What was shocking in the entire episode were the ***multiple internal touch points*** the bank had for getting a simple thing done. ***Not that the customer would have minded these multiple touch point if they were well co-ordinated and didn't affect his service delivery,*** but they did. And the front line bank staff was unable to explain where the process delay lay. And the worst was the ***rigidity in policy*** of not allowing the customer the convenience of picking up his card from the bank if he so wished. Organisational bureaucracy at it's worst.

Just to contrast this incident, a friend of ours who had a similar problem with an ATM card of another bank had a pleasant experience. He also proactively requested for a fresh card. A similar condition was quoted, that two ATM cards could not be active for the same account at one time. But the bank person attending to our friend told him, ***"You can keep and continue to use the existing card. The moment you receive the new card from our end, you could destroy the old card yourself. We trust you to do that much."***

A similar situation, so beautifully handled. And if one bank could think of this, why not the other?

Compare the rigid attitude of the first bank with an endearing example of an organisation called ***Burgmann India Ltd.*** Burgmann is in the engineering sector, primarily into the manufacturing and installation of seals in machinery. Some of these seals are humongous, weighing over a tonne. A representative of this organisation mentioned to us how a customer of theirs, a petroleum refining organisation, once had a problem where a seal on a piece of equipment had failed, causing leakage and stoppage of production. The staff of the refinery was in panic mode. Their previous supplier of seals had taken a week to rectify a similar problem and they anticipated that Burgmann would take the same period of time. (Burgmann was not their current supplier of seals.) A week's loss of production for the refinery would have been catastrophic.

But the Burgmann team swung into action with the precision of a military operation. They had a spare seal of those dimensions available in their stores, (it weighed over a tonne.) They immediately got it airlifted by helicopter to the customer's refinery. The two engineers who went along to install it were both Catholics, and although the episode occurred on Christmas eve, they gave up their religious festivities, spent the entire day at the refinery, and ensured the equipment was up and running in a day's time. The refinery management was so grateful, it immediately signed a long term contract making Burgmann India their premier suppliers for seals. And obviously any other product that Burgmann has to offer which this refinery uses, the refinery will think of Burgmann as their first choice supplier.

The contrast in the above two episodes (between the bank and Burgmann), is more striking than that between chalk and cheese. The excuse that Burgmann have comparatively fewer customers while the bank has thousands just doesn't hold water. Remember ***the Circle of Influence?*** Any ***one*** of these thousands of customers of a bank could wield sufficiently large influence to cause the bank to lose a large number of key accounts.

And if the bank (or any organisation), doesn't HAVE the capacity to adequately service large numbers of customers, it should first be developing the capability and infrastructure to do so before adding more customers to their customer base.

That's a logical sequence of activity.

A truly customer oriented organisation will never think in terms of - ***"Since our volumes of customers is large, therefore some customers getting poor service is inevitable and tolerable."***

A truly customer oriented organisation will think of the welfare of ***EVERY*** customer it generates revenue from, and how that customer would benefit from transacting with the organisation.

A truly customer oriented organisation will not treat an individual customer as just another faceless statistic to be boxed into a neat little compartment for later analysis.

Statistics Never Lie? Think Again

Most organisations, when queried about the prevailing levels of their customer's satisfaction tend to say, ***"On an AVERAGE, our customers are satisfied."***

As any good statistician will tell you, averages are one of the most misleading concepts in statistics. Imagine the following scenario:

A man is made to stand with one foot in a bucket of icy water and with his other foot on burning coals. A statistician would say, ***"His temperature is average and therefore normal."***

Only the poor guy would know what he is going through.

This is the reason why true marketers would never use such language and reduce an individual customer to a mere statistic. We have heard internet service providers say - ***"On an average, our customers in that region are getting a sufficient bandwidth."***

That's good. But what about the customers who are getting poor bandwidth at the cost of other customers who are getting an excellent bandwidth, which is ultimately what makes your ***average*** good? That factor is rarely considered.

Once an organisation starts considering customers as individuals, then it will start being more tuned to their specific needs and problems. ***It will become more flexible and considerate to individual requirements.***

Aren't specific individual requirements, needs and problems the reasons that get customers to approach an organisation in the first place?

(We have never heard of a customer with a ***generic*** requirement. For every customer, his own need is a unique one, and not to be mixed up with the need of any other customer.)

Then why ignore these specific needs and requirements now that organisations have been given a chance and opportunity by the customers to address and service them?

"We ***have*** to deliver the ATM at your residence. We don't care what ***the customer's*** problems are. It's ***our organisational policy.*** And ***that*** takes priority over ***customer*** needs." – ***The Friendly Bank***

That's why we say, "Hats off to organisations such as Burgmann India Ltd. As was said about Abou Ben Adhem in the poem - ***May their tribe increase."***

Pull down fences that serve no purpose

One of the ***primary reasons that rigidity exists in many organisations*** is that policy framing is being done in an ivory tower with total disregard for realities at the operational level.

Also, policies which were once made with a specific objective and a reason in mind continue to remain functional long after the purpose for which they were created has ceased to exist.

Take the example of the universal typewriter keyboard with which all of us are familiar. The positioning of the alphabets on the keyboard begins with the weird combination in the top row going as - Q W E R T Y U I O P.

What's the logic for this positioning? Definitely not user convenience or operational efficiency. At least, it's not convenient from the current point of view.

Let's get back into history and examine the origin of this strange positioning. This system of this alphabet positioning on keyboards dates back to the era when the first manual typewriters were produced. Being slow machines with physical keys, if the typist was fast and could type rapidly, the keys jammed and the machine stalled. ***At that point of time, for those circumstances, this weird positioning of keys was useful in that it slowed down a fast typist, thus preventing the keyboard from jamming.***

Today with no physical keys present to get stuck even during rapid typing, the reason for this weird positioning no longer exists. In fact it's estimated that it takes a person not used to the positioning of keys on the keyboard at least three months to become comfortable with it. Today, the best positioning from the customer point of view would be the logical ***A B C D E F G.*** But inertia has set in. The keyboard manufacturing industry refuses to realise that the reason for this weird positioning no longer exists. The attitude rather is:

"Don't rock the boat."
"Let sleeping dog's lie."

And as a result, the customer unknowingly suffers.

That's how lack of flexibility and responsiveness to changing environment and customer needs, negatively affects everyone concerned and results into a lose-lose scenario.

But it's important to note that while fences which are no longer of use should be brought down, ***before*** pulling them down it's important to get back into history and understand ***why*** the fence, (or the rule or policy), was put up in the first place. The reason may still be alive and valid, in which case the policy could be retained, but modified for customer convenience.

Stay committed to your decisions,
but stay flexible in your approach.

- Tom Robbins (American novelist)

We are also not advocating that an organisation be flexible and accommodate a customer when he asks the organisation to do something UNETHICAL or ILLEGAL.

No way.

That's a very clear line which cannot be crossed under any circumstances. In such cases, the customer must firmly but politely be told where to get off.

But in most cases of customer request which are turned down by organisations, we have seen that there's nothing that the organisation really has to do to comply and satisfy the customer, apart from restructuring it's own working systems. And this is something most organisations appear reluctant to do.

Such organisations resist change. They avoid moving outside their self created comfort zone. We realise its human tendency to do so, but that's why organisations need to focus upon the aspect of lack of flexibility so strongly to ensure that it is overcome and this human frailty on part of organisations and their staff does not hinder customers from getting an experience to their personal customised satisfaction.

A Great Brand should be HARD as well as SOFT.

Hard, as far as the brand's rock solid foundation of dependability, systems and reliability are concerned. In these areas, there can be no compromise.

But soft, in terms of the brand's flexibility to find the way to, and enter, customer's hearts.

- Cyrus M Gonda, Kalim Khan

Sorry. No sharing of Ice Cream Allowed

The other day, the two of us went to a mall and picked up two cups of ice cream from a counter of a well known ice cream brand. Since we each wanted to taste the flavour the other was having, we asked the salesman at the counter if he could give us an extra cardboard cup each so we could put a portion each of our ice cream in the extra cup and exchange it with each other. ***"Sorry Sir. I am not permitted to give out extra cups. They are all counted before my shift commences and all cups have to be accounted for. Then the cups are tallied against the money I have collected to count the total sales made during my shift."***

Utter nonsense.

For the sake of the organisation's lack of faith on its staff, why should the customer suffer? We had paid Rupees Sixty each for a single scoop of ice cream and we couldn't even be provided the flexibility of exchanging half of it comfortably with each other? Ridiculous.

If organisations want to keep track of their salesmen's honesty, surely there are other methods? We could suggest a few. Some cups could be kept with the message printed in bold on them, ***"These are for sampling purpose only. Please report to the management if you have paid for ice cream in this cup",*** or cups of a smaller size could be made and provided for the purpose of sampling. So many options are possible. But no. Operational realities, ground level situations and customer requirements appear to be the last thing on the mind when such policies are framed. It's not enough for a brand to know how to make and distribute good ice cream. These things are the least that the customer expects.

And what sort of a message about the brand does the customer get - knowing that the organisation doesn't even trust its own staff, and that the staff does not even have the authority to provide a customer an empty cardboard cup?

'*Just Around The Corner*' Excels at Flexibility

As a counter to the above, the other day we experienced a fantastic experience of flexibility. We had visited the food chain, ***Just Around The Corner,*** to pick up a parcel order of salad. They have a ***make your salad counter,*** and they offer the takeaway salad in two sizes of containers. A small box for around a Rupees Hundred and Forty, and a large one for around Rupees One Hundred and Ninety. The system followed is that the customer pays the money at the counter, gets the empty box of the size he has paid for, fills it up with the salad items of his choice from the salad counter, and takes it away. The day we went there and asked for the small size takeaway box, the person at the counter politely told us,

"Sorry Sir, we are out of small boxes for takeaway. But you can take this large one instead and fill it up. You just need to pay for the small portion, since it's our fault that the small size container is not currently in stock."

Terrific flexibility. We were thrilled with this organisation.

The story doesn't end there.

The day after we experienced this terrific example, the two of us were conducting a Sales Training Programme for the sales team of an FMCG organisation, and we brought up this incident as a case study to the participants and asked them how they would have responded if they were in the position of the salad bar counter salesman who had run out of small size containers. Would they have done as he did and wowed the customer, or would they have said that they were sorry they were out of stock of the small container; but if the customer wanted, he could take a large container at full price. We thought it was a no brainer. Imagine our surprise when more than half the participants responded with statements such as:

- **"No way."**
- **"It will set a bad precedent."**
- **"The customer will expect it everytime."**
- **"Why should we pamper the customer?"**
- **"Why should he get extra just because we are out of stock of a small size container?"**
- **"What about the extra food cost. Who will absorb it? How can it be justified?"**

All these and many more similar responses came from sales and customer service professionals who are apparently geared up to service customers. No wonder organisations seem to have such a tough time retaining their customers today.

These responses are part of an organisation's DNA and culture.

If on the other hand, the top management stresses and emphasises to all front end staff that flexibility and customisation be the order of the day, that a customer should never go away disappointed if it can be prevented, then customer delight is the obvious and logical result of the customer getting things ***"His Way."***

And if these positive messages are repeated and seen to be put into practice over and over again by the management at every opportunity they get, and if employees practicing this are rewarded for the same, then this culture of customisation will leave every customer with a happy taste and a fond memory and a yearning to return.

Radio Ga-Ga

Contrast this with a recent service scenario we were involved in. We had scheduled an early morning meeting with a client at an outlet of a well known coffee shop chain. We were to meet our client at nine. We reached there fifteen minutes before time. The coffee shop was open, with a solitary employee running around doing the cleaning as well as the set up. The moment we sat at a table, he informed us without glancing in our direction, "It will take some time for any order to be served."

We were fine with that, but wondered why the shop was open in the first place if they were not ready for service. The table we sat at was dirty, and since we were the first guests that day, obviously the dirt was left over from the previous night. The tables hadn't been cleaned when the shop had shut the previous night. We requested the man to come over to our table and he wiped it clean. There was a radio playing, and it had been tuned in to a blaring rock music channel. We were in the mood for something soothing, so we requested him to switch over to an old Hindi music channel. We even told him which frequency it would be on. We were flabbergasted when he said, ***"Sorry Sir, I'm not permitted to play that channel. We are not allowed to play slow or old music as it is the policy of the entire chain not to do so. The latest music is what most of our customers, the teenage crowd, prefer."*** With that one statement, he had already made us feel that we were not wanted here, that we were the odd ones out. Anyway, we tried reasoning with him, pointing out to him that we were the only customers in the entire coffee shop, and in case someone did walk in, he could always change it back to the rock channel. Again the response was, ***"Sorry Sir, I couldn't take that risk. If someone from our management came in for a surprise check, I would be in trouble for breaking a rule."***

That said all we wanted to know.

We wouldn't blame the employee. It is the management which is not customer oriented.

The focus is not on the customer.

It is on their own set of rules, and many of them seem to make no sense.

What is important to the management is not customer delight, but the organization's own policy.

No flexibility has been given to the employees to exercise their discretion. Neither has the necessary situation based training been provided. Instead the staff work in an atmosphere of fear.

And it is very clear where the management priorities lie. As the employee said, the management representative would be upset if the radio channel were different from the one they had instructed.

But the employee was not worried about the management being upset about tables left dirty overnight, and guests having to sit at filthy tables first thing in the morning. Or about the restaurant being open, but no orders capable of being served. Oh, no. Apparently, the management was not concerned with such trivial issues. What they were concerned about was that at no time should soothing music be heard on their premises. They might as well have kept a notice at the entrance – ***Entry only for persons aged below thirty five.***

(And the average price of a cup of coffee in this outlet is around Rupees Seventy, taxes extra.)

A Brilliant Example of Flexibility

To counter the above, let's learn from a superb example of flexibility, displayed by the airline SAS, led by Jan Carlzon, whom we discussed earlier.

Carlzon mentions in his book, ***Moments of Truth,*** about Randy Peterson, an American businessman, who was staying at the Grand Hotel in Stockholm, Sweden. He checked out of the hotel and headed for Arlanda airport, north of Stockholm, on an important business trip for a day to Copenhagen. After he arrived at the airport, he realised he had forgotten his airline ticket back at the hotel. He had put it down on his dressing table in the hotel room while putting on his overcoat, and had forgotten to pick it up.

He realised he would have to miss his important flight, as obviously no passenger could board the aircraft without displaying a valid ticket. Sadly he explained the situation to the person at the check-in counter. Imagine the pleasant surprise he received when she smiled and said, "Don't worry, Mr. Peterson. Here's your boarding card. I'll insert a temporary ticket in here. If you just tell me your room number at the Grand Hotel and your destination in Copenhagen, I'll take care of the rest."

What the check-in person did was immediately contact the Grand Hotel and explain the situation. A bellboy at the hotel checked the room and found the ticket on the dressing table. The check-in person at the SAS ticket counter then sent across an SAS vehicle to the hotel to retrieve the ticket. The airline staff moved so quickly that the ticket arrived at the SAS counter before Mr. Peterson's flight had even taken off. The check-in person approached Mr. Peterson in the passenger lounge and politely handed his ticket over to him. (In such a similar situation at most other airlines, the passenger would definitely have missed his flight.)

Mr. Peterson was gratitude personified at this flexibility and out of the way service and helpfulness displayed by the lady at the counter.

There was no way Mr. Peterson would ever travel by any other airline ever again in the future. He was a fan of the brand for life.

The question is, in this entire episode, ***who deserves the praise?***

The lady at the counter?

Of course she does.

But the lion's share of the praise belongs to the organisation which permitted and empowered her to use her discretion and good judgement, and provided her the necessary resources to go out of the way to help a customer in need.

If the lady had a boss, who bluntly asked her, ***"Why did you go so much out of the way for that passenger? How is he connected to you? Is he a relation or a friend of yours? Who gave you the permission to take***

such a decision?" - do you think the lady would ever have gone out of her way for another passenger throughout her entire career?

No way.

It is the airline that deserves the praise for the way in which it trained and empowered the front line staff and encouraged them to be flexible in such situations, judiciously using organisational resources to ensure that the customer was delighted.

This is what empowerment and flexibility truly mean.

WOW is rarely the result of superior technology.
WOW is usually the outcome of healthy organisational attitude.

- Cyrus M. Gonda, Kalim Khan

Being flexible enhances the scope of your business and generates revenue

Understanding your customer also means being flexible in your viewpoint. Trying to see things from his point of view. A simple example will prove the amount and volume of business lost from looking at things only from the organizational and industry perspective. It concerns the garment industry. Many times we have liked the texture, colour and design of what is popularly termed as a Party Shirt. One of the distinguishing features of a ***Party Shirt*** is that it does not have a pocket, for whatever reasons best known to designers. (No sales attendant has ever been able to explain why.) But many prospective purchasers of party shirts, (including ourselves), have many times ***not*** bought a party shirt which they otherwise liked very much, ***only*** because it had no pocket. Well, if a party shirt is supposed to have no pocket, then it must have no pocket. ***But what prevents the manufacturers from being flexible and providing a little extra material for a pocket with the shirt, and if the customer desires, he can have the pocket stitched on later.*** This would involve no cost for the manufacturer, but absence of this leads to so much loss of revenue in terms of lost sales from customers who need a pocket for at least keeping a pen.

Flexibility can be recognised when a front end staff tells a customer, ***"Officially I can't do this for you, but.....",*** and then he proceeds to helps out a genuine customer in need.

Which is very, very good.

The question is, if ***officially*** (according to company rule and policy), the staff is not authorised to do what he has done, yet he does it, the customer benefits, and obviously no harm or damage accrues to the organisation in the process, ***why does the hindrance exist in the first place***? Organisations need to focus as a priority area on training and empowering staff to use their discretion while handling customers.

Ding Dong Bell

One of us authors recently went shopping for a wall clock. In the shop was an eye catching piece, which also had a lovely musical chime to mark the hour. It was a very pleasing sound, one which we would have found very pleasant to listen to, day or night. Unfortunately, no customer could listen to the chimes at night, even if he had wished to. The makers of this clock have wrongly assumed that all people go to sleep at eleven p.m. and don't wake up before seven in the morning, every day. They have also assumed that no customer would want to listen to pleasing chimes continuing the night through. This is apparent because the clock had been designed in such a way that the chimes have been blocked between these hours. For some people this may be fine, but there are many like us who love to listen to the chimes even at night. No flexibility in the machinery had been provided for activating the chimes during these hours. The factory setting was fixed and rigid. After we expressed to the shopkeeper that it was a wonderful clock with lovely chimes, but this was the sole reason we were not purchasing it, he said in frustration, "You are the fourth set of people who have said the same thing. That's the fourth sale I have lost."

Think of it. Such a small feature which could easily have been incorporated by the clock makers, which would have provided the flexibility to both sets of customers - those who wanted the chimes on at night, and those who did not.

By itself, the thought process of the manufacturer is very good. They have considered a need that some customers could possibly have. One set of customers could find the chimes disturbing at night. So far, this is the true marketing philosophy at work. But this is where the thinking gets cloudy. Flexibility to accommodate preferences is not incorporated, (which could so easily have been done by adding a simple setting), and a huge chunk of customers with a slightly different set of needs is totally ignored, resulting in loss of sales and disappointed customers.

Empower your Employees

As in the case of the law, where justice must not only be done, it must be ***seen*** to be done, the same is the case with flexibility.

Flexibility in an organisation must not only exist, it must be seen to exist.

And the way the customer views flexibility in an organisation is on the basis of the level of genuine empowerment that has been provided to the front end employees.

Even considering making the organisation flexible is not possible if the employees are not genuinely empowered.

Empowering employees is ***step one*** when it comes to building a customer-centric, flexible organisation.

The Americans have their own way of speaking. Their accent is unique. For example they don't say ***them,*** they say ***'em.*** Considering this accent, consider the message of this tenet as meaning: ***'Em Power,*** or ***Give 'Em Power. 'Em,*** (or ***'Them'***), here, refers to employees.

Another way of looking at it would be to consider ***Em***, as a short form for ***Employees***.

Thus, Empower would translate as - Give ***Em***ployees ***Power.***

What we mean when we say – "Empower Employees"

When we talk of empowering employees, we definitely don't mean that the reins of the organisation need to be handed over to the employees.

But since it is an organisation's front end employees who have maximum contact with the customer, they definitely need to be given some healthy amount of flexibility in deciphering the rules and norms of the organisation on a case to case basis.

'BRAINS TRUST' DEFINITION OF EMPOWERING EMPLOYEES:

Does the work structure permit front end employees to take non-strategic, simple decisions, favouring customers, to facilitate customer service without harming the organisation, but which may be beyond existing convention, norms and regulations, or which may be a request which is being made for the first time by any customer.

\- Cyrus M Gonda, Kalim Khan

Each employee should be informed and aware as to what discretion he has, and should possess good situational intelligence for evaluation which will thus result in a healthy, win-win decision.

This can be achieved through making employees undergo customer sensitivity training, role plays, situational analysis, behavioural training, understanding non-verbal communication and messages, and so on.

The idea of empowering employees is to make them confident and capable of taking basic, practical, customer-related decisions and not decisions pertaining to rocket science.

The basic root cause and reason for employees in organisations not being empowered is that organisations don't trust their employees.

And if an organisation cannot trust IT'S EMPLOYEES, (who are the internal customers), such an organisation will NEVER be able to trust its external customers.

Let's first briefly examine the reasons why organisations tend to NOT trust their own employees:

1. No person or organisation can ever completely trust someone with whom they know they are going to have a short term relationship.
2. Most organisations today utilise contract labour at the front end to interact with customers.

3. Contract labour by it's very nature will have a short term relationship with the organisation.

4. Since these front end staff are rarely given necessary facilities such as Provident Fund and medical benefits, rarely are good staff looking for a secure career likely to stay for any length of time.

Now let's examine WHY organisations need to trust their employees:

1. It's the only cost effective way of functioning and running a business in the long run.

2. You can't provide terrific service to your customers if you operate by remote control.

3. When trust is placed in people, most people respond positively and reciprocate.

4. The front end employees are the ones who are interacting with customers.

5. The only way to earn trust is to give trust. Don't you want your employees to trust you?

6. Customers can notice and understand when an organisation doesn't trust its front end employees. Customers would tend to be far more cautious and careful while dealing with such organisations.

7. If trust in front end employees is lacking, sustainable growth is simply not possible.

We once again refer to Jan Carlzon, the originator of the concept of Moments of Truth. Jan was very clear that Moments of Truth do not occur in the Boardroom of an organisation. These moments occur on the shop floor, where the rubber hits the road.

And Jan therefore, advocated delegating of responsibility to middle managers for analysing problems, managing resources, and most importantly supporting the needs of frontline employees.

He was very clear that frontline employees need to be bestowed the trust and authority to respond to the needs and problems of individual customers and be trained thoroughly, so that they could respond to the customer's unique needs with speed and courtesy. ***As Jan said, "By apportioning responsibility in this way, companies can maximise***

their positive moments of truth. They will multiply their happy, satisfied customers, and therefore secure an important competitive advantage."

Trusting employees is one of the greatest investments an organisation can make

In most factories, hotels, and retail outlets worldwide, workers are randomly frisked when they leave work to check and see if they are pilfering any goodies from the work place. In spite of this frisking, a lot of pilferage and petty theft still occurs.

The same was the case in the ***Semler Corporation***, a family run business in Brazil. This continued till young Ricardo Semler took over and initiated his own unique style of ***Super-man-agement*** (a term we at ***Brains Trust*** have coined to indicate an enlightened level of leadership.)

Ricardo Semler was absolutely against the concept of frisking and bodily searching the employees when they left work to see if they were carrying company property away with them. His logic was crystal clear. His logic ran on the following lines:

Agreed, there is pilferage carried on by some employees of my organisation. But not all employees are involved. It's a small percentage of employees who indulge in it. The majority of the employees in any environment will always be honest, unless given reason to be otherwise. I am stopping the practice of frisking employees in my organisation. I don't mind if pilferage goes up, but I will not tolerate an honest employee to be embarrassed and humiliated in this manner.

The frisking stopped as per Ricardo's instructions, and within a couple of years, ***pilferage rates in his organisation DROPPED.***

Unbelievable?

Not really.

Most people respond positively to being trusted. Also, the honest employees were now so happy, that they acted like a check and balance on the few employees who used to pilfer, preventing them from doing so. And all this happened in Brazil, not in a first world country. Brazil is a country similar to India in terms of poverty and illiteracy. If trust can beget trust in Brazil, there is no reason to feel that in India it would be otherwise.

Those who trust us educate us.

- T.S. Eliot

In certain Western countries, when children give exams, they are sometimes put on the "Trust" system. The supervisor gives the children the exam papers, gives them instructions, ***makes them solemnly promise not to copy or use unfair practices,*** and then leaves the room for the duration of the examination.

It is not that the authorities want to save on the cost of a supervisor. They are, along with testing the student's knowledge of the subject, imparting a most valuable lesson in the area of ***trust.***

Children learn at a young age what the concepts of solemn promise, honour, and trust really mean.

Think of it. Which child can really understand what it means to be trusted if there is a supervisor keeping an eagle eye on him throughout the examination?

The feeling of how to respond to trust is simply not allowed to flower and blossom.

The same holds true for most employees in organisations today.

If organisations wish to be able to successfully empower their employees for ensuring front end flexibility and customer delight, demonstrating a sense of trust towards them is the number one imperative.

It is trust that leads to empowerment,
and empowerment that leads to flexibility.

- Cyrus M Gonda, Kalim Khan

Organisations need not give the keys to the family jewels to the employees, but they at least need to be provided with limited resources and petty cash which they can use at their discretion in case of emergencies.

The following example will better explain what we mean to say.

The "Great" Experience – WOW? Or OWW?

The concept of coffee shops as a place to spend time and relax is fast increasing in urban environments. Very recently, the two of us had time to spare on a Sunday evening and we decided to walk into a posh outlet of a leading coffee shop chain in Mumbai. (Coffee shops are getting very popular and mushrooming in urban areas in India.) This particular chain of coffee shops guaranteed in it's Marketing Communication that what it offered was not only varieties of coffee, but moreover an entire experience to go along with the coffee. ***Damn right we got an experience, but not the type we would want to repeat.*** We ordered two cold coffees with ice cream, costing around a hundred rupees each. The coffees arrived. Tall glasses of coffee with a big scoop of luscious, creamy ice cream on top.

To have that coffee, we were provided a ***puny plastic spoon,*** which wouldn't have been sufficient to stir a teacup. We tried to have the ice cream with that spoon, it just didn't work. We got a miniscule portion of ice cream on the spoon after Herculean attempts. The first bite we had with difficulty, as the ice cream dripped upon the short stem of the short spoon, making the stem sticky and extremely inconvenient to hold. The second spoonful, an even tinier one, although the mouth of the spoon was filled to capacity, dropped on the table and a little fell on our clothes as well. That's when we went up to the counter, (the shop was horribly short staffed and no person was attending to any table at that time), and asked the guy if he didn't have any long handled, metal sundae spoons, the kinds used for this beverage. His response floored us. ***"Do you really need long metal spoons?"***, he queried. Seeing our faces reddening with indignation, he hurriedly said, ***"Just wait. I'll get you some."*** We returned to our table and shortly he brought over a couple of long handled metal spoons. By now the ice cream had half melted. We asked him why he didn't provide them in the first place, instead of spoiling our experience by imitating beggars having coffee at rupees hundred a glass. The next response floored us further. ***"We're almost out of water for washing utensils and spoons. We're conserving water and only use water if it's absolutely needed. So we are using disposable spoons as far as possible"***, he mumbled. We couldn't believe our ears. Well, anyone can run out of water, but this was six in the evening, and the coffee shop was open for a further few hours. What would all the other guests experience? We asked him if his superiors had been informed about the situation. We had to ask this question twice before getting a mumbled, "No", in response. "Can't you pick up a twenty litre large keg of Bisleri water from a nearby grocery store if you've run out of water? A tumbler would barely cost Rupees Sixty", we informed him. ***"Two such kegs should see you through till you close,"*** we added.

"We don't have authority to spend that amount", he replied.

WOW.

Premium coffee chain. Promising a great experience and charging heavily for the same.

Why on earth is there no chain of communication to pass on the gravity of the situation to a regional manager at a time like this?

"This type of thing happens quite often," the staff added. No apology or anything of that nature was forthcoming. "Customers," as he put it later, "were supposed to understand and co-operate."

Double WOW.

Or rather, OWW.

The staff had been given no authority to act to ratify the situation either.

No immediate petty cash or spending power provided or permitted, (even a measly rupees sixty), even for such situations.

The person heading such a chain ought to put in his resignation papers. Sitting in a Head Office somewhere, glorying in a fool's paradise that his customers are getting an EXPERIENCE. He must be spending much more time with the guys in his advertising agency compared to what he spends in moving around his outlets. Forget being proactive, he's not even reactive. It's a clear case of telling his staff, "Don't burden me with your problems. And don't expect the system to support you either."

Compare this with Sam Walton and Jan Carlsson and our very own dabbawalas. In Wal-mart and SAS, such incidents could never happen to even one customer in a billion under the stewardship of Sam Walton and Jan Carlzon. It's all a question of having one's organisational priorities in place.

> *It is an absolute must that service organisations have customer service as their top priority.*
>
> \- Cyrus M Gonda, Kalim Khan

It's rarely a question of mere money. There are many other forms which empowerment can take to ensure that the customer feels satisfied with the organisation at the end of the day. ***Organisations can also empower their employees to give an honest opinion about the range of products and services they offer so that the customer can make a wise and informed choice as per his needs.***

We were recently at a store belonging to a leading electronics chain as one of us wanted to purchase a laptop. We saw five brands of laptop displayed and we asked the salesperson attending us as to which brand had the reputation for being the toughest and most durable. This toughness and durability was the parameter we were most interested in, and we asked the salesperson to help us out on that parameter. His response didn't help us in the least. He said, "***All five brands are tough***." We then asked, "Which brand has had the least complaints coming in from customers?"

Again, his response was not helpful. "***Even if you buy the most expensive piece, it could still get spoilt***." We said, "Our parameter for purchasing a laptop is toughness. We would like you to guide us as to which brand is the most durable." Again his response was, "***All are equally durable***."

Then we decided to speak to the store manager and told him that our parameter for selecting a piece was first and foremost its durability. High end features were not our priority. We said we were ready to make an immediate purchase if he could guide us on that parameter. The manager's response was similar to the salesperson's response. He said, "I can't comment on that. I have no data on durability. No customer has ever asked me to evaluate the brand on the parameter of durability."

Ridiculous. Instead of looking at things from the customer's point of view and giving him information on a parameter important to him so that the customer could make an informed choice, the store staff preferred to focus on their own convenience and protect themselves by being non-committal. This displays clear lack of empowerment to genuinely guide the customer. It cannot be lack of data as a manager of a section in the store would definitely have this basic data with him, if not formally, then at least through experience. It was clear that the top management had instructed staff not to mention the negative aspect of any brand they stocked, and the staff then carried this policy to ridiculous extremes, hesitating to even guide and help a customer to make an informed purchase decision. A clear case of rigidity and following the selling mindset.

FAQ's and NSFAQ's

Customers want to deal with people who have the authority to take decisions.

Empowerment is a process. Unless your organisation has the right people at operational level, and has trained them well on customer orientation and requirements, provided them in-depth knowledge on aspects of product and service, organisational capabilities and processes, possible situations and scenarios, and frequently as well as

Not So Frequently Asked Customer Questions; empowerment in the organisation can never occur. If you're looking at maximising positive Moments of Truth for your customers and becoming a benchmark brand, you can't be satisfied with generating only a list of FAQ's.

The focus has to be on NSFAQ's. Even if a few customers could have a particular query, your staff needs to know how to deal with it.

Every organisation needs to keep an FAQ booklet and train its employees to answer these FAQ's or ***Frequently Asked Questions,*** which customers tend to come up with.

This is essential in order to ensure that standard queries are attended and addressed by the first staff member whom a customer approaches with such a query. At the same time, we feel that while having an FAQ booklet is necessary, it definitely is not enough. How responsive an organisation is to individual, out-of-the-way, and one-off customer needs can be determined by the importance the organisation pays to ***NSFAQ's.***

We at ***Brains Trust*** have developed a model of ***NSFAQ's*** - The ***Not So Frequently Asked Questions.*** These are the queries that would not currently be the concern of the vast majority of customers, but a few key customers may have them as queries or areas of concern. And if the front end staff is unprepared and not geared up to handle these queries which come up once in a blue moon, they could result in unpleasant, negative Moments of Truth for the organisation, leaving key customers with a bad taste in the mouth.

As part of our ***Brains Trust*** consulting assignments, we have developed industry and organisation specific lists and booklets of NSFAQ's for some oganisations we have advised, and these organisations have found the list of NSFAQ's and resultant booklets a very valuable and useful tool to prepare their front end staff to be more flexible and knowledgeable while handling out-of-the-way customer queries. Multiple organizations we have assisted have found it an extremely useful tool of knowledge management and a terrific method in which to understand the diverse needs of current and future buyers of their brand.

What is YOUR Organisational Hierarchy of Empowerment?

In certain Hotel chains, the junior most employees, for example the bellboys and the waiters, have been given the authority and have been empowered to waive off up to fifty dollars from a guest's bill without taking permission from their superiors, if they feel that a guest has a legitimate and justifiable grievance or complaint. The next higher level of hierarchy has been provided a limit of up to a hundred dollars for the same. The idea of empowering them to do so is to provide the guest with an immediate feeling of relief and proving to him that the hotel is willing to go to lengths to make amends to rectify negative experiences. But empowering employees without providing them with situational training serves little purpose, and may do more harm than good. The employees need to have the insight to understand and evaluate the situation and the guest they are handling. The employee need not use his discretion to waive off a bill each time, which is precisely what will happen if the employee has been empowered without sufficient training being provided. And this is the reason most organisations are sceptical about providing staff this level of empowerment, as the staff lack relevant and sufficient situation evaluation training.

It has to be understood that true empowerment is a process, not a gimmick

For any process to function at peak efficiency, due importance needs to be provided to each step in the process, and not just to the final result.

The empowered employee need not 'give away the house' each time a guest is upset or complains. ***But the equation should be tuned to ensure that no guest goes away with a feeling that injustice was done to him.***

Increasing the time that it takes to resolve his query by shuffling him around from one level of authority to another will only increase the customer's level of frustration. All front end staff must learn and be trained to shoulder responsibility for handling customer situations of all types as an important part of their training.

For example, in many call centres when a customer has a query, it takes a minimum of twenty minutes for a supervisor to come on line after a junior staff expresses his inability to help, as he has not been sufficiently trained and empowered. Even once the supervisor does come on line, in most cases he also expresses his inability to assist after listening to the whole story, citing lack of authority and empowerment.

Shirking of responsibility in many organisations has thus become endemic.

Even certain top layers are not immune from this malaise.

We have even read in newspapers of certain top executives making the comment, "***What can I do. I am only the Chairman of the Board***", as if he were at an insignificant level in the hierarchy.

All this is of vital importance in the context of marketing, as customers tend to get alienated when the employee interacting with them appears to have no decision making power. The more the distance between the organisation's decision making seat and it's customers, the more exponentially the customers move away from the organisation.

In this regard, ***Richard P Feynman***, the famous physicist, mentioned – The pull of any two objects is proportional to the mass of each and varies as the square of the distance between them. ***Bill Bryson***, in his work ***A Short History of Nearly Everything,*** simplifies Feynman's point and explains, ***"If you double the distance between two objects, the attraction between them becomes FOUR times weaker."***

The same is so true when the distance between the brand and the customer increases.

Your procedures should facilitate and enable your customers to have excellent experiences

The best organisations understand that the customer doesn't care about organisational hierarchy and procedures. He is really not bothered about who the boss man is. All that the customer wants is for his work to be done smoothly, swiftly and efficiently through a one-point contact he is interacting with. That's a great motivator for securing a customer's loyalty and repeat business. Organisational systems and procedures have to be structured keeping this vital point in mind. It is not an impossible task, but it requires management focus, discipline, and a customer oriented philosophy.

Even countries have realised the importance of this customer need as a marketing tool for inviting and retaining foreign investment, and are focusing on creating one point windows for project clearance. This is being advertised and used as a USP by countries to attract foreign investors. It's a crucial parameter on which countries are rated as to how investor friendly they are.

Flexibility in Retail

Many retail stores spend huge amounts on creating an ambience and on promotional activities to attract clientele, but provide very little leeway to a front end staff to enable him to take a customer oriented decision. We strongly feel that unless this area is focused on, the ambience and promotional activities undertaken to attract customers would by themselves be wasteful expenditure. Employees in retail outlets should be empowered to take basic decisions and handle immediate requests, such as requests for exchange, without having to refer to supervisors, who may not even be around.

The extremes to which this can be taken was unfortunately displayed to one of us authors recently at a leading book store, where the concerned author had accumulated points on the store's loyalty card, which could be redeemed against further purchases. When the author approached the cash counter with the books he wished to purchase, handed over the loyalty card and mentioned that he wished to redeem the points already accumulated against the current purchase, the cashier left the counter and dashed off somewhere into the store without mentioning what he was up to. He came back more than five minutes later, saying, "Sir, the manager has gone for lunch, and I need his sanction to redeem your points."

Unbelievable.

These were points already earned against past purchase, which clearly reflected on the loyalty card, and yet the cashier had to wait for the store manager to authorise redemption, and the customer had to wait till the manager arrived.

When such incidents happen, very often customers perceive (and rightly so), that a large amount of the rules, regulations and policies applicable to them when they interact with an organisation have been devised to protect the interests of the organisation at the cost of inconveniencing customers. The moment this perception takes root, the organisation's relationship with customers who have suffered the brunt of such rules, policies and procedures, tends to rapidly weaken.

The twelve tasks of Asterix

Customers today primarily want speed and efficiency from their service providers.

Customers dislike playing the role of the parcel in an organisational game of passing the parcel.

- Cyrus M Gonda, Kalim Khan

Readers who are fans of the ***Asterix and Obelix*** series of comics may recall a story titled ***The Twelve Tasks of Asterix***.

The hero of the story, Asterix, is given a set of twelve near impossible tasks to perform as a challenge by the Romans.

One of these twelve tasks involves Asterix entering an organisation as a customer and getting some information from the help desk of that organisation. It turns out to be one of the most difficult tasks for Asterix, and one of the most hilarious tasks as far as the readers are concerned.

Asterix is made to run from pillar to post, from top floor to basement, from department to department, seeking information. Finally, in frustration, he himself resorts to some trickery to confuse the staff in the organisation and gets the information he is required to get. We are sure there must be many customers who wish they could emulate Asterix in real life. Although the tales of Asterix are set in a mythical world around two thousand years ago, we seriously believe that even in the world of today, it could be considered one of the twelve most difficult tasks in the world to interact with a front end executive in a multinational organisation who has the knowledge and the authority to immediately help and assist you, without sending you around the place.

Customers rightly feel that they should not be made to run a marathon to get basic information and requests attended to efficiently.

- Cyrus M Gonda, Kalim Khan

Rules Versus Principles

Flexibility as a way of working would get a strong boost if organisations understood the fundamental difference between being ***RULE BOUND*** and being ***PRINCIPLE BOUND.***

Our experience across organisations has been that organisations lack flexibility primarily because they are rule bound, or pretend to be so.

We do not say that rules are bad. Rules are necessary. But good rules come into operation when there are good, sound principles behind them. And if employees were to understand the principles on which the rules were made, flexibility in organisations would never be an issue. Thus, the onus is on the management of the organisation to explain to the employees the underlying principles which form the building blocks of the rules.

Organisations should therefore ensure that they keep the fewest possible rules, and these rules ought to be the ones which are absolutely essential, which make good sense to customers, and management should take care to explain in detail the rationale behind these rules and policies to their staff, so that they in turn can explain them clearly to the customers they interact with.

As an example, when one visits certain wildlife parks, very clear rules exist which mention that a visitor to these parks should not even pick up a stone from one place and put it in another. By itself the rule doesn't seem to make much sense. But, not only the rule, but also the rationale behind it is explained politely and clearly to visitors. The rationale behind this rule being – ***Don't disturb nature. Think of the entire park as the home of the wildlife who reside here, and please realise that any shift in the environment, however minor, impacts the delicate ecological balance of the wildlife preserve.***

Now, this rule makes perfect sense. And visitors respect it and abide by it now that they understand it.

Or, for example, even in a simple issue such as a dress code, organisations have five page chapters in their Personnel Manual regarding the same. This dress is what one ought to wear for meetings, this is the dress code on a regular day, this is the dress code when on tour, this is what can be worn on weekend, these are the shoes to be worn during the monsoon, and so on.

When employees are treated like children,
it is no wonder that they behave like children.

- Cyrus M Gonda, Kalim Khan

Contrast this with the Dress Code at the Semler Corporation in Brazil, run by Ricardo Semler, whom we mentioned earlier on. His organisation does have a dress code for its employees. ***It consists of the following two words:***

'DRESS SENSIBLY'

Semler says that if he can trust his employees to represent his organisation to the outside world, surely enough he can trust their judgement on basic issues such as choice of suitable attire.

Thus, we strongly feel that when an organisation is rule bound, it will be rigid, and when it is principle bound, it will be flexible.

It will be flexible in its functioning because front end employees understand the principles on which they operate and function.

By blindly obeying a rule, an employee does not
display knowledge of the principle behind it.

But by understanding the principles, he will automatically follow the right rules in the right way, and have the knowledge and confidence as to in which situations and with which customers they can be relaxed.

- Cyrus M Gonda, Kalim Khan

Tenet 13

TRUST YOUR CUSTOMER

When in your customer you trust,
Loyalty from his end will be a must

Little happens in a relationship until the individuals learn to trust each other.

- David W Johnson

Do unto others as you would have them do unto you.

This is such a time worn phrase. But years have only added to its lustre. It has flowered and blossomed with the test of time. If there is one phrase that sums up the essence of this tenet in a nutshell, and indeed sums up and encapsulates the entire marketing philosophy, (this is the reason we have kept this tenet in end position), it is ***this*** phrase: ***Do unto others as you would have them do unto you.***

Who does not feel a warm glow of pride from within when his word is trusted? And conversely, who does not feel devastated and crushed when his word is doubted, even though he is speaking the truth. We all have undergone and experienced such feelings only too often to well understand and empathise with the positive and negative emotions that the memories of such situations evoke.

It need not be a reputed brand alone which can create positive impact through the ***simple tool of trust.*** Even a small sole trader can display this vital act of genuine trust towards his customers. To illustrate, there is a fruit vendor in our locality who has a small stall on the street. His stall doesn't even have a name. His prices are not lower than other vendors. The variety and range of fruits he sells are not wider than nearby vendors either. But we regularly purchase fruits from him and not from other vendors nearby for one main reason. Fruits being fruits, it is difficult to know by just looking at them whether they could possibly be spoilt from within. This happens quite often with apples, and also mangoes and watermelons. Fruits are quite an expensive commodity. But we don't need to worry if the fruits we buy from this particular vendor ***do turn out*** spoilt, as this particular fruit vendor tells us very clearly at the time of purchase - "If you find any of the fruits are spoilt once you take them home and peel and cut them, ***I'll replace them."***

And he actually does replace them.

And he does this without any grumbling or muttering or hemming or hawing. He even apologises for the inconvenience caused to us. And, he doesn't even ask us to get the spoilt fruits to show him as proof. He scorns the very idea. ***"Your word is good enough for me. Why do you take the trouble to get me the spoilt fruit as proof? Aren't you my regular customers? If I can't trust your word, I have no right to be in business", he tells us.***

THAT, is the epitome of trust.

It doesn't matter to which industry your organisation belongs. It doesn't even matter how large or small your organisation is. ***What matters is the amount of trust you have lying within the heart and the DNA of your organisation.*** It's just that for some brands and some people, trusting others is a philosophy, a way of life.

A couple of contrasting examples will better cement this point. Every book lover in the city of Mumbai is familiar with ***Strand Book Store***. It's a store located in the commercial district of the city, having a ground floor and a mezzanine floor. The staff at the store is very friendly and know almost all the regular customers by name. But the main point is, ***any*** customer who walks into the store with a carry bag, whether large or small, whether he is a regular customer or a first time visitor, ***is allowed to carry his bag with him inside the store***, whether he browses on the ground floor, or goes up to the mezzanine. No staff member follows him around with an eagle eye, waiting to see if he is a potential shoplifter.

Contrast this with book stores who make you leave your bag at the entrance. Nothing wrong with that, you may say. After all, they are only protecting their interest. And we agree. But Strand Bookstore, being in the same industry, having a similar set of customers, thinks differently. And Strand Bookstore has survived. And has thrived over the years. Point to ponder. And, book lovers being book lovers, almost the same set of individuals will have visited all the bookstores in the city. If they were going to shoplift at one bookstore, they would do so at Strand as well. Logical, isn't it? Yet Strand trusts this same set of people whom most other bookstores view with a wary eye.

There is yet another bookstore, one which prides itself on being an elite and upmarket one. It is of a similar size as Strand. It too, has a ground floor and then there are steps leading up to the first floor. This is where the bulk of the books are displayed. When a customer enters, he is asked to leave his bag at the counter on the ground floor before he goes up to browse. Fair enough. But when the customer asks for a counter-token in lieu of the bag so he can remember to collect it later, he is bluntly told, ***"We have no token system. Just leave your bag here. It is safe with us."***

WOW.

So the brand doesn't trust the customer, but the customer is expected to trust the brand with his belongings, without even being given a token for the same.

This brings us to the concept of ***LEVELS OF TRUST.***

At ***Level One,*** we feel, stand organisations, such as Strand bookstore which trust their customer unconditionally. (Take your bag with you, don't leave it at the counter.) They trust their customers as they would trust their own dear family members. We have always seen such brands move from strength to strength.

At ***Level Two*** are brands which say - "We don't trust you, you don't trust us. Let's play safe. Leave your bag at the counter, take a token, collect your bag when you leave. Let's just keep this relationship at a purely professional level."

And at ***Level Three,*** stand, (or rather fall), brands which have as their philosophy - "We won't trust you, but you have to trust us. (Leave your bag with us, but don't expect a token for it.) The choice is yours. Take it or leave it. In many instances, customers leave it.

CUSTOMERS RECORD, REFLECT UPON, AND RUMINATE ON ALL THESE THINGS.

Trust is like a vase, once it's broken, though you can fix it, the vase will never be the same again.

- Unknown

The above example of customers made to leave their bags at the counter are meant to represent the atmosphere of trust that a brand will generate or will refuse to generate towards it's customers.

Obviously in every industry a similar parameter cannot be used to identify levels of trust. But each industry has it's own ways of working and processes, and hence it's own unique measures on which customers evaluate the amount of trust an organisation displays in it's dealings with them.

Organisations that are at the forefront in trusting their customers reap the largest chunk of business in their industry over a period of time.

- Cyrus M Gonda, Kalim Khan

In our experience, genuine trust is rarely betrayed by the recipient. But the way that some organisations operate when it comes to this vital aspect of customer relationships, it appears that ***lack of trust, rather than trust***, is the first thing that comes to the minds of some organisations when it comes to hearing out or interacting or creating policies with reference to customers.

Many organisations that go overboard in welcoming the potential customer as king, emperor, and even God, immediately classify him as a crook and a trouble maker the moment he complains about something or wants to return or exchange a product.

- Cyrus M Gonda, Kalim Khan

The first impulse from such an organisation's end is one of disbelief, then denial and ultimately outright cynicism, that something could be wrong with it's own processes and functioning. The customer is made to feel like a liar. The organisational defence mechanism immediately swings into play. Rather than the organisation keeping an open ear and an open mind and truly listening to what the customer has to say, it tends to switch off. And that does no good to either party. After all, one can only learn something when one is actually listening.

"This could not have happened at our end."

"It is just not possible."

"It was not broken when you took it from the store."

"No other customer has ever faced such a problem with us."

These are just some of the standard phrases that the customer receives when he tries to get a grievance redressed or attempts to provide some genuine but critical feedback to the organisation of which he has been a customer.

Remember, Lack of Faith Seals Favourable Fate

This is the reason why so many customers are hesitant to register a complaint with organisations in the first place. (It is a proven statistic that at least ninety eight percent of customers who have reason to complain, don't bother to complain. They just don't come back.) ***And the organisation remains complacent under the impression that all is well, as no complaints are coming in.*** This continues till the time that the customer base of that organisation shrinks to such an abysmal level, and word of mouth reaches such negative proportions, that it is almost impossible for the organisation to reach previous glory.

Indians who have travelled and shopped overseas marvel at the discrepancy between the ease with which returns and exchanges are done in the Western countries and the way they are handled by most brands in India. When top management of brands in India are questioned as to why there is so much distrust displayed in most cases when a customer comes to return or exchange a product even when it is under guarantee or warranty, a typical answer we hear is, "By and large if consumers in India are given similar facilities as those given to consumers in Western countries, ***they will take undue advantage of the same."***

Nonsense.

We are proud to be Indians and feel we are at least as honest a people as other nationalities are.

In this context, we would like to bring to light some sterling work that the brand ***More,*** (the retail arm of the ***Aditya Birla Group***), is doing.

Speaking to ***Mr. Harshvendra Soin, the Chief People Officer*** of the ***More*** retail chain, really enlightened us.

Mr. Soin strongly feels that it is incorrect to believe that Indian consumers would take undue advantage of lenient exchange and return policies and guarantees. He gives an example of the More chain of retail outlets, where although they provide a one year, no question asked guarantee on their mixers, grinders and similar products, rarely do even one or two percent of their customers return to claim that the piece does not function. And even this minute percentage of customers come because they face a genuine problem with the product. He cannot recall any of their customers ever taking undue advantage of the guarantee and the return policy. And even if a minuscule few do so, it is easily outweighed by the huge volumes of positive goodwill the brand generates from genuine delighted customers.

According to Mr. Soin, ***"A test of organisational credibility and repute is how fast and how trouble free is the process for fulfilling the guarantee provided."***

We genuinely feel that the more individuals like Mr. Soin we have at the helm of corporate affairs in India, the sooner will Indian Industry take her rightful place among the world leaders in Consumer Delight.

Trust your Customer's Judgement

We were at a Tibbs Frankie stall at Linking Road, Bandra, treating ourselves to a ***frankie***, (an Indian wraparound snack), when a customer came up to the counter and effusively thanked the owner, Mr. Kamal, for having trust and faith in her judgement. As a matter of professional curiosity, after she left, we asked Kamal what had happened.

He mentioned that she came to the stall accompanied by her three teenage children, one of whom wanted to have a frankie. They selected a vegetarian cheese frankie, and it was served to them. The customer handed it over to the daughter, who sniffed it and made a wry face. She whispered something to her mother, who then came to Kamal and asked if the cheese was fresh. He guaranteed that it was indeed fresh, as they use one of the best brands of Indian cheese, (Amul), and said that many other customers had just been served cheese Frankie and they had no complaints. The mother apologised and said that maybe there was nothing wrong with the cheese, it's just that they'd recently come to Mumbai from America, and the smell of the cheese they used to have there was different. It was just that she didn't feel her daughter would have the frankie because of the smell of the cheese. There was nothing that the service provider had done wrong, but Kamal immediately said, "***No problem. What is important is that you enjoy the Frankie. I'll make a fresh one for you without cheese, just the vegetables. And there will be no charge. We want you to be happy.***" The lady was thrilled, the daughter enjoyed the frankie very much, and they bought six more vegetarian frankies and carried them away as a parcel order. That's when we heard her thanking Kamal. Truly, it pays to have faith in your customer's word and in your customer's judgement. ***Customers can have their own idiosyncrasies, but they don't display them with the intention of troubling you. Take them in your stride with a smile, and you'll be more than glad you did so***. As Kamal told us, "Of course I was glad of the extra business she gave, but the real treasure was the genuine thanks she left me with. And even if I look at it from purely monetary terms, (which I don't), for the cost of one frankie, I have gained a customer for life. I'm confident that even if my competitor gives her a product for free, she'll still come back to my shop. Service providers tend to forget that a customer is a very important part of the business. You as a service provider comprise fifty percent of your business, and your customer comprises the other fifty percent. Without him, there would ***BE*** no business." Thanks Kamal, and may your business grow and prosper.

Learn a Lesson from the Game of Baseball

Admittedly, there ***ARE*** some customers which the organisation would be better off not having. ***But the FIRST time that a customer complains is NOT the time to mistrust him.***

There is a rule in the American game of baseball, called the ***three strike rule.*** Unlike in the game of cricket, where being bowled once means you are out, in baseball it's slightly different. The first time you miss the ball, it is termed as strike one. The second time, it is strike two. You are still not out. It is only the third time when you miss are you considered out. Thus, the first and the second occasion that the batter misses the ball, he gets the benefit in his favour. Only the third attempt going against him puts him back in the dugout (pavilion). Transferring the same principle into the realm of marketing, the first time a customer complains; give him the benefit of the doubt. The same goes for the second time. But keep a track of the complaints. Only the third time he complains or it appears that he is trying to take undue advantage of the organisation in some way, is it okay for you to begin to doubt his word. ***Come to think of it, why should we distrust a customer who has given us no previous reason to do so?***

Trusting is easy when your heart and soul is in it.

- Cyrus M Gonda, Kalim Khan

We recently experienced a terrific example of trusting the customer. We received a card from a friend as a New Year's Greeting. The card had been painted by an artist representing the ***Indian Mouth and Foot Painting Artists Association.*** We really liked the card and wanted to encourage the artists of this association, so we wrote to the association asking for details of where to purchase these cards, stating that we would prefer cards depicting nature scenes. We were really amazed when within a week, we received a dozen assorted cards of the nature scenery variety from their end, along with a bill for Rupees Two Hundred and Forty. (Rupees Twenty per card.) The organisation didn't know us from Adam. They had never interacted with us before. They had no reason to trust us. Yet they sent across the cards while we had merely made an enquiry as to where the cards would be available. It was a wonderful gesture which won us over. We later went to their office, paid the bill, bought a few more cards, and also recommended them to other friends of ours. It was a rare gesture which first won our hearts, and ultimately a share of our wallets.

(We would like to take this opportunity to promote the ***Indian Mouth and Foot Painting Artists Association*** and the artists representing it as they are truly world class. Their paintings bring a tear to the eye. The cards are tastefully made and reasonably priced with sensible words suitable for any occasion. It is difficult to find a sober card with lovely views or scenery depicted on them in the branded greeting card showrooms. But with the cards of the Mouth and Foot Artists Association it's a different story. Each card is lovelier than the other and we would like to pass a message to all corporate houses to consider these cards for their bulk greeting purposes.)

In contrast to the Mouth and Foot Artists Association, there are organisations whose regular customers may have given them business worth thousands or even more, yet the moment it comes to an issue of trusting these very same customers, organisational policies are quoted which act as hindrances to the trust factor.

But such need not be the case, if organisations take the time and effort and train and ***empower*** front end organisational staff to ***identify trustworthy customers*** and use their discretion while dealing with them. After all, these are customers of repute who would be an asset to the brand, if treated with the care and understanding that they deserve.

If you want your customers to trust your brand,
the first step is for you to trust your customers.
TRUST CAN NEVER BE A ONE WAY STREET.

- Cyrus M Gonda, Kalim Khan

Country Music shows the Way

A beautiful country music song, reminiscing about the times when personalised relationships were the hallmark of human interactions, has the following lines as the heart of the song.

"Dad was a quiet man, whose gentle voice was seldom heard.
He could borrow money at the bank, SIMPLY ON HIS WORD."

It's not that ***every*** customer was permitted the luxury of borrowing money simply on the strength of his word even in those far off days. But organisations took the time and effort to identify certain customers as ***trustworthy, (worthy of being trusted.)***

A Veterinary Surgeon Speaks Sense

As John McCormack, a country veterinary surgeon in America, said, "When I shake hands with a ***farmer with calloused, work worn hands,*** I find that a vet or any other professional they summon for services, gets his bill settled promptly. However, if the farmer feels he's been overcharged, there is no invitation to return."

What McCormack's experiences tell us is that we need to identify certain characteristics and certain personality traits among customers, which enable front end service providers to trust customers who possess these traits. John McCormack has identified the ***farmer's calloused, hard working hands, roughened with honest toil, as a parameter of customers who can be trusted to settle their bill promptly and honestly. And John's judgement has never failed him.***

Have you identified such parameters which will exist in customers worthy of trust in your own industry? Invest time and effort looking for and identifying such parameters. They definitely exist. Retention and loyalty from the customer's end will be your reward for the effort you take.

In Beethoven we Trust

The best way to sum up this tenet is through an anecdote we read in the Reader's Digest a few years ago. An individual wrote an anecdote to the Reader's Digest saying that he was once passing by a new music store for the first time. He walked in, found a Beethoven symphony CD that he liked, then realised that he wasn't carrying sufficient cash, nor did he have a credit card. But he ***was*** carrying his chequebook with him. He hesitantly requested the cashier if he could pay by cheque, and was obviously expecting a negative answer. (Normally, people would not accept a cheque payment from someone they did no know.)

But the cashier smiled, and said, ***"Sure Sir, we trust you. People who listen to Beethoven don't write bad cheques."***

Imagine the warm glow that must have passed through the customer. Hats off to the cashier, and more so to the organisation he represented for allowing him the freedom to use his discretion and judgement, and take this noble decision. And what a lovely way of putting it, making the customer feel special, and appreciating the customer's taste in music at the same time.

Until and unless we genuinely trust the customer, developing a relationship, a rapport, a bond, and close ties with him; getting positive access to his ***Circle of Influence*** is simply not possible.

Think of all the personal relationships that you as an individual have developed over the years. The ones you feel most comfortable about would be the ones where there is a very high element of trust between you and the other party involved. The same holds true for business. And without this strengthened relationship and rapport which comes through the medium of trust, repeat business and retained customers will simply remain a pipe dream.

The beauty of the concept of trust is that it is reciprocal. If you trust your customer, he will learn to trust you. Gradually at first, like a man stepping into a pool, cautiously testing the water temperature with his toes, till confidence sets in that the temperature is comfortable, and slowly the entire body sinks in and relaxes. The man has found peace and comfort, which are important outcomes of trust.

Once a brand has attained the trust of its customers, and continues to earn and retain this trust ferociously, through every action of the mind, body, and soul of the brand's DNA, we GUARANTEE that the customer would be a fan of the brand for life.

Guarantee is not a word we would lightly use, and no better example of earning trust can be given than that of the proud, royal Siamese cat.

The Siamese cat, considered a royal animal in Siam, (modern Thailand), has a kink or a sharp bend, about an inch in length, at the edge of its tail. There is a very interesting story relating to how this particular species of cat acquired the kink in its tail. The ancestors of today's Siamese cat were given the proud privilege of guarding the Siamese princesses. When the princesses came to bathe in the palace lake, they put their valuable rings on the tail of their guardian cats for safekeeping. The cats were proud of being given this honour. The story goes that these cats, to justify the trust reposed in them, bent the last joint in their tails so that the rings would not slip off. And through generations, this now genetic kink or bend passed on, becoming part of their DNA, and the faithful Siamese cat's tails have become crooked for all time to come.

To be trusted is a greater compliment than being loved.

- George MacDonald

EPILOGUE - A WORD OF CAUTION

"Those who aim to give the public what the public wants begin by under-estimating the public taste and end up by debauching it."

- T S Eliot

"A leader takes people where they want to go. A great leader takes people where they don't necessarily want to go, but ought to be."

- Rosalyn Carter

At the end, let us say that truly great organisations and brands don't merely provide customers what they want, as what they want may not be necessarily good for them. Great brands tend to act as guides for their customers. That is the least that a professional brand can do for customers who provide the brand with the fuel and lifeblood of revenue.

For example, a doctor cannot prescribe shiny, colourful pills to a patient simply because the patient says that they look nice.

An architect cannot permit a customer to dictate design elements which would compromise on safety.

Newspapers ought not to say that we focus on the glamorous elements of news because readers tend to prefer such news. The media is the Fourth Estate. The guardian of democracy after the three pillars of the legislature, the executive and the judiciary. News which has genuine value needs to be given pride of place.

A chartered accountant cannot permit a wrong entry to be passed in the books of accounts he certifies, merely because a customer so demands.

The two quotations above, by T. S. Eliot and Rosalyn Carter very clearly and in no uncertain terms state that the first job of a strong brand and the primary job of marketing is to keep the customer's interests uppermost at all times, even though the customer may not be aware where his own interests lie. That is the reason that service providers are termed as ***professionals.***

Having clarified this, we would like to pass a message to all readers and marketers that business ought to be simplified rather than made unnecessarily complex.

The following seven points could sum up the philosophy that all marketers need to follow, to attain success and generate customer loyalty.

1. ***Identify your strengths and genuine capabilities as an individual or as an organisation. Too often we have seen brands entering areas of business and overextending themselves in ventures in which they lack thorough knowledge and capability, simply because business opportunities apparently currently exist in those areas. It is like an MBA student opting to specialize in the area of Finance even though his strengths do not lie there, simply because the current market scenario depicts that the job openings in finance are currently at their peak. Career choices based on such temporary external factors are doomed to failure, as are decisions of organizations to enter sectors and industries based on current market demand without considering innate capabilities.***

2. ***Identify areas where genuine customer needs gel with your strengths and focus on business in those areas by developing robust product or service offerings. The needs may currently not be being fulfilled by any existing service provider or even if they are, you may feel your strengths and capabilities would enable you to provide them in a better manner.***

3. *Manufacture products and design services in the areas of your expertise which match genuine customer needs in as effective a manner as possible.*

4. ***Price your products and services reasonably, which will ensure that you get a decent but not abnormal profit. This is essential else the customer may not then get Value for Money and then it would not be possible to retain him. Also, reasonable profits and***

not abnormal profits would ensure that only serious competitors and not fly-by-night operators would enter the sector in the future.

5. *Take genuine proactive customer feedback on all elements of your product, your service, your organizational processes, your delivery systems, your points of customer contact, and act on this feedback to customise your offerings and add enhanced features in product and service delivery which provide genuine benefits to even a small segment of your customers. These improvements and innovations need not be earth shaking discoveries and that is not what customers expect either.*

6. *Don't treat your customer base as one solid mass, but treat them as the individuals they are. Maintain relations with these individual customers, finding out as many details about them as possible, which will enable you to wow and delight them better, often in unexpected ways.*

7. *Provide as strong a guarantee as possible with regard to your product and service, and strive to provide and give great after sales service, and stand behind your product as you would stand behind your own child.*

Nothing else is required for success in any type of business in the world.

The HOW may differ from Industry to Industry and Organisation to Organisation.

But the WHAT and the WHY will remain constant.

Whether you're making rockets or rat-traps, if these seven points are followed, the WHAT and the WHY are taken care of.

The HOW is the missing component in the above seven points, and we feel that without providing knowledge of the HOW, the recipe is incomplete. HOW you achieve the above in the best possible way as far as your unique customer base is concerned is by following our THIRTEEN TENETS.

(Some of our readers may believe in the power of numbers and numerology at least to a certain extent. That too, is a part of human nature. A strange fact regarding the Number Thiteen. Contrary to normal belief, it is ***NOT*** by itself a number associated with negative events. It is in fact ***The Number of Truth***. This means that any activity which is undertaken by any individual or organisation which involves the number Thirteen, if done honestly, with a clean conscience and to the best of one's abilities, is bound to give the desired results. But if the activity is done half-heartedly and with not the right intentions, it would be better not to commence the activity in the first place.)

If all the tenets which have been enumerated in this book are implicitly and whole-heartedly followed; if an organization can honestly say it scores at a considerably high level on all of them as far as customer perspective is concerned; it's a recipe for organizational success. And the beauty is that none of these tenets cost a lot to implement. ***In fact most of the tenets would help organizations to lower their costs (Advertising, Brand Endorser), while simultaneously generating the enumerated benefits.***

Our ***Brains Trust Management Consultancy model and training programme*** (which has been highly appreciated and profitably implemented at several leading brands), is centred and built around these tenets to provide any organization with a scorecard through quantified research to show where it currently stands on the vital parameter of customer retention. No special equipment, technology or additional investment is required to implement these tenets. Rather than provide cosmetic USPs to an organisation, following our tenets and the subsequent scorecard based thereon enable any organisation to develop genuine USPs.

Last few words:

What we've enumerated in our tenets is not rocket science. No genius is required to comprehend the message. But ***implementing*** it? Aha! ***That's*** where the problems begin. And end.

The tenets seem and sound easy enough to put in practice, but ask a person who's not used to exercising to follow a strict regime of going to a gymnasium six days a week without missing a single turn.

Or ask a poor man who's found a loaded wallet on the streets. It's an easy thing to tell him to return it, but the proof is in the doing. And not only once, but if he finds himself in that situation a second and a third time, his response hopefully should be the same.

Or we can learn from a housewife in the kitchen who does not compromise on her cooking methods by using short cuts even though that would be so convenient, especially when she has a hundred other tasks to perform

It is a curious but true tenet that a passion for profits may not lead to profits. But passion for the product and service and customer will always lead to profits. It would not be incorrect to say that a person or an organisation whose focus is on profits may well end up making a loss.

If, after going through the thirteen tenets, we are labelled by some as being unnecessarily ***ORTHODOX, we would take that as the supreme compliment.*** For though today, the word orthodox has wrongly acquired negative connotations, and is used in a sarcastic, derogatory sense to refer to someone or something as being old fashioned and hopelessly out of date, the reality is the opposite. The roots of the word ***ORTHODOX*** lie in the prefix ***ORTHO*** (which means CORRECT), and the suffix ***DOX*** (which means PROCESS or PROCEDURE). So someone who is labelled as orthodox is merely ***someone who is following the correct or the right procedure. In the same way, the terms and tenets we have elaborated in this book (USP, Public Relations, Marketing and so on), have genuine goodness associated at their roots, but have become diluted, distorted, contaminated and compromised with the passage of time.*** Therefore the subtitle ***– Remaster the lost art of Marketing.***

If some readers have felt that positive examples in the book are comparatively less in number, that's because that's the way it is in real life. Again, some may feel that there is not much that is exceptional or earth shaking in the positive examples of certain brands we have provided. They may feel that these brands are only doing what all other brands also claim but don't do. That is precisely the point. These positive examples stand out and become USPs only because all brands who advertise and claim similar service quality and should be doing these things ***DON'T*** do these things.

We would like to conclude by emphasizing that the examples we have provided are merely representative samples out of a huge database and that they are all replicable by other organisations which wish to do so. These tenets can never be undertaken by accident. We feel that if something is not replicable, it is not worth imparting.

Our tenets can be followed by all brands across industry and we would be more than happy to provide assistance to brands and organizations which wish to streamline their processes and systems and attain the ultimate objective of any organisation, which is ***Customer Retention***.

Brains Trust Management Consultancy

The success of every organization depends on how efficiently it solves customer problems. But while doing so, several organisations encounter their own set of problems. And with increased awareness of global trends, customers have become more discerning than ever before, thereby leaving the onus on the organisation to exceed customer's expectations from time to time. So while customers turn towards these organisations to solve their problems, these organisations themselves encounter multiple obstacles along the way, as in the process of focusing on their day-to-day operations, they often lack time to observe their entire operation as a holistic process. Also, the solutions to their problems may not lie within the documented sphere of their industry operations.

At Brains Trust, we consider every business unique and derive customised solutions to optimize results. We render professional advice and work closely with our clients to help them implement the suggestions in a partnership approach. Our multidisciplinary expertise across industries has enabled us assist several organisations in the service and manufacturing sectors to streamline business operations, enhance processes, improve customer satisfaction levels and directly contribute to a healthier bottom line. Our experience has also demonstrated that one of the key determinants of the value that we can bring to an organisation is our extensive 'real world' experience of operating both in and with major organizations. This has also resulted in our understanding the need to deliver practical, measurable and realistic solutions to the organisations with which we work.

At Brains Trust, we firmly believe training should be an on-going process and not a one time experience. If done properly, training need not be a cost but can be one of the best and soundest investments an organisation can ever make. A systematic training effort will lead to a lower attrition rate, lesser wastage, higher productivity, superior quality of product and service, healthy inter and intra organisational relationships, enhanced customer satisfaction, word of mouth publicity, larger market share and ultimately increased profitability.

Our core competency lies in the fact that we don't outsource our Training or Consultancy assignments to others as we have a strong in-house knowledge base in the areas we specialize in, namely Customer Delight, Systems Enhancement, Corporate Communication and Total Quality Management.

For any professional assistance regarding Customer Experience Management workshops and consultancy, branding and market research related queries, kindly visit *www.brainstrustindia.com*